Breaking Free

Overcoming Self-Sabotage

Edited by Linda Ellis Eastman

Professional Woman Publishing
Prospect, Kentucky

Breaking Free Overcoming Self-Sabotage

Published by:
Professional Woman Publishing
Post Office Box 333
Prospect, KY 40059
(502) 228-0906
www.pwnbooks.com

Please contact the publisher for quantity discounts.

ISBN 13: 978-0-9886462-3-0

Library of Congress Cataloging-In-Publication Data

Cover Design and Typography by:
Sential Design, LLC — www.sentialdesign.com
Photo credits: cienpies design/illustrations/dreamstime

Printed in the United States of America

Table of Contents

Table of Contents
—Continued—

Table of Contents
—Continued—

ABOUT THE AUTHOR

LINDA ELLIS EASTMAN

Linda Ellis Eastman is President and CEO of The Professional Woman Network (PWN), an International Training and Consulting Organization on Women's Issues. She has designed seminars which have been presented in China, the former Soviet Union, South Africa, the Phillipines, and attended by individuals in the United States from such firms as McDonalds, USA Today, Siemens-Westinghouse, the Pentagon, the Department of Defense, and the United States Department of Education.

An expert on women's issues, Ms. Eastman has certified and trained over two thousand women to start consulting/seminar businesses originating from such countries as Pakistan, the Ukraine, Antigua, Canada, Mexico, Zimbabwe, Nigeria, Bermuda, Jamaica, Costa Rica, England, South Africa, Malaysia, and Kenya. Founded in 1982 by Linda Ellis Eastman, The Professional Woman Network is committed to educating women on a global basis regarding, self-esteem, confidence building, stress management, and emotional, mental, spiritual and physical wellness.

Ms. Eastman has been featured in USA Today and listed in Who's Who of American Women, as well as Who's Who of International Leaders. In addition to women's issues, Ms. Eastman speaks internationally regarding the importance of human respect as it relates to race, color, culture, age, and gender. She will be facilitating an international conference where speakers and participants from many nations will be able to discuss issues that are unique to women on a global basis.

Linda Ellis Eastman is also founder of The Professional Woman Speakers Bureau and The Professional Woman Coaching Institute. Ms. Eastman has dedicated her businesses to increasing the self-esteem and personal dignity of women and youth around the world.

Contact:
The Professional Woman Network
P.O. Box 333
Prospect, KY 40059
(502) 566-9900
lindaeastman@prodigy.net
www.pwnbooks.com
www.protrain.net

Introduction

Let's face it, women are shackled by many chains in life. But the most important factor is that women often sabotage themselves and maintain a ball and chain that holds them back from personal and professional success, and a feeling of freedom and joy.

What are those areas of self-sabotage? Consider over-spending, addictions, jealousy, bitterness, unforgiveness, gossip, the 'I'm not good enough syndrome", and other behaviors that are poisonous and create a downward spiral for women.

The authors of this book have written powerful chapters filled with steps to live a life free of emotional burdens and strategies to begin creating the life of your dreams. The choice is yours. If you are ready to break free and embrace new, healthy behaviors, then read on, my friend.

This book is dedicated to YOU.

Linda Ellis Eastman

Breaking Free

Overcoming Self-Sabotage

ABOUT THE AUTHOR

JURACY JOHNSON

Juracy Johnson is an expert in Self-Growth. She has studies in Life Coaching, Holistic Coaching, NLP and currently working on her thesis in Business Coaching to help develop a person's full potential.

A National and International Workshop Leader from Mexico with a M. Sc. in Seismology and a passion for life and self discovery, she is the author of more than 100 Scientific and Self-Help articles.

"As a cancer survivor since 1993, I made a choice: I absolutely refused to be a victim. I love life and I am grateful for the support I received from my husband, my family and friends at that difficult time. I love people and helping them to reach their dream is one of my goals".

Currently Juracy is a Coach, a Professor at the State's University and also a caregiver to her husband who sustained a Traumatic Brain Injury in 1999. She Coaches and offers Workshops for Latin American Women. She also participates in Conferences regarding Natural Hazards all over the world. She is the Founder of "Mujeres Líderes Latinoamérica" (Women Leaders Latin America). She has been offering Workshops and Coaching Services since 2003. "I have a passion for helping people overcome their challenges and guide them into having a joyful life".

Contact:
Websites: www.juracyjohnson.com
www.CoachingMujeres.com
juracy@coachingmujeres.com

ONE

Regaining Self-Confidence as a Latin American Woman

Juracy Johnson

As a Latin American Woman you struggle to stand out, to achieve your goals and to combine your professional life with your role as a mother, a wife, a caregiver, a cook, a server etc. The pressure we put onto ourselves combining the multiple tasks we are involved in and do them with perfection is humongous. When a Latin American woman fails to comply with her standards in any of her roles, she punishes herself with her thoughts and this reduces her self-confidence. No matter if she was not at fault, her ideal self is to be a Super Woman. It is crucial to let go of the need to have everything in perfect order.

To recover your self-confidence it is necessary to concentrate on "*the self*", and this means concentrating on YOU! Getting to know yourself again, and then act as you really are in each of the important areas of your life and not respond as you are expected to do so can be relearned. Also, it is important for you to remember that the greatest obstacles that women have are classified in two categories: external and internal. External obstacles are the ones we absolutely cannot control and we must take notice of that. Examples are: "machismo (the macho man)", violence against women, etc. Internal obstacles are the ones we do to ourselves because of lack of self-confidence. Some examples include: Eating or drinking too much, not buying the dress you like because "I am too fat/ugly", not doing things because of your age, of what others will think, etc. You can empower yourself and change the limits you internally put in yourself and to do so, you first have to regain your self-confidence, your self-worth and your self-love.

The following questions will help you get to know yourself again and regain self-confidence. Please take all the time you need to answer each one. It is important that you let your inner-guidance flow and avoid judging yourself as you write. If your internal dialogue starts to come up, thank it for being here, for trying to protect you and then let it go.

You do not need to answer all the questions at once, you can do it at your own pace. The most important thing is to have enough peace and quiet surrounding you so you can listen to yourself as you think them through.

Have a Journal or a notebook at hand. And let's begin!

1.- We are overwhelmed by all the tasks we must complete and most of the time we cannot possibly do them all; instead we must prioritize. So, first you must distinguish which roles are important to you and which roles are important for you to do. Please limit yourself to 3.

ROLES THAT I LIKE	ROLES THAT ARE IMPORTANT FOR ME TO DO

Now, read them carefully and notice your thoughts… just let them flow and avoid any judgment. Take a glance at the first column and then at the second column. Notice your feelings. Now open your journal and write what you feel without censoring or editing. Write until you are finished.

2.- We sabotage ourselves when we take actions that are against our own benefits. Why we do this comes from our childhood experiences. The good news is that we have the power to change that! Take a minute to recall your internal dialogue. What do you usually say to yourself?

____

____

____

____

____

Whose voice is this? Can you recognize your mother, father, any of your grandparents or maybe an older sister or brother? Are they helping you? Do they want to protect you? What is the hidden benefit of having these levels of anxiety? Please take an opportunity to answer these questions in your Journal. Your internal dialogue has a profound impact on your experiences in life. When you become aware of the thought patterns that run through your mind, you can interrupt them and change them.

When your internal dialogue starts to emerge, you can see that maybe your eyes and/or your face are looking down. So, the first thing to do is to look straight ahead with your chin slightly up and thank your internal dialogue for being here to help and protect you. Tell it you don't need it anymore and that you are in control. Immediately change your thoughts to a more positive ones. If for the moment you can't do this, then fill in your mind with any type of neutral thoughts like "how green the leaves on the tree are" or "how beautiful the little bird you see outside your window is", etc. Just keep on allowing these kind of thoughts to come into your mind, and breathe easily, don't start breathing fast and think that the faster you breathe, the faster the thoughts will go away. This has nothing to do. Keep your calm, remember that the internal dialogue was there to help you but you no longer need it.

3.- We all have things that we would like to change. This doesn't make you a bad person. Please know that you are perfect just the way you are and from that point of power, state 3 things you would like to modify or change to feel better with yourself (instead of feeling better about yourself); you see, feeling better <u>with</u> yourself is helping your-*self* because you matter to you, and <u>about</u> could mean you are doing it to please others. For the moment, just state

3 things.

a) ____

b) ____

c) ____

Now, open your journal and write an action in terms of small steps you could take to help you get to each one of the goals stated above. For instance, if you want to change your eating habits you could say: "For dinner, today I will serve myself an extra portion of green beans and skip dessert". You see, breaking down our goal into small steps that you can easily do, and taking one at a time, lets your brain know that you are in control and helps you regain your self-confidence in a way that it will stay with you because you are achieving lots of goals in a continuous manner. After you've reached your desired status, congratulate yourself, take a break and when you feel like you want to start over again, write another three things you would like to do. It is important to take a break because you don't want to put yourself to more stress, and feel like you must change lots of things about yourself; that is not the point. The objective of this exercise is to empower you!

4.- Now about what you like about yourself. We all have qualities in ourselves we like, but most of the time, we Latin American women are so busy taking care of others that we don't think about them. Please take a moment to state 5 things you like about yourself.

a) ____

b) ____

c) ____

d) ____

e) ____

Can you think of another 5? Please write them in your Journal and include for each of your ten qualities, how these have helped you to become who YOU ARE. Have you used them to avoid becoming a victim? Did they help you get that job you wanted? Write, write, write. This is a very empowering exercise that assists you in recalling things you have accomplished in the past, and you know what it is said: "If you did it once, you can do it again!"

5.- We all have our moments when we have felt powerless, not knowing what to do or where to go. Can you remember those times? Please write three of them down. Be brief.

a) ____

b) ____

c) ____

6.- There have been times when you have felt strong, empowered. State 5 times when this occurred.

a) ____

b) ____

c) ____

d) ____

e) ____

Notice if the situations are similar, if they all belong to the same category or if they can be classified in different categories. For instance, "I felt strong when I got promoted", "I felt strong when I got congratulated for a job well done after I presented my thesis" can be put in the same area: profession or career. How many categories did you find?

How would you have used these strengths to solve the things you wrote down on point 4? Write them in your Journal.

7.- Write 3 things you are most passionate about doing; it doesn't matter if you are not doing them at the moment, just jot them down.

a) ____

b) ____

c) ____

Can you incorporate them into your current lifestyle? What changes could you do to fit them into your life? Are you willing to do so? Write the answers in your Journal.

8.- Did you ever sabotage a relationship? If so, name 3 persons in your past, that could have brought you joy, peace or financial security. This could have been be your best friend, your boss, etc.

a) ____

b) ____

c) ____

Write in your Journal what you could have done better at the time and ask for their forgiveness coming from the heart to your mind. They don't have to be there and you don't need to call them up. Just to this exercise in your mind and bless them away. This is a very liberating exercise.

9.- Learning to accept your value. We must learn to recognize our needs and our wants.

Please complete the following personal questions in your Journal.

a) I am capable when I …

b) I am happiest when …

c) My future perspective …

d) I feel safe when …

e) My achievements make me feel I have self-worth because…

f) I feel self- confident when I …

Close your Journal and keep it in a safe place. Read it again so it continuously builds your self-esteem up and makes you aware of the YOU that lives and matters the most. Your greatest attractiveness is self-confidence. Women with self confidence generate and irradiate incredible energy, impossible to resist. Avoid putting a label on to yourself and having to live up to that (i.e. "we, Latin Women are..." "we, Latin Women must..."). The more freedom you allow yourself to have, the more universal you become.

Remember we all have a magical place that we can go and this is inside our minds. Go there as often as you can, it is your exclusive place and it always works on your behalf.

Golden Nuggets for your life.

The following tips are valuable tips that you can easily implement in your life-schedule. They will help you build your self-esteem up:

- ✓ Take 20 minutes each day to get in touch with yourself. This will be your "Me-time". It doesn't need to be at the same hour of the day; it is understandable that you are starting to regain your self confidence and you need to set your own pace. It is OK if you start with 3 times a week and upgrade to a daily basis. Don't rush yourself up. Rushing will only frustrate you. Find things to be grateful for. Spend a few moments feeling love in your heart and enjoying your own company.

- ✓ Learn to say "no, thank you", until you feel that the words come naturally out of your mouth. You can start going to the store or to the mall. When someone asks you if you need any help, pay attention to yourself when you say "no, thank you" and make it a part of your vocabulary for self-growth. I am not saying that you will be saying "no" to everything, but just start to feel comfortable with the word *no*.

- ✓ Have a Journal at the side of the bed and write just the good things that happened to you during the day and/or how you made those good things happen. Thank yourself for this and immediately go to sleep. Don't allow worrisome or negative thoughts to take over your bliss.

- ✓ "Pick your battles" as they say. Choose to ignore the unimportant details so you may pay attention to what really matters. Just let go. You will achieve a level of peace you hadn't believed it could be possible.

- ✓ Exercise. When you are depressed, you might not want to even get up in the morning, but believe me, exercise will lift you up even if you don't want to! So, you need to do this, especially when you are feeling down.

- ✓ Visualize. Visualizing yourself in happy situations generates a new film that if done well, can erase the subconscious program. Before you start your visualization exercise, stand up straight and lift your chin up a bit, then close your eyes and go to a place you like, surround yourself with the people that love you, and start envisioning a mental picture where you are the main character. Live it. Don't see yourself "down there" as if watching a movie, be IN the movie.

- ✓ Join a group that has the same hobby as you have. If you can't find a group in your area be a pioneer and start one! Whatever your interests are, there are people out there who share them and will want to take part.

- ✓ Although changing your external image does not guarantee you will make changes on the inside, you can try different clothes (you don't need to buy them) and see what you look like if you ever decide to change your style or the colors you usually wear. If you don't want to cut your hair for the moment, then try a pony-tail or have fun with a friend and try wigs. See how you look before you make a drastic change.

- ✓ Write yourself 'reminder notes' of how wonderful you are and keep them in your lunch box. Just write one word: "marvelous" or "exciting" and complete a statement in your mind (I am marvelous). No need to tell your co-workers about this. If they happen to see your note, and ask you about it, just tell them you were playing with your children on writing down positive words that start with the letter "m" or something similar. If they don't ask, you don't have to explain yourself.

Other suggested readings are:

Empowering Women. *Every Women's Guide to successful Living.* By Louise L. Hay

ABOUT THE AUTHOR

Rachela Leonello

Rachela is a psychotherapist, coach and Managing Director of the London based consultancy, LionsPond, with associates in Europe, South Africa, Australia and the United States. Her core focus is empowering clients to move closer to their potential and she does this with "great compassion, energy, vitality and clarity". In addition to her commercial work in private practice and business/educational sectors, Rachela is a qualified Yoga teacher, specializing in yoga for depression and anxiety. She is also passionate about giving back to the community and has worked with numerous London based charities including Help Counselling, MIND, Brent Bereavement Services and FreshStart Psychotherapy, with whom she is a Trustee and Director. Rachela worked as a lawyer for 15 years, 10 years of which were in-house as a senior legal director with one the largest entertainment companies in the world, the Walt Disney Group. During this time, Rachela built up a wealth of knowledge and experience in relation to management, working relationships, training, development and accomplishment, which she utilizes in her current work.

Some testimonials about Rachela...

- "Rachela has a beautiful combination of head and heart and a natural way of engaging people. I felt completely at ease with her."
- "Rachela made me feel so relaxed and I will not forget the trust and comfort she gave me. I learnt to find courage and light which will never leave me."
- "Rachela taught me to recognize my own strengths and faults and helped me muster the courage to work through material that I never would have before."
- "The work with Rachela changed my life and without it I would not have been able to move on."

Rachela is available for lectures, workshops, self-development programs, retreats, corporate and private coaching, psychotherapy and yoga therapy.

Contact:

Rachela Leonello
Managing Director, LionsPond Reflecting & realizing potential in people.
www.LionsPond.com
T: +447764863953 E: rachelaleonello@gmail.com

TWO

How to Build a Healthy Self-Esteem & Stand Up to Your Internal Saboteur!

Rachela Leonello

WHAT DOES SELF-ESTEEM ACTUALLY MEAN?

When I was growing up, I was often told by teachers that I had "low self-esteem". After hearing this several times, I finally asked what it meant. What I was told was that I had great potential but lacked confidence and didn't believe in myself .

It took me a long time to address my self-esteem issues. Not only were they difficult to understand. They also felt so big, bottomless and deeply programmed in me and I wasn't convinced coaching, therapy or anything else would help me. So I decided to accept them as part of me.....there goes Rachela...she has brown eyes, brown hair and self-esteem issues. End of story!

Unfortunately that wasn't the end of the story. Ignoring my self-esteem issues only made matters worse and they began to sabotage almost every facet of my life: my job, my relationships, my happiness and my dreams.

It was during my training as a psychotherapist and coach, that I finally decided I had enough. It felt wrong trying to help others when I wasn't doing anything about helping myself. In the spirit of walking the walk and not just talking the talk, I decided to address my own self-esteem issues once and for all.

Even though I was familiar with the term "self-esteem", I was confused about what it actually meant given that it is used so widely in relation to all sorts of people suffering from problems related to Self. So the first step for me was to understand this term a little better. I read everything I could on the topic of self-esteem and discovered the following.

Firstly, I came to understand that self-esteem refers to what I believe about myself deep down. If these beliefs about myself are rational, balanced and constructive, they are "***Helpful Beliefs***" (e.g. "Not everyone I meet will love/like me"). However, if they are not, they are "***Unhelpful Beliefs***" and may lead to self-esteem issues (e.g. "I'm unlovable, bad and unworthy").

To my relief, my second finding was that it is entirely normal and natural to experience some Unhelpful Beliefs/self-esteem issues and these only become a problem if they start to overshadow who I really am and my potential.

Thirdly, I discovered that Unhelpful Beliefs are often found under layers of "***Unhelpful Thoughts***". Unhelpful Thoughts are thoughts that are not rational, balanced or constructive (e.g. "if he doesn't call, it means he definitely doesn't like me"). They are different to Unhelpful Beliefs in that they are more fleeting and conscious, whereas Unhelpful Beliefs are deeper and more constant... similar to belief in religion.

Fourthly, I realized that Unhelpful Beliefs and Unhelpful Thoughts fuel and keep each other going in a vicious circle e.g. The Unhelpful Thought... "There is no way he will call".... is a natural bi-product of the Unhelpful Belief... "I'm unlovable". If the Unhelpful Thought is confirmed (i.e. he doesn't call), the Unhelpful Belief is reactivated and confirmed as though it were fact.

Next came the hard bit of working through my self-esteem issues. I tried all sorts of therapies, tricks and techniques, some more useful and effective than others. It was a long and difficult journey and I almost gave up a number of times, but I persisted and can finally say that I now have a much healthier self-esteem.

In this chapter I want to share with you some of the key steps that worked for me. There are 20 steps in total and each one, on its own, is enough to make a real difference to what you believe about yourself deep down. If you have also had enough of your own self-esteem issues, I would strongly encourage you to READ ON, work your way through these steps and stand up to your internal saboteur once and for all.

April Simpson www.fat-duck.com
Copyright © 2012

STEP 1 – CHALLENGE UNHELPFUL BELIEFS

If Unhelpful Thoughts come up (e.g. "There is no way that I will get promoted to a manager"), keep asking yourself over and over again "what does this mean I am?" until the Unhelpful Belief underneath the thought is revealed (e.g. "I am not good enough").

Exercise: When you have a list of your Unhelpful Beliefs, understand and challenge them by completing the statements in the space indicated below (see shaded examples).

- My Unhelpful Beliefs are:
  "I'm stupid" & "I'm not good enough".

- This belief often sits under Unhelpful Thoughts such as:
  "I'm not very good at my job" and "Someone is going to realize this one day and I will lose my job".

- My Unhelpful Beliefs and Unhelpful Thoughts are not rational, balanced or constructive because:
  no one has ever fed this back to me, I have achieved good results and much success.

- To cope with this belief:
  I work very hard and aim for success at all costs.

- This belief usually gets triggered when:
  I say something without thinking it through properly, find something difficult to accomplish, fail at something, someone questions or challenges me or when I feel unheard.

- It is understandable that I have this belief because:
  the rest of my family is super bright and I felt like the dumb one.

- The advantages of holding on to this belief are:
  it keeps me on my toes and ahead of the game – this makes me become a doer, an achiever and more successful.

- The disadvantages of holding on to this belief are:
  I don't live life in the moment and get stressed, depressed and exhausted.
- This belief would be a Helpful Belief if it was reframed to:
  I am reasonably intelligent and am good enough.
- To help me believe in this Helpful Belief, I will:

  (i) make a list of evidence in support of this belief and keep it under my pillow; and

  (ii) repeat this belief when I wake up and before I go to bed as a daily affirmation.

STEP 2 – TAKE RESPONSIBILITY

The bottom line is that you choose the beliefs you have. To prove this, consider the following scenario. Three women go for a job, two of which (Linda and Abbey) are not successful. Even though they experience the same result they choose to adopt different beliefs. Linda adopts the Unhelpful Belief: "I am no good!". Abby, however, adopts a more Helpful Belief: "I am disappointed, but I cannot expect to succeed at everything and I will try harder next time."

Unless you are ready to step up and take responsibility for the beliefs that you choose about yourself, it is unlikely that you will see any positive changes in your self-esteem. Remember, it was Einstein who defined insanity as doing the same thing over and over while expecting a different result. So why don't you agree to do something different, starting now?

Exercise: Swear a formal and solemn oath to yourself that you will start taking ownership and responsibility for the beliefs that you choose to adopt about yourself from this day onwards.

STEP 3 – STOP MAKING ANXIOUS PREDICTIONS

Do you make anxious predictions such as... "There is no way I can support myself after my divorce". Then if they happen, do you say to yourself with glum, yet smug satisfaction "I told you so"? Even worse, if your predictions do not happen (i.e. you get a job and can support yourself), do you continue to make similar anxious predictions in the future? If the answer to these questions is "yes", you may be:

- Attracting the result that you anxiously predict, based on the "law of attraction";
- building evidence in support of your Unhelpful Beliefs if your anxious predictions become a reality; and
- ignoring evidence to the contrary if your anxious predictions do not come true.

<u>Exercise</u>: Next time you catch yourself making an anxious prediction, imagine pressing the "re-wind" button in your mind. Instead of planting seeds for the anxious prediction to grow in the future, try making a different prediction, which is open to all sorts of positive outcomes, such as success, happiness, abundance and joy. If these positive outcomes become reality and take root, ensure that they continue to grow by acknowledging them and practicing gratitude. You can practice gratitude for any positive outcome by taking a few minutes to simply breathe it in and out until there is a sense that your body has fully absorbed the outcome.

STEP 4 – RELAX PERSONAL RULES

"***Personal Rules***" are rules that you set for yourself and often start with "I must" or "I should" (e.g. "I must always look young"). If you suffer from an unhealthy self-esteem you may create Personal Rules as a way coping. However the big problem with Personal Rules is that they are often impossible, unrealistic or extremely difficult for us mere mortals to maintain. So why don't you do yourself a favor and avoid stress, resentment, failure or burn out by relaxing your Personal Rules?

<u>Exercise</u>: Prepare a list of all your Personal Rules and ask: what is the worst thing that could possibly happen if I relax them? Often the answer is not much at all. Have a go at reframing each Personal Rule to something more helpful, rational, balanced and constructive i.e. "I must always look young" ...might be relaxed to..."I don't like getting older, but it is a fact of life so I will try and age gracefully and embrace all the wisdom and experience that goes with it."

STEP 5 – MAKE THE MOST OF QUALITIES

One of the most important steps to building a healthier self-esteem is to know your core qualities and make the most out of them. Core Qualities are generally qualities that you are born with. However, they can also be developed in life. They include qualities such as being curious, creative, determined, energetic, courageous, honest, caring, generous, joyful, observant, wise, and intuitive.

<u>Exercise</u>: Identify your core qualities and specify:

- How each one serves you (e.g. if the quality is determination it may lead to much success);

- What happens if this quality gets out of control (e.g. if you become too determined, you may become exhausted and burn out); and
- How you can better manage this quality to make the most out of it and keep it balanced (e.g. you might practice relaxation techniques and limit time allocated to work).

STEP 6 – BUILD UP INTELLIGENCE

Unfortunately, intelligence is commonly associated solely with cognitive intelligence (i.e. clever, academic people). However, intelligence incorporates much more. It includes - without limitation - emotional, interpersonal, social, creative, moral, spiritual, and physical intelligence. Intelligence can be natural, learnt in life or a mixture of both. People who hold on to Unhelpful Beliefs like "I'm not smart" may be focused only on cognitive intelligence, denying their other forms of intelligence.

Exercise: In what ways are you naturally intelligent? Going forward, how will you make the most out of this natural intelligence and build up other areas of intelligence?

STEP 7 – ADOPT OPTIMAL WORK & LEARNING STYLES

Many people believe they are stupid or no good, when what is really going on is a lack of understanding about how they work and learn best. For example, if you know that you learn better with others, you might set up a study group to "top up" and compensate for your work and learning style rather than just reading books to complete your assignment.

Exercise: Ask yourself the following questions to discover your optimal work and learning style:

- Do you prefer to work and learn using diagrams, pictures and images, sound and music, speech and writing, your body, hands and sense of touch or your logic, reasoning and systems?;
- Do you prefer to work and learn on your own or with others?;
- What useful tricks (i.e. word, alphabet and number associations, rhymes, songs, mind maps, repetition and/or testing) do you use to remember information?;
- What factors impact your ability to work and learn? Factors may include motivational levels, time of day, light, place, emotions, comfort, background sound, consumables (such as food, liquid and medication), sleep, energy, stress and anxiety levels, people and distractions (such as TV, phone, Internet, housework, personal administration, socializing, friends and family); and
- What will you do, going forward, to manage each factor directly above based on your experience of what has worked well and not so well in the past?

STEP 8 – REACTIVATE PASSIONS & HOBBIES

Passions and hobbies help build a healthier self-esteem by giving you fresh energy, vitality and life force. Do you know what your passions and hobbies are? They might include reading, walking, animals, dancing, music, travel, theatre, cooking, exercise, time with friends and family, art, fashion, community and charitable projects and/or competitive sports.

Exercise: Starting from today, what passions and hobbies will you reactivate in your life? If you don't know what your passions or hobbies are, dig out some photos of when you were younger and as you look at them, reflect on what you used to love doing and how might it translate into an adult passion or hobby. Alternatively, why not try a few new hobbies until you find one that you like.

STEP 9 – ADOPT A HEALTHY MANAGEMENT PLAN FOR DIFFICULT EMOTIONS

Difficult emotions are feelings that are hard to cope with (i.e. sadness, anger and boredom). If you don't know how to manage them in a healthy way, they can sink down and become toxic, producing self-esteem issues and physical and mental ailments and symptoms such as stress, anxiety and depression.

Exercise: You can do this exercise anywhere, anytime whenever difficult emotions come up. Close your eyes if appropriate. Scan your body and notice any sensations i.e. racing or heavy heart, tense shoulders, churned up gut, dull headache, blocked or dry throat. Sit with the sensation(s) until you notice what emotion comes up. Breathe the emotion in and out of the body for as long as it needs to burn off naturally. Afterwards, ask your inner wise self:

- Who or what triggered this emotion?;
- What it is about your past that made you react to this trigger?;
- If you could let this emotion run wild, what would happen?; and
- What could you do instead of letting the emotion run wild that is rational, balanced and constructive and will move you closer to your potential?

STEP 10 – BECOME BETTER AT GIVING AND TAKING FEEDBACK

Giving and receiving feedback constructively helps build a healthy self-esteem by building confidence in communication, assertiveness and authentic expression. When receiving feedback constructively, it also makes the feedback feel less like criticism or an attack and more about learning and moving closer to your potential.

Exercise: The next time you give feedback, try the following:

- Agree a time and place with the person to whom you are giving feedback and let them know roughly what it's about;
- Communicate in a way they will understand;
- Say why the feedback is important to you/what you want out of it;
- Be authentic;
- Back it up with clarification, evidence and/or examples;
- Focus the feedback on behavior or performance rather than the person themselves;
- Make sure your tonality and body language are not aggressive or critical;
- Own your own thoughts and emotions;
- Don't tell the other person what they think and feel;
- Check out any suspicions, hunches, intuition or imaginings;
- Be open to all possible reactions/responses without attachment to any expectations;

- Allow space and time for the recipient to give his or her feedback; and
- Follow the technique below when receiving feedback.

The next time you receive feedback try the following:

- Listen carefully and manage any difficult emotions that come up for you – STEP 9;
- Reflect back your understanding to check you have heard everything correctly;
- Ask for clarification, evidence and/or examples if needed;
- Dig deep and ask yourself whether there is anything constructive that you can take from the feedback, even if it only something small;
- Always remember that feedback often says more about the person giving it than you, so keep it in perspective; and
- Provide feedback following the technique above, or if you need time to reflect/respond ask for time out before getting back to them.

STEP 11 – NURTURE & SOOTHE YOURSELF

Nurturing and soothing are important to do and practice for the simple reason that they help you feel better about yourself. Nurturing and soothing might be as simple as having a warm bath, lighting a candle and getting to bed early.

Exercise: Starting from today, how will you nurture and soothe yourself better and how and when will you do this? If you don't know what nurtures and soothes you, think back to what nurtured and soothed you in the past or try and few new and different things until you find what works for you.

STEP 12 – DON'T DEFINE YOURSELF BY ANYTHING THAT COULD CHANGE

If you define yourself by things that could change in life (i.e. "I am young, I am a lawyer and I am a happy person") then there is a risk that you will feel a loss of identity and existence if you ever lose these things (i.e. get older, your job changes, you become unhappy).

Exercise: Write a list of all the things that you think you are. If you define yourself by anything that could change in life, have a go at re-wording each one so that they no longer define who you are. (i.e. I turned 38 this year, I currently work as a lawyer and sometimes I experience happiness). The change is only subtle and may even challenge traditional ways of communicating, but may help you build and fortify a stronger and more accurate sense of self that is not dependent on anything that might change in your lifetime.

STEP 13 – GET YOUR PRIORITIES STRAIGHT

"***Life Priorities***" are what you choose to spend your time and energy on and are forever changing. Life Priorities help build and sustain a healthy self-esteem if they are in tune with who you really are, your core values and your potential.

Exercise: Imagine that you only have a certain amount of time left to live and ask yourself what you would do with the remaining time. Start with 20 years left, then 15 years, then 10 years, then 5 years, then 1 year, then 6 months, then 1 month, then 1 week and then 1 day. As the remaining time gets less, it will reveal your Life Priorities in order of importance. Ask yourself: (i) how much time you currently allocate to these priorities (as a rough percentage); (ii) how much of your time and energy you would like to allocate to each priority; and (iii) what you are going to do to move this forward?

STEP 14 –COMPLETE TASKS, MAKE DECISIONS AND SOLVE PROBLEMS MORE EFFECTIVELY

If you don't do anything about an unhealthy self-esteem, then like a boat rudder, it steers you away from who you really are and your potential by making you feel less worthy, confident and capable. This may impact important decisions in life (i.e. whether or not you go for a job), how you solve problems and whether or not you set and accomplish tasks.

Exercise: The GROW model is a results-orientated model, extensively used by coaches around the world to help move clients forward. Follow a simplified version of this model below to set and achieve tasks, make decisions and solve problems productively and effectively.

- What is your **GOAL**?
- When you achieve it what will you do, be and have?
- What is your current **REALITY** ?
- Which **OPTIONS** are available to you?
- How will each option serve you and not serve you?
- Which one will steer you closer to who you really are and your potential?

- What is the first step if you choose this option?
- Which obstacles could get in the way and how will you manage them?
- How are you going to **WRAP UP**? i.e. what are you going to do, how will you do it, when will you do it and who and/ or what could help you?

STEP 15 – CELEBRATE FAILURE

One thing that successful people always agree on is that failure is critical to success. This is because the best lessons are usually learned from failure. It gives you important information about what works well for you and what doesn't. There is no such thing as a last chance, so why not celebrate failure and use it as a good opportunity for growth rather than fuelling an unhealthy self-esteem?

<u>Exercise:</u> Next time you think you have failed, call it an "outcome" instead of a "failure" and ask yourself what you have learnt from this outcome and what you will do differently as a result of this learning.

STEP 16 - PRACTICE SELF-SHRINKAGE

If you suffer from an unhealthy self-esteem, one way to make yourself feel better is to improve yourself. However for some self-esteem sufferers, the pressure to look better, work harder and be better can get out of control. The concept of self-shrinking is not about going backwards. Rather it is about counter-balancing the natural drive to improve self. Self-shrinkage includes downtime, sleep, rest, being still and just being, without doing or planning.

<u>Exercise</u>: Reflect on an average day and calculate how many hours you spend on self-shrinkage (including sleep time) and how many

hours you spend on doing, growing and striving. If the time spent on self-shrinkage is less, what could you do to practice more self-shrinkage going forward?

STEP 17 – PRACTICE MEDITATION

If you spend too much time in your mind and not enough time connected to your physical body, spirit and soul, you may lack the inner strength and consciousness to tackle your unhealthy self-esteem effectively. Meditation is a very effective way of achieving these connections and has a number of health benefits (Ornish.D. 1990).

Exercise: There are many different meditation techniques. It is important to try a few to find one that works for you. For a simple technique to get you started sit comfortably. If appropriate close your eyes and bring awareness to your natural breath in and out of the nose. Feel the belly expanding with every in-breath and collapsing with every out-breath. Scan your body from head to toe, toe to head and so on. As you scan, notice any physical sensations (i.e. tension, heaviness, tingling, tightness). If you detect a sensation, acknowledge it without attachment and then keep scanning. If your mind wonders off into thoughts, acknowledge them also without attachment and simply come back to the scanning. Continue for whatever length of period feels right for you i.e. 10 mins, 20 mins, 1 hr etc.

STEP 18 – BE COMPASSIONATE

If you experience an unhealthy self-esteem, it is very important to be kinder and more compassionate towards yourself. Working through these 20 STEPS will achieve this, but it is also useful to practice the compassion exercise below.

Exercise: Every morning when you wake and every night before you go to bed, breathe in all your pain, shame, anxiety and suffering. Breathe out an affirmation in the form of white light, making it compassionate, comforting and true to you. For example..... "despite my pain shame and suffering:

- I still love and respect myself;
- I am working on loving and respecting myself;
- It is normal and natural to have pain, shame and suffering; and/or
- It doesn't mean I can't also experience love, happiness and joy."

STEP 19 – ACCEPT THE PAST

If you are haunted by something in your past and can't seem to move on from it (i.e. loss, death, abuse, pain, shame or suffering) it could impact your self-esteem. For example, you might adopt the following belief: "I will always be a sad and miserable person". For some people, what helps is to treat it like a wound somewhere on the body that may be with you for the rest of you life and not something to get past, through or over. Rather, it is something that you need to live with and learn to treat and manage from time to time. Only when you start to accept a wound in this way will it be easier to live with and not overshadow who you really are and your potential.

Exercise: Imagine your wound somewhere on your body. It is not part of your unique personality or soul. Nevertheless it is something that happened to you and may stay with you until the day you die. Like any wound, it needs to be managed: checking it from time to time, keeping it clean, airing it out, allowing it to heal naturally and soothing it with ointment. Remember that if you look after your wound well, it can produce scar tissue, which is far stronger than the normal skin you had in the first place!

STEP 20 – TAKE GOOD CARE OF YOUR HEALTH

Tackling your inner saboteur and building a healthy self-esteem requires a certain degree of physical and mental health, strength and will power. For example if you are sick, tired and stressed, it might be harder to challenge your Unhelpful Beliefs. Taking good care of your health might include: doing exercise, eating healthy food, taking care about what you read, see and listen to (i.e. books, magazines, radio, TV, films), getting the right vitamins and minerals you need through food, supplements and sunlight, avoiding unhealthy toxins, chemicals and pollution, practicing stress management and relaxation techniques such as meditation and doing activities that boost energy and vitality.

Exercise: Write down the ways in which you currently take care of your physical and mental health? What will you do going forward to take even better care of your physical and mental health?

CONCLUSION

In order to really tackle self-esteem issues, you need to take a deep interest in yourself. By using these STEPS to practice important life skills and examine your inner reality, you will achieve mastery

And transform not only your relationship with yourself, but also your relationships with others, your dreams, goals and your life as a whole. As per the ancient quote....."As above so below, As within, so without" (The Emerald Tablet, circa 3000 BC),.....it is through hard work and deep inner exploration that we create and shape our lives in a way that is authentic and in line with our truest selves. Go within, or go without!

ABOUT THE AUTHOR

Michelle Lewis

Michelle has been working in the mental health field since 2001. She has a Bachelor's degree in Psychology from Weber State University and a Master's degree in Social Work from the University of Utah. She has spent her career working with adolescents and adults in a variety of treatment settings. Michelle is skilled at treating a variety of mental health issues, but specializes in emotional barriers to weight loss, emotional eating, binge eating, relationship issues, codependency, self-esteem and stress management. She has also worked as a health and wellness coach helping clients achieve their health goals.

Michelle is a contributing expert for GoodTherapy.org writing articles about weight loss, relationships, motivation and self care.

When she is not working, Michelle enjoys cooking, hiking, traveling and spending time with her husband and dog.

Contact:
7105 S Highland Dr. Ste 303
Salt Lake City, UT 84121
(801) 907-1391
www.slweightcounseling.com

THREE

Negative Self Talk and The Sabotage Cycle

Michelle Lewis

Negative self-talk is the accomplice to self sabotage. It is the little voice in your head that tells you all of the destructive statements that create the pattern of self sabotage. We consciously and unconsciously talk to ourselves continuously. Every time an event occurs, we have thoughts about them. At times, they are so automatic; we may not even notice them. Where do these thoughts originate? For most of us, negative self-talk can be a culmination of lack of resilience and past history which then leads to thoughts referred to as Cognitive Distortions. This literally means deformed thought and the terms thought distortion or thinking errors are used interchangeably. These thoughts become so much of a part of us, we struggle to separate ourselves which ingrains these beliefs to our core sense of self. These are the most common cognitive distortions described by psychiatrist David Burns, MD (1980) in his book "Feeling Good: The New Mood Therapy":

Common Cognitive Distortions

1. All-or-nothing thinking
2. Overgeneralization
3. Mental filter
4. Disqualifying the positive
5. Jumping to conclusions
    - Mind reading
    - The Fortune Teller Error
6. Magnification or minimization
7. Emotional reasoning
8. Should statements
9. Labeling and mislabeling
10. Personalization

From: Burns, David D., MD. 1989. The Feeling Good Handbook. New York: William Morrow and Company, Inc.

These thoughts are not pathological. In fact, we all have them from time to time, but when they occur in great frequency, they can crush our self-esteem and confidence. Left unchecked, these thought distortions lead us to believe the worst about ourselves and the world around us. This can create chaos in all areas of our lives. For the purposes of this chapter, I will focus on relationships and weight management.

Relationships

Negative self talk diminishes our self-esteem to the point that we don't feel like we are worth having healthy and positive relationships. We end up settling for friends and romantic partners who don't treat us well. This is often why people who grow up in abusive homes end up in abusive relationships as adults. Dysfunctional patterns have been role modeled early in their lives and the destruction creates life long consequences. When we are not shown healthy relationship dynamics in our childhood, we begin patterns of recreating those relationships throughout the rest of our lives. In our relationships, we teach people how to treat us. When we show people we can be treated badly, there are some people that will take advantage of that. We choose relationships with individuals who consciously or unconsciously recreate their own dysfunctional relationship patterns with us. Every time someone treats us badly and we don't say anything, we have just taught them that we condone their behavior and it is likely to continue. All too often, people do not have the confidence to stand up for themselves. We make such degrading comments in our heads that the words and actions of others just reinforce those statements and vice versa. This becomes a cycle that occurs over and over again.

Common thought distortions used in relationships are:

- **Disqualifying the Positive** - we shut down compliments people give us, we minimize the positive attributes we have to offer in relationships, and we can also minimize the positive things about our partners. When we disregard positive feedback, we feel even worse about ourselves. This also creates distance in our relationships because we never trust that our partners really mean the kind words they say. We do not believe that we deserve positive feedback and reject anything that does not fit with our negative self image.

- **Mind Reading** - we assume we know what our significant other is thinking and react accordingly. Often, we have incorrect information and it can have devastating consequences. In relationships we take words and behaviors out of context, misunderstand and assign arbitrary meaning. We think that it is too good to be true, so there must be something wrong with this person. We think that if they actually find out how awful we are, they will leave. Left to our own devices, we may notice that our partner is quiet and assume they are angry with us. Because we "know" they are angry, we will start to fume because they have no right to be angry, we have done nothing wrong. How dare they? When our partner does speak up, we bite their head off. Of course, they are taken aback because they have no idea that we have just created this entire situation in our head. In reality, your partner may have had a rough day at work and it has absolutely nothing to do with you.

- **Should Statements** - we think someone "should" or "shouldn't" behave in a certain way. When you direct should statements toward others, you feel anger, frustration, and resentment. Often, when we have patterns of self-sabotage that manifest in relationships, we don't feel like we deserve to stand up for ourselves and end up feeling resentful. This also often results in us behaving in passive-aggressive ways to indirectly vent our frustrations. We also think that our partners "should" do things exactly as we would like them to. We they don't, which is nearly guaranteed, we find ourselves boiling.

- **Fortune Teller Error** - if you have had a history of unsatisfying relationships in the past, you may feel that your current or future relationships are destined to end badly. Often when we struggle with self-sabotage, we will consciously or unconsciously sabotage our relationships in order to fulfill a self-fulfilling prophecy. In the case of self-fulfilling prophecy, you anticipate an outcome (usually negative) and look for evidence that reinforces that belief. The result is almost always what you anticipate because you actually create the outcome you fear out of your own anxiety.

- **Overgeneralization, All or Nothing Thinking and Mental Filter** tend to be varying degrees of perfectionism. We expect our partners or ourselves to be perfect and when we/they fall short, there is conflict. We are all human. No one, at least to my knowledge, is perfect. Yet, so many of us expect that of ourselves and/or our partners. If they make one mistake, we attack them with the words "always" or "never". How likely is it that they NEVER take out the trash? Well, if it is true, why do you keep asking and setting them up for failure? In happy relationships, it is said that there is a 5 to 1 ratio of positive to negative statements or interactions. In unhappy relationships, it is likely to be the opposite and people tend to underestimate the number of positive interactions even further.

- **Personalization** - we take responsibility for things that we did not cause. This often comes up in codependent relationships because we always feel responsible for our partners' feelings, mood, failures, etc. When you take on this responsibility, where does which leave them? Where does it leave you? Once you take responsibility for another person's problems, they have no incentive to take care of it themselves. Why should they when you have clearly taken care of that for them?

Weight Management

Food is love. At least that is what it feels like. Food can be a powerful drug to heal all wounds, at least temporarily. When that intoxicating feeling wears off, watch out.

Here are the common thought distortions that contribute to emotional eating and weight loss sabotage:

- **All or Nothing Thinking-** you see yourself as good or bad based on what you have eaten. You see yourself perfect in your eating and exercise habits or you are a failure. This is probably the most dangerous thought distortion with regard to weight loss and emotional eating. The difficulty with this distortion is that as a human, it is impossible, impractical and downright foolish to expect perfection. By engaging in this thinking, you will likely throw yourself into a binge cycle that will feel impossible to break. Once you take that first bite of ice cream, you may as well finish the whole carton and maybe start another. Overgeneralization and the Mental Filter feed into this as well. When you succumb to this perfectionistic thinking, you will never measure up and you will always be disappointed in yourself because no matter how much progress you make, it will never be enough.

- **Disqualifying the Positive**- someone says you look great and all you can think about is the ten pounds standing between you and your happiness. You only think about all of the things you hate about your body or think that the person doesn't really mean it, but only give you compliments to be nice. This puts you at risk for falling into the All or Nothing thinking pattern as well. We say things to ourselves that we would never say to another person. If you wouldn't think of saying something to another person, don't subject yourself to those criticisms either. Failing to recognize your positive attributes can lead to hopelessness.

- **Magnification and Minimization**- you exaggerate the importance of one action like overeating at lunch. You berate yourself which then tends to lead to more overeating. In the grand scheme of things, what is one lunch? You also minimize your progress. You have been working for months and have only lost five pounds. You compare yourself to someone at your office that has lost twenty. This will only lead to disappointment, anger and despair.

- **Emotional Reasoning**- you feel it and that makes it fact, right? Wrong! You may feel like a failure, but that doesn't make you a failure. Emotions are not evidence, yet so often we take them to be truer than anything in black and white. By challenging this distortion, you are able to see yourself and the world more clearly.

- **Should Statements**- you "shouldn't" eat that and you "should" exercise. When we create these expectations, we condemn ourselves when we don't follow through. Deep down, we are all oppositional teenagers. When told to do something or not to do something, we rebel. By using should statements, the likelihood you will follow through is slim. The likelihood you feel guilt, shame and disappointment his high. This will continue a cycle that will further diminish your self-esteem and confidence that you can succeed. Often should statements come out of what we think others will expect of us. So many people think that they should go on a diet or exercise because that is what society expects of them. For many women, diet and weight loss are among the top topics of discussion with their friends. There is so much pressure around this, the expectations feel insurmountable.

Of course, all of the Thought Distortions can show up in eating and relationships, but these examples tend to be the most prevalent. As you can see, they tend to create disastrous emotional consequences. The longer the pattern prevails, the more pervasive the damage becomes. Learning the cycle of the self-sabotage will help you understand why you behave in certain ways and you will learn to see your patterns ahead of time which will enable you to make changes.

The Behavior Chain below illustrates the pattern of self-defeat that is so commonly the result of distorted thoughts.

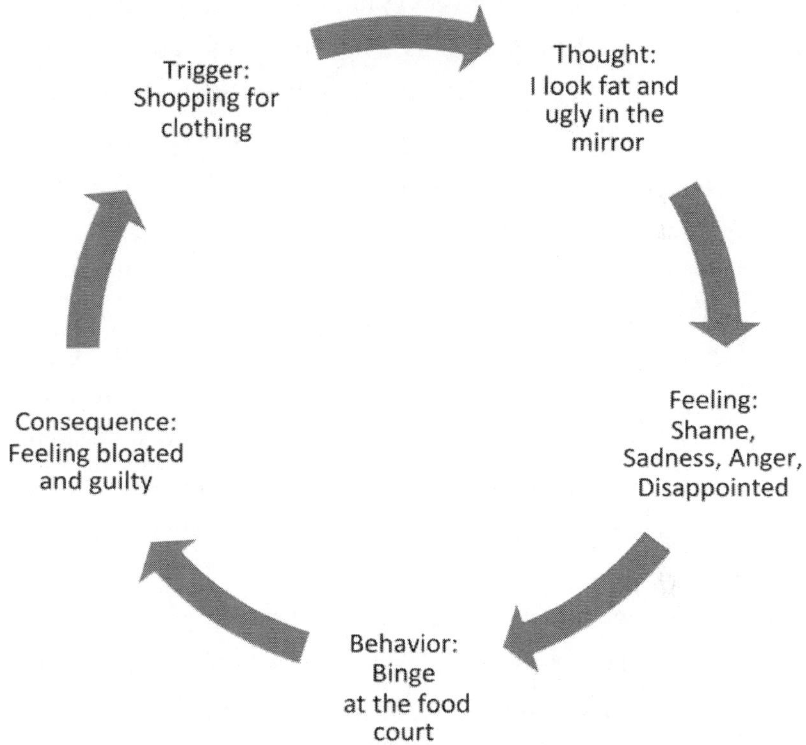

There are five elements to The Behavior Chain:

Trigger - the trigger is the catalyst or stimulus that begins the chain reaction. The trigger can be a person, place, memory, etc. In the example below, we will look at a trip to the mall to shop for clothing. As you know, shopping for clothing when you don't feel confident about your body can create a barrage of negative thoughts and emotions which sets the stage for self-sabotage.

Thoughts - often thoughts are initially missed in this chain. We are not consciously aware of many of our thoughts. They become so much a part of the ongoing chatter in our heads, that we are consciously desensitized. We are so connected to them, it feels impossible to separate ourselves. Although they are not conscious, they continue to do a fair amount of damage to our self-esteem. In situations where you find yourself feeling a strong negative emotion, the thoughts that we do experience in relation to the trigger are almost always distorted. If they are not distorted, the chain will not continue.

Feelings - we tend to notice feelings directly following the trigger. We tend to jump directly from the stimulus to negative emotions. We often see the trigger as the cause of our emotional state, but it is actually the thoughts that influence the negative emotions. In the example below, if you did not tell yourself you were fat and ugly, you would not feel the shame, sadness, anger and disappointed, you would not feel compelled to continue the cycle and act out. There would be no reason to engage in self-destructive behaviors if you were not attempting to soothe the intense negative emotions.

Behavior - as a result of the negative thoughts and feelings, we often feel the need to act out. This serves as a release for the built up negative emotion and serves as a temporary distraction from the feelings. A binge in the food court feels really good initially. It is an outlet for all of the angst you feel. Yet, it is only temporary. When you use something external, like food, to fill a void or soothe you emotionally, the effect will not last long and will only create more pain.

Consequences - after you act out as a result of the negative emotions, there are always consequences. Sometimes you may not notice them at first. The consequence of this example initially may be bloating and guilt, but the longer term consequences would be more shame and could ultimately lead to depression. The biggest consequence is that this perpetuates the cycle and becomes a new trigger. The longer you stay stuck in the cycle, the harder it will feel to escape it.

So, where do you break this cycle? The easiest place to create change is with your thoughts. Once you can identify the distorted thoughts, you can begin to challenge them. By challenging the thoughts, you decrease the intensity and frequency of painful emotions. Without the painful emotions, you will not have the urge to act out to avoid them. Without the behavior, you will not experience negative consequences. Alternately, the positive consequences you will experience will be an increase in your confidence due to your ability to challenge this pattern which will improve your self-esteem. By learning your patterns, you can begin to "play the tape through". This allows you to understand how your cycle, if left unchecked, will turn out. Understanding the chain of events in your pattern will enable you to make changes when you see the warning signs arise. By continuously challenging these thoughts, you will find more peace and contentment in your life. If you were able to let go of this negative image, what would change? For most people, this changes everything. Without the distorted thinking, you will feel more motivated and confident. Your self-esteem will reach new highs and you will feel hope to accomplish your goals. The key here is practice. Your negative self-talk did not form overnight and your new positive self-talk won't change as quickly either. By actively challenging these distortions, you can create a positive cycle of self-talk. Be patient with yourself and enjoy the journey to your new sense of contentedness!

References:

Burns, D. (1980). Feeling Good: *The New Mood Therapy.* p 32-41. New York: William Morrow and Company, Inc.

ABOUT THE AUTHOR

HUEINA SU

Hueina Su, MS, BSN, CEC is an internationally recognized expert in helping heart-centered, high-achieving women find the missing PEACE and POWER in their stressful lives. What sets her apart from other speakers and coaches is the 5,000 years of ancient Chinese wisdom behind her, and 4 generations of doctors, dentists and nurses in her family. She transformed herself from a painfully shy, insecure and suicidal young girl from Asia to a Black Belt, 10-time gold medalist, international keynote speaker, bestselling author and certified life coach. She is the bestselling author of *Intensive Care for the Nurturer's Soul*, and costar with Jack Canfield, Marci Shimoff and John Gray in the award-winning transformational movie *The Keeper of the Keys*. With 24 years of experience in nursing, counseling, coaching, speaking and consulting, Hueina is known for her wisdom, compassion, and the way she graciously blends Eastern philosophy and Western training in solving modern day problems. She is on a mission to inspire one million heart-centered, high-achieving women to nurture their true self, succeed on their own terms and create a life of their choice. Visit www.HueinaSu.com for more info about Hueina's programs, products, and free resources to help you claim your Peaceful Power for more inner peace, self-confidence and sustainable success.

FOUR

Taming the Invisible Chaos

Hueina Su, MS, BSN, CEC

Last summer, when I went to Taiwan to deliver a keynote speech at a medical conference, I came across a game show on TV in which teams from different organizations competed in various obstacle courses. One of the games had contestants cross a narrow bridge made of wood planks connected only by ropes -- with no railing or other support. As if balancing on that bridge wasn't hard enough, there were people under the bridge throwing dodge balls at the contestants, and a huge "wrecking ball" swinging back and forth in the middle of the bridge. So, the contestants had to cross the bridge, while trying to avoid being hit by the flying dodge balls or the swinging wrecking ball. How's *that* for a test of balance and agility?! Granted, the risk of injury was not as high as one would imagine, since the wrecking ball was probably made of heavy duty rubber, and there was a safety net underneath the bridge. Still, I'm sure it's nerve-wrecking to cross that bridge. Not surprisingly, very few people completed this challenge.

As I was watching the show, I couldn't help but think about how similar our modern life is to crossing that bridge. As a high-achieving, professional woman, you have so much on your plate. It's hard enough to keep *everything* in balance, while you are standing still. However, you can't stand still. As a high-achiever, you have to keep moving forward in order to reach your goals. Now, imagine yourself as one of the contestants in that game show. You have to keep your balance while attempting to arrive at the other side of the bridge (i.e. your goals). The dodge balls coming at you from all random directions are the little challenges along the way, and the wrecking ball represents the bigger setbacks and adversity you might encounter. Any one of these, big or small, could throw you off balance or, worse, knock you off the bridge.

Now, let's bring it to the next level. Imagine: while you are crossing the bridge, balls are flying, and you have a powerful tornado swirling *inside* of you. Does this make it easier or harder for you to keep your balance and cross the bridge? I bet you'd think it is harder. The internal tornado represents the invisible blocks and barriers that sabotage your success. You cannot see this internal tornado, but you can completely *feel* its power and see the devastating damages it leaves behind. That's why I call it the ***Invisible Chaos***.

After twenty some years of working with high-achieving professional women (and men), I have identified 8 major Invisible Chaos that almost everyone has to some degree, including myself. These Invisible Chaos are universal -- they affect people from all different age, gender, racial, cultural, economical, educational and professional backgrounds. Even the most driven, successful and wealthy people fall prey to the Invisible Chaos. In fact, I'd argue that the Invisible Chaos is *the* underlying root cause of stress, negative emotions, self-sabotaging behaviors, and a host of emotional, relationship or even health issues. **Chances are, you also have some of these Invisible Chaos. You have certain mindset, emotional and behavioral patterns that are counter-productive for achieving what you want in life and business. Otherwise, you would've achieved everything you have ever wanted, wouldn't you?**

If you were to change your self-sabotaging behaviors and achieve better results, it's not enough to treat the symptoms of the problem. That's like putting on a Band-Aid when you have a serious infection. **You must identify and treat the root cause of the problem, which is the Invisible Chaos.** I will show you what it is, how to identify your own Invisible Chaos, and the powerful 3-R process you can use to tame your Invisible Chaos.

Invisible Chaos

So, what is the Invisible Chaos? The Invisible Chaos is the internal, often invisible (subconscious) blocks and barriers that cause you stress, self-doubt and self-sabotaging behaviors. As I mentioned, I have identified 8 major Invisible Chaos that are commonly seen in almost everyone I've come across and worked with. They are:

1) I'm Not Good Enough

There are many variations of this belief, such as "not smart enough", "not pretty enough", "not young enough", "not thin enough", "not enough credentials or experience", etc. When you boil it down, the core belief is "I'm not good enough." I see this in many successful, high-achieving women. Despite all their impressive credentials and achievements, they never feel good enough inside. When you don't feel good enough, you often feel anxious, insecure and inadequate. You might try even harder to achieve more, in order to prove yourself (often at the cost of your own wellbeing). Or, you might feel resigned and sabotage yourself. Note that either way is self-sabotage for your long-term success and happiness.

2) I'm Not Worthy

You feel unworthy of your achievements, wealth, loving relationships, recognition, promotion, or anything good that comes your way. Even when you do accomplish something good, you quickly attribute it to luck or fluke, instead of acknowledging your own talents or efforts.

3) I Have to Please Everyone

It's hard for you to say no and you'd bend backwards to please and take care of *everyone*, even at the expense of your own wellbeing. When you disappoint others, you feel tremendous guilt and anxiety. The underlying message is, you are not as important as other people.

4) I Have to be Perfect

Perfectionism is prevalent in high-achievers. You feel that you have to be perfect all the time, or you are not good enough. Perfectionism often goes hand in hand with procrastination, because if you don't finish that project, nobody will know you're not perfect.

5) I Have to Compare with Others

When we compare with others, we tend to compare our less-than-perfect qualities or achievements with other people's Oscar-worthy performances. Instead of challenging ourselves based on our own goals and abilities, we feel inadequate and sorry for ourselves, beat ourselves up, and sometimes even sabotage ourselves to avoid competition.

6) The Four Fears

There are four major fears that hinder our success: fear of failure, fear of success, fear of rejection and fear of judgment. You might hold yourself back, sabotage your efforts, procrastinate, or not put in 100% efforts, in order to avoid disappointment when you fail. If you have fear of judgment or rejection, you might not go after that promotion, play small so you don't have to stand out or outshine others.

7) Past Traumas and Dramas

We all have negative experiences, emotional traumas and dramas. It's all part of the human experience. Problems arise when you cannot (or will not) let go of the past. You are not willing to forgive (yourself and others), let go of the negative emotions, and release the fear of repeating the mistakes and pain. Can you see how holding on to your past traumas and dramas can seriously sabotage your success and happiness?

8) Self-Limiting Beliefs

Here I am referring to beliefs that are limiting to your success. For example, because I am a woman (or certain age, race, educational background), I cannot be, do or have __________. Because it didn't work out for me in the past, it will never work out. You get the idea. For me, I used to believe that because I don't speak perfect

English, I cannot be a professional speaker or author; and because I'm not strong enough, I cannot learn martial arts. Today, I'm an international keynote speaker, bestselling author and champion Black Belt, because I released those self-limiting beliefs.

The 3-R Process for Taming the Invisible Chaos

Here is the powerful 3-R process that I use with my private coaching clients and audiences to help them tame the Invisible Chaos. It contains 3 steps.

- Step 1. Recognize the Invisible Chaos
- Step 2. Release the Invisible Chaos
- Step 3. Reclaim Your Peaceful Power

Step 1. Recognize the Invisible Chaos

Recognizing your own Invisible Chaos is your first step to changing your self-sabotaging behaviors. Can you see which of the 8 major Invisible Chaos is affecting your life and work? If you can't pinpoint which one, the following symptoms are tell-tale signs that you have the Invisible Chaos: frequent anxiety, self-doubt, feeling like an impostor, hard to rest or relax, can't say no to other people's requests, stuck in analysis paralysis, afraid of making mistakes or taking risks, procrastination, can't start or finish your projects, using distractions or addictions (such as food, alcohol, drugs, TV, Internet) instead of working on your projects, feeling inadequate, difficulty acknowledging your own merits and accomplishments, putting everyone's needs before your own, believing that people only like you for what you do/have but not who you are, etc.

Step 2. Release the Invisible Chaos

Now that you have identified your Invisible Chaos, you can work on releasing them. After twenty some years of working with high-achievers, I've found that even though there are many symptoms of the Invisible Chaos, there is a simple and graceful way to release them. **As I have illustrated earlier with the Band-Aid analogy, we must identify and treat the underlying root cause. When we treat the root cause, the symptoms disappear.**

What is the root cause then? Our self-sabotaging beliefs and behaviors may manifest in many forms; however, at the deepest root of roots is the belief "I'm not good enough". **This is the mother of all Invisible Chaos, the deepest root cause of self-sabotage. This is the core belief that produces all the other self-sabotaging and self-limiting beliefs and behaviors. And when you drill down to the deepest core of "I'm not good enough", you will find self-rejection. Plain and simple.**

Before your mind protests and tries to argue, complicate and over-analyze this concept, let's take a deep breath together and consider this: **If you truly love and accept yourself *unconditionally*, would you ever think or feel "I'm not good enough"?** Would you ever feel the need to please and compare with others, to always be perfect, fear criticism or rejection, afraid of making mistakes, do things that sabotage your own health, happiness or success, feel unworthy, speak of or treat yourself unkindly, or believe in any negative ideas about yourself?

The problem is, all of us, when we were very little, invariably received the message "I'm not good enough" from our parents and other care-givers. We accepted the belief without questioning, and internalized this and all the other messages derived from this core belief into part of our identity and self-concept. They became part of who we are. Sometimes you might even take pride in these self-concepts. For example, you might see or describe yourself as someone who is a hard worker, high-achiever, perfectionist, CEO of the company, or someone who is always supportive and available for everyone. Asking you to change is like asking you to get rid of a part of your self. This is why it is so difficult to change your self-sabotaging beliefs and behaviors.

Since who we are is fundamentally flawed, we try many different ways to become "good enough". Instead of focusing on who we are, we attempt to feel good *through* what we do and what we have. For some it might be more credentials, achievements, bigger house, corner office, more money, plastic surgery, working harder and longer hours, changing yourself in order to fit in a certain mold, etc. None of these tactics work in the long run, of course.

A much simpler and more graceful solution is to understand the truth about who we are, and release that which is NOT part of our true self. Let me use lotus flowers to illustrate. Lotus flowers grow in muddy water, however, they are never tainted. They remain pure and beautiful because they have an amazing self-cleaning ability to get rid of dust, mud, bacteria and other impurities in their environment. Our true self is like a lotus flower, and the Invisible Chaos is like the mud on the flower. When we were very young, the Invisible Chaos overwhelmed our inherent self-cleaning ability, and as a result, we were left with all the mud that landed on us. Over the years, the mud grew thicker, until we totally forgot what the flower actually looked like

without the mud. We now believe that the mud-covered lotus flower is who we are. If we can wash away all the mud, we will reveal once more the lotus flower with its magnificent beauty and purity, and we will understand that who we are inherently is more than good enough.

When you are stopped by self-sabotage, first, recognize which of the 8 Invisible Chaos is at play (there may be more than one). Then, ask yourself these coaching questions: Is this belief part of my true self or the mud on the lotus flower? Is it true? What evidence do I have that it's NOT true? Could the opposite be true or truer? If it is not true, what are other possibilities? What can I think/feel/do instead? Challenge your limiting beliefs. Chances are, you'll realize they are not true, and you can make a conscious choice to release them.

Step 3. Reclaim Your Peaceful Power

After identifying and releasing your Invisible Chaos, it's time to reclaim your Peaceful Power. **Peaceful Power is a state of being when you are fully aligned with your true self. When you are deeply rooted in your true self, nothing and nobody in the world can disturb your inner peace, and you are most powerful.** It amps up your own power and confidence but doesn't overpower others. That's why I call it Peaceful Power. In my work, I use many ways to help my clients connect with their true self and reclaim their Peaceful Power. For example, coaching questions and exercises, meditation, breath work, visualization, journaling, martial arts principles and movements, energy medicine tools and techniques, etc. My years of training and competition in martial arts taught me how to be calm, centered and confident no matter what, and I'm teaching the techniques to my private coaching clients. Everyone is unique and I've found that there are different combinations of tools and techniques that work for each person. Having a mentor/coach guide you through the process will be most beneficial.

One of the exercises I often do with my clients, is to visualize yourself as a mud-covered lotus flower, imagine growing deep roots into the core of the earth to ground yourself, and have the Spring shower gently wash away all the mud on you. Then envision yourself being embraced in pink healing light, surrounded by a group of beings representing unconditional love for you. They could be Buddha, Jesus, Kwan Yin, any religious or historical figures, or your own grandma who loves you unconditionally. Imagine seeing yourself through their eyes, and see how much love and admiration they have for you. Ask them for a message you most need to hear right now. When you get the message, thank them and return to here and now. Ask yourself: *"If I were good enough, I would __________"* and write down your answers.

Stopping self-sabotage is not a one-time event. The recognizing, releasing and reclaiming 3-R process is an ongoing process for personal growth. Every time you go through the process, you will become more confident and at peace with who you are. With practice and hopefully guidance from a mentor, you will advance on your journey of reclaiming your true self, inner peace, confidence, and all the success and happiness you truly deserve.

ABOUT THE AUTHOR

Gabriela Eikeland

Delivering nurturing care has been a long time priority for Gabriela Eikeland, founder of Womyn's Path of Healing center and Your True Strengths Life Coaching in Campbell River, British Columbia, Canada.

Ms. Eikeland offers a variety of healing and bodywork services, as well as life coaching and stress management coaching services to her clients. In addition to facilitating women's support groups, she conducts numerous meditation and healing workshops.

Prior to founding her center , Ms. Eikeland provided compassionate care to developmentally and physically disabled young adults.

A native of Germany, Ms. Eikeland brings a high degree of specialized knowledge to her clients. Having received her formal education at business college in Germany and Athabasca University, Alberta, Canada, she also trained, and holds diplomas and certificates, in Swedish massage, advanced reflexology and spa aesthetics.

In addition, she holds a doctorate in Naturology, and is certified in various holistic healing modalities including reiki level IV, hot stone therapy, sacred lomi lomi massage, iridology, lymphatic drainage, yogic stress management, yoga, and counseling. She also holds certificates in relaxation therapy and initiations in shamanic healing.

In addition to providing coaching services at her center, she also provides life coaching services to Fresh Start Health Retreat Center , Oyster River, BC, Canada.

Having raised three beautiful children, Ms. Eikeland resides in Campbell River, BC, Canada, with her husband Mark and she is proud grandma of two wonderful grandchildren.

FIVE

Empower Yourself through Stress Management

Gabriela Eikeland

Stress is defined as mental or physical tension or strain (Webster's New World Dictionary, 2000) and is a factor that happens to affect everyone's life. How various stress factors affect different people, however important such studies are, is not the objective of this paper. It is also not the objective of this paper to discuss stress as only relevant to work, relationships, finances, or time management issues.

The purpose of this paper is to look at the stress factors that are rooted in the patriarchal societies' interpretations of women's emotional competency. The paper will then continue to discuss beneficial stress management tools and strategies, including the significance of breath work .

Whether through dynamics that can go back as far as early childhood or through societal conditioning at large, we, as women, frequently hand over our power to notions that we are not in control of our emotions and, consequently, the many stresses in our lives. If we fail to understand the possible concepts of gender biases lingering behind those notions we will be left feeling dis-empowered to take charge of our emotional as well as physical well-being. We continue the learned behaviour of helplessness that keeps us questioning our emotional competency.

While it is true that we often have no control over what kinds of the stresses we will be confronted with on a daily basis, we do have control over how we manage those stresses. We must empower ourselves to take charge - and managing stress is all about taking charge: of our thoughts, emotions, and the way we deal with problems. We no longer can give in to a learned believe that allows for power-over dynamics.

The first step toward change is that we must allow ourselves to admit that some methods of coping with stress are not beneficial to our emotional and physical health. The important factor here is to pay attention to how we think. Approximately 60,000 thoughts that are running through our head every day (DeVillers, Julia. 2002) and all thoughts have certain qualities but some thoughts produce more stress by leading the attention toward doubts, fears and skepticism. Each time we think a negative thought about ourselves, we dis-empower ourselves and our body, mind , and spirit is affected negatively.

If we keep ourselves stuck in a thought pattern that is dis-empowering and depreciating of our experiences and of who we are, we remain stressed and we self-sabotage the required change in coping strategies. Knowing that as women we are in control and able to implement relevant coping strategies is the very foundation of effective stress management .

Adapting healthy stress management strategies is a process. It requires consistency and oftentimes it seems too big of a mountain to climb and hence, procrastination, a common obstacle, comes into play and serves as an excuse. We tell ourselves, consciously or subconsciously, that we need to do other things that a far more important than self-nurturing and taking care of our well-being. At this point it is imperative not to judge ourselves for it. We need to be aware of what is happening and recognise it for what it is: another negative thought pattern that does not belong to us – we have internalized years of conditioning and the time for change is now.

When women nurture and care they commonly extend nurturing and caring to family and loved ones.

Nurturing and caring for the "Self" often does not receive the same level of attention. This encourages the cycle of unhealthy and negative thoughts to continue and it limits women's opportunity for authentic self-expression. Establishing, and giving attention to, a healthy stress management routine plays an essential part in creating an authentic and healthy relationship with the "Self" that is free from biases and self-destructive thoughts and behaviours.

A woman's journey of discovering what healthy and effective stress management means for her and how to manifest it in daily life is a journey of reclaiming her inner power. It provides for the inspiration to break free from the shackles of limiting belief pattern and conditioning. It is a journey that brings forth the strength within. We are free to take charge and we are accountable for our own thoughts, experiences and behaviours – we reject the idea to be spoon-fed information that will have us conditioned to think according to standards that are not our own.

So how do we engage in a stress management process that is relevant for us women? This step entails that we look at some basic facts related to stress in general. Essentially, stress can be positive or negative. Positive forms of stress, or "eustress", is usually related to positive and desirable life events. "Eustress" provides the means to express motivation in our personal and professional life and feels exciting (Mills, Reiss, Dombeck.2008)

Negative forms of stress, or "distress", has negative implications and is often synonymous with anxiety or nervous tensions. The impact of stress can be physical, mental, emotional, and behavioural. The important thing to understand is that the body cannot physically make the distinction between "eustress" and "distress".

Both forms of stress, if experienced over a period of time, can cause exhaustion. As the body responds to physical or emotional stress, changes occur and the sympathetic nervous system prepares the body for action (unlike the parasympathetic nervous system which aids in the relaxation response) - a mechanism commonly known as the fight-or flight response.

These changes include increased heart rate, increased blood pressure, and secretions of hormones such as Noradrenaline, Serotonin and Dopamine. These reactions occur whether the stress is positive or negative in nature.

The body's fight-or-flight mechanism is absolutely essential if we are faced with an emergency situation. Continual exposure to stress, however, can compromise our ability to think clearly and can deplete the body's vital organs of nutrients and adequate blood supply.

Over time, this lowers the body's ability to cope with any additional forms of stress and lowers the functions of our body's immune system, which, in turn, provides for ill-effects on our physical, emotional, and spiritual health.

We now continue to look at what women can do to actively engage in a relevant stress management process that will alleviate the ill effects of stress on body, mind and spirit. It is important to remember that there cannot be a "one fits all approach". Each woman must find what resonates with her.

For the purpose of this paper we will explore two powerful stress management tools to help you get started on your journey.

Meditation

Meditation is the process of experiencing a state of complete awareness. It allows for complete clarity and can play a significant role in self-empowerment. It allows you to connect with your inner truth, with emotions and feelings that represent your authentic self.

The many emotional and physical health benefits may include:

* Reducing anxiety and aids in eliminating phobias

* Reducing stress and reverses the fight-or-flight reaction

* Creating a sense of inner calm

* Reducing cardiovascular problems

* Strengthen the immune system

* Decreasing chronic pain

* Lower blood pressure

But here again is it important to consider that there cannot be a "one fits all approach". The style of meditation and your meditation routine must resonate with you.

Reluctance toward meditation is often rooted in the idea that meditation sessions should be lengthy. This is not so. The key to reaping the benefits of your meditation routine is consistency. Start out slow – even if you only invest five or ten minutes each day – you will begin to notice a positive difference.

Another obstacle is that it can be difficult to stay focused during meditation as the mind tries to preoccupy itself with something else. Fortunately there are tools available to help you with this. Foremost, be gentle with yourself. Remember that your mind is designed to think. Telling your mind to stop thinking would be like telling your eyes to stop seeing. Don't try and force anything.

Here the use of an "anchor" word is helpful. An anchor word is a mental object you associate with a particular state of mind, in this case meditation. It could be the name of a person, a color, or a place. The important thing is that whatever you choose for your anchor word is something you associate with peace, calmness or anything else positive. The anchor word is not something you meditate on but rather it is used in order pull yourself back into meditation in case distracting thoughts should arise.

At this point, let's bring our attention back to some of the benefits of meditation. As listed, meditation can help reduce anxiety and aids in the elimination of phobia, it reduces stress and reverses the fight-or-flight response and creates a sense of inner calm. All of this may well warrant the question "Why".

The reason for it is that it all ties in with proper breathing habits: diaphragmatic breathing is one of the most important foundation practises for meditation. Diaphragmatic breathing triggers a relaxation response and allows for maximum inter-change of oxygen and carbon dioxide, maintaining the correct balance of both.

Shallow chest breathing on the contrary, the type of breathing we have become accustomed to, actually induces the fight or flight response in the body because this type of breathing signals the brain that a stressful situation is imminent and triggers secretion of large amounts of stress hormones in the adrenal glands. Shallow breathing can also disrupt the balance of oxygen and carbon dioxide, which makes us feel a need for more air and aggravates anxiety and stress symptoms (Moore, Shelley.2010)

Another profound aspect is that our bodies are designed to expel 70 % of toxins through breath! Looking at this number makes it self-explanatory just how important proper breathing is for our health and well-being.

All of this means is that we do not have to feel powerless when it comes to dealing with stress. Meditation practise and implementing meditation tools in your daily life will re-establish an internal balance; wholeness on the physical and emotional level.

Give yourself permission to try different meditation styles, such as guided meditation, walking meditation, candle gazing meditation, or silent meditation. There are great many choices and it is important that you find what works for you. One single most important aspect to remember is that the only thing you can do wrong is to think that you are doing it wrong. Rest assured that there are no wrong ways to meditate.

Yoga

Yoga postures tie together meditation and breathing exercises and serves as yet another tool on the stress management journey as it greatly benefits body, mind and spirit. Specifically, research shows that yoga can help manage anxiety, chronic fatigue, depression, stress and many other conditions. Yoga exercises do not have to be complex and strenuous to be effective. Here again - there cannot be a one fits all approach applies. There are many different styles of Yoga and it is well worth exploring the choices.

Yoga, as well as meditation, provide for great tools for self-empowerment because both practises teach how to take care of one's health on all levels: emotional, physical, and spiritual. These practises encourage a sense of self-worth and they also necessitate self-responsibility. Ultimately, these stress management tools are incredibly self-empowering because they allow us to manage and control different emotional states in healthy ways – as opposed to destructive ways. Most importantly, they encourage the process of transformation. Transformation is a process that must start from within and it may take time. This in itself might sound discouraging – but remember you are not alone. You are never alone in your struggles; women are connected through a bond of strengths that has, as her/history has shown, defied even the worst of insults.

We as women are often very familiar with the concepts of self-doubt. Society has taught us the dynamics of second guessing ourselves for far too long. It is time to take back, and take control of our emotional competency. We have the power and the ability to take charge of our emotional, physical and spiritual well-being. It is a choice we must permit ourselves to make. This is what stress management is all about: It is all about energy and where we choose to put that energy. Yes – we do have that strength! As soon as you engage in this process and you hold yourself accountable for following through – you are on your way to stress management that is authentic and therefore empowering.

Self-doubts and second guessing ourselves result in coping techniques that are destructive and self-sabotaging and are made of nothing other than the energy of fear. This fear has been entrenched into our hearts and souls by means of patriarchal ideologies. It does not belong to us. If we allow this fear to dictate what directions in life we are taking then it becomes the dis-empowering entity that keeps us from moving forward and from taking charge of our well-being.

We have the power to guide ourselves to think and act in ways that benefit us emotionally, physically, and spiritually. Our thoughts affect how we feel and our emotions are deeply implicated in the restoration of health (Mate, Gabor. 2003) on all levels. There is an abundance of resiliency and strengths within each woman and we must empower ourselves to scrutinise our surroundings as well as actions that are conducive to self-sabotage. This will allow us to engage in the necessary changes. It is a process that requires us to take one step at the time. Positive changes may not come overnight but through relevant stress management we have the ability to bring back to its rightful place our authentic self - authentic self that is free from the restraints of patriarchal misinterpretations.

References:

DeVillers, Julia (2002). *GirlWise: How to be Capable, Confident, Cool, and in Control.* California.

Prima Publishing

Harry Mills, Ph.D., Natalie Reiss, Ph.D. and Mark Dombeck, Ph.D. (2008). http://www.mentalhelp.net.

In *Types of Stressors (Eustress vs. Distress)*. Retrieved July,10, 2011, from http://www.mentalhelp.net/poc/view_doc.php?type=doc&id=15644.

Gabor Mate M.D (2003). *When the Body says No.* Toronto Vintage Canada

Moore, Shelley. (2010). www.livestrong.com. In *Benefits of Diaphragmatic Breathing.*

Retrieved September 08, 2011, from http://www.livestrong.com/article/93768-benefits-diaphragmatic-breathing.

Notes:

ABOUT THE AUTHOR

Janet Stevenson, BA (Hons), Cert FE

Janet Stevenson is founder and owner of Train2Grow Consultancy and Achieve Insight Coaching. She is a professional Training Consultant and qualified Teacher, Coach and Counselor. Her passion is to help people grow, become more fulfilled and achieve success in every aspect of their lives.

Janet specializes in personal development and has empowered, trained and coached individuals and groups to set and exceed goals, find fulfilment, and realize their dreams both personally and professionally. She is a licensed Springboard trainer - a personal development program for women - and runs Leadership for Women, 'Kickstart' and 'Empower' women's programmes.

Other seminar topics include Leadership, Management, Counselling, Coaching, Mentoring, Building Better Relationships, Doing Business Across Cultures, Train the Trainer, Interpersonal Skills, Influencing, Assertiveness & Managing Conflict, in addition to the women's programmes above. Janet's training style is highly participative, using brain-friendly techniques, and her coaching style has been described as "life-changing, intuitive and insightful". Her clients are from both the private and public sectors, and include banks, hospitals, universities, councils, as well as small businesses.

She has been published in Training Journal, Executive PA and Families First magazine. She is also a contributing author to The Power of Woman, How to Break the Glass Ceiling Without a Hammer, Madam CEO, Leaders in Pearls and The Power of God. Janet is a Master Practitioner of NLP and Non-Verbal Intelligence, a member of the Institute of Leadership and Management, member of the British Institute for Learning & Development, member of the Academy of Professional Coaching, member of International Coach Federation, member of European Mentoring & Coaching Council & member of the Professional Woman Network.

Contact:
Mrs. Janet Stevenson
info@train2grow.co.uk
www.train2grow.co.uk
www.achieveinsight.co.uk
Tel + 44 1293 614624 or +44 7801 479801

SIX

Steps to Self-Awareness

Janet Stevenson

'But I do nothing upon myself, and yet I am my own executioner'
—John Donne

We could all do with the ability to overcome self-sabotage and stop being our own executioner. What does it mean to do this? Alyce P Cornyn-Selby says, *'Self-sabotage is when we say we want something and then go about making sure it doesn't happen'*. It sounds crazy that any of us should do this, but we do!

This chapter enables you to overcome self-sabotage by taking you on a journey to greater self-awareness. This, according to Billie Jean King, '*is probably the most important thing towards being a champion.*'.

Step #1 Become Consciously Aware

We all self-sabotage to some degree, but we need to be consciously aware that we are doing so if we are to address it. '*Until you make the unconscious conscious, it will direct your life and you will call it fate*' – Carl Gustav Jung.

The following questions are designed to bring self awareness. Check those that are true of you.

Do you have grand plans to do things 'one of these days' but fail to get going on them?	
Have you been working on something important which is still outstanding, when you've had more than enough time to complete it?	
Do you often find yourself making excuses and blaming people, situations or circumstances, when explaining your lack of progress to others?	
When you make a mistake, do you beat yourself up with self-criticism and then use it as a reason to stop trying?	
Do you spend too much time on social media or other things, or put trivia before what's important, and then feel guilty for not achieving what you wanted?	
If you have managed to stop a negative habit and have achieved your goal, do you then slip back into old habits a few weeks or months later?	
Can you be relied on to do the things you say you are going to do (whether said to yourself or others)?	

Do you conform to how you think others want you to be, and then feel uncomfortably inauthentic for not showing the real you?	
When you are asked to do something that you don't want to do, do you find yourself agreeing and then feeling resentful? Or guilty if you refuse the request?	
Do you regularly rebuff compliments and encouragement, when you'd really prefer to receive and embrace what's being offered?	

Step #2 Be curious

Give yourself the permission to ask questions, to be curious, to explore, to wonder. *'Who looks outside, dreams; who looks inside, awakes'* – Carl Gustav Jung. Plan some undisturbed 'me' time every day to do this, without personal criticism but out of pure curiosity. Ask for input from those who know you well too, because their perspective will provide you with insights and awareness of blind spots. I strongly recommend you record your thoughts in a journal.

Day 1	What sort of things do I put off doing? What's my earliest memory of doing this? What am I saying to myself when I put things off?
Day 2	What is important to me about the issue that I've been slow to progress? Is it really important to me or is it someone else's?

Day 3	How often do I say "should" and "ought" and "must" when talking about things I plan to do to? Who says I ought to do them? What would happen if I didn't?
Day 4	What issues have I been making excuses about? How often do I do this? Do I need to excuse myself anyway?
Day 5	How often have I complained about people or things in the past week when things went wrong? Does the fault really lie with them? What's my part in it?
Day 6	When I make a mistake, what is my response? Whose voice from the past do I hear criticising me? When is something good enough?
Day 7	If I had access to unlimited resources and I knew I could not fail, what would I do? What resources would I tap into? Whose brains would I pick?
Day 8	I've been keeping this journal for a week now. What am I noticing? What am I learning? What am I allowing to get in the way of doing it?
Day 9	When am I at my most creative? What words do I hear or what do I say to myself when I am in the flow? Where do these words come from?
Day 10	When do I feel de-skilled and useless? What words do I hear or what do I say to myself when I'm feeling like this? Where do these words come from?
Day 11	How often do I lose or misplace things that are important? When does it happen? What stops me from putting them away where I'll find them again easily?

Day 12	What gives me the greatest satisfaction in my life? How often do I make time for this? What gets in the way? How much control do I have over it?
Day 13	What have I agreed to in the last few days that I'd have preferred not to? How often does this happen? What stopped me from saying no? What would happen if I did?
Day 14	How often do I struggle on when I could really do with help? What stops me from asking for help? What do I imagine would happen if I did?
Day 15	How often do I say I'm going to do something and then don't do it? What do I say to myself when I don't follow through? What would help me to do so?
Day 16	How frequently do I agree with others, rather than say what I really feel? What do I gain? What price do I pay for not voicing my opinion?
Day 17	I'm halfway through the month of writing my journal. What am I aware of that I wasn't aware of before? What insights have I gained? What's difficult?
Day 18	When someone pays me a compliment, how do I tend to respond? How do I think the other person feels when I do that? How would I like to respond?
Day 19	When someone invades my space/gives me unwanted attention, how do I respond? What happens to my self-esteem when I do that? What would I prefer to do or say?

Day 20	How often do negative things or misfortune happen to me? What's my response to this 'bad luck'? What part do I play, if any, in enabling them to happen?
Day 21	To what extent do I find myself adapting to how I think others want me to be? How would it be if I let the real me out? What would I gain/lose?
Day 22	When I've set myself a target (e.g. getting fit, stopping smoking) and achieved it, how quickly do I slip back into old habits? What do I say to myself?
Day 23	I'm now three-quarters of the way through the month. What's most significant thing that I've become aware of? What's surfacing for me?
Day 24	How frequently do I feel unworthy or unloved? What triggers this? What reinforces it? What do I need to feel worthy or loved?
Day 25	How often do I start things enthusiastically and then give up? To what extent do I make the task harder than it needs to be? What stops me from succeeding?
Day 26	To what extent do I take too much on and then have to rush to get things done? What effect does this have on the quality of what I do? How would it be to do less?
Day 27	How much do I allow others to know what's going on inside me? How would it be to voice my feelings more openly? What do I think would happen if I did?

Day 28	To what extent do I avoid challenges? When do I do this? Whose voice do I hear stopping me? What do I fear would happen if I took on a challenge?
Day 29	How aware am I of stress in my body? How do I release stress? How helpful is that strategy? Who could help or support me?
Day 30	What do I consider to be my strengths? What do I think are my weaknesses? How would others describe me? How would I like to be described?
Day 31	What are my hopes for the future? What would I most regret not having done in ten years' time? How do I want the rest of my life to be?

If you've been doing this conscientiously, you'll now be at the end of your first month of journal writing. Take time to review what you have written, and highlight key insights.

Step #3 Know what drives you

'Behavior is the mirror in which everyone shows their image' —Johann Wolfgang von Goethe. Drivers – or working styles – are distinctive behaviors that we consistently display. Knowing our key drivers provides insight into ways we may self-sabotage. To identify yours, read the statements below and score as follows: 2 – very true of me; 1 – somewhat true; 0 – not like me at all. The total for each set of statements goes in the emboldened box.

1

Things must be done right and I'll often rework them until they are		
People would describe me as a perfectionist		
I like to prepare things thoroughly and well		
I like to make sure I've crossed all the *t*'s and dotted the *i*'s		
I have high standards and expect them of others too		Total
I get irritated when others pay scant attention to detail		

2

I get frustrated when people pay too much attention to detail		
I have a fast work rate and achieve a lot in a short space of time		
I usually arrive barely on time or late to appointments or meetings		
I get things done quickly and don't like wasting time		
Sometimes I make avoidable mistakes rushing to complete on time		Total
I get bored when things go on too long		

3

I am naturally empathic and intuitive of people's feelings		
I find it hard to say no when people ask me to do things		
I prefer working in groups or teams to working alone		
I am concerned about the well-being of others		
I like to build good relationships and to get on well with people		Total
I believe harmony and friendliness are important		

4

It's important to be tough and resilient if you want to survive		
I believe logic is more important than feelings		
I'm the one who can be counted on to keep a cool head in a crisis		
I value fairness, honesty and directness		
I prefer to keep my feelings to myself		Total
I prefer to work by myself most of the time		

5

I enjoy challenges and the prospect of starting new projects		
People would describe me as keen, motivated and enthusiastic		
I get interested when I hear what others are involved in doing		
I often start new tasks, even when others aren't completed		
I often multi-task or have several projects on the go at once		Total
I tend to start things with enthusiasm and then lose interest		

Scores of 8+ are strong drivers. You may have just one that stands out or several, and it's the combination that makes you unique. None is better than another, as they all have advantages and disadvantages. Here are the descriptions of each driver:

1 Be perfect You don't like making mistakes nor do you like having others point them out. You're critical of yourself and others, and notice anything that falls below par quickly. You don't like delegating and do not tolerate fools gladly. You're accurate, efficient and thorough but cannot be relied on to produce work to deadlines. You expect high standards of yourself and others but may fail to recognise when something is good enough.

2 Hurry up With one eye on the clock, you work quickly and get lots done in a short time. You respond well to short timescales, as your energy peaks under pressure. You tend to take on too much, juggle tasks and miss some deadlines. While your output is high, quality suffers in your haste to finish. You can come across as impatient with 'slower' people. You find it difficult to relax and feel guilty when you do have some leisure time.

3 *Please others* You're a good team player, and enjoy being with others. You are naturally empathic and understanding of others' needs but often don't recognise what your own are. You strive to keep everyone happy and don't like saying no. As you're considerate and sensitive to people's feelings, you tend to hold back from giving your opinion or challenging ideas (even if wrong) and are reluctant to criticise.

4 *Be strong* You are rational, reliable, steady and calm. You see inability to cope as a weakness, and feel you should be able to manage whatever comes your way. You're resilient and will work long hours on your own, often pushing yourself to extremes. Your independence and pride stop you accepting or asking for help, even when you need it. While you handle people firmly and fairly, you come across as emotionally detached and aloof.

5 *Try hard* You love new projects and tasks and tackle them enthusiastically. However, you're more committed to trying than succeeding, and your interest wears off before the task is finished. You tend to turn small jobs into large ones, as you investigate all possibilities and aspects. You're great at motivating others, but they can become frustrated and confused when you sidetrack and play havoc with the time schedule.

Our drivers can help us to achieve. However, perfectionism, haste, pleasing others, avoiding emotions, procrastination, refusing help, multi-tasking, having too many things on the go, etc can also be forms of self-sabotaging behaviour. When do your drivers push you too far? How can you stop them driving you to self-sabotage?

Step #4 Be present

It is easy to lose present focus by worrying about some future event; or by reflecting negatively upon the past for what we said, did or did not do. With our mind elsewhere, we switch to 'autopilot', paying scant attention to the current moment. When we do this, thoughts, feelings and sensations trigger more easily old and unhelpful patterns of self-sabotage.

Being present means bringing your attention to the now. It means being mindful of what you don't normally notice, aware of the present moment with its rich mix of sensory details, thoughts and emotions. Try to do this regularly, noticing what your body is feeling, the sounds you hear, the colours and shapes you see, the inhaling and exhaling of your breath. When thoughts intrude – as they invariably will – simply observe them, and then bring your attention back to the present.

The more you practice this, the easier it will become, and you will start to notice how thinking patterns and feelings build up towards a reaction. This awareness equips you to decide consciously what you pay attention to and how you want to respond.

Step #5 Make conscious decisions

Both conscious and unconscious decision making can leave us open to self-sabotage. For example, you may have consciously weighed up the pros and cons, come to a conclusion about what was best, and then done the very opposite. Was it your decision or was it someone else's? Did you really want to do it, or was there a 'should' in there somewhere?

We make unconscious decisions all day long, such as which fingernail to paint first, or where to dip our spoon in a bowl of cornflakes. This is just as well because if we pondered over every decision, we'd get nothing done! But when we fail to make a conscious decision, such as how to spend our time, we drift aimlessly through the day spending our precious moments on trivia.

Conscious decision making is an antidote to self-sabotage, but there are some conditions attached to it. It must be what you want, aligned with your values and you must follow it through. However it's not a straightjacket. If further information comes to light and you realise you made the wrong decision, then consciously change it! '*You are in control of your life ... You are what you are because of the conscious and subconscious choices you have made*'—Barbara Hall.

Step #6 Make yourself accountable

When you make a decision, following through becomes much easier when you make yourself answerable to someone.

- Ask a friend or colleague to be an 'accountability partner' to check in with you and follow up on your progress.
- Consider working with a coach to keep you on track and help you overcome blocks and obstacles that stand in the way of your progress.
- Give yourself a date for completing your tasks and put them in your schedule. No deadline = opportunities for self-sabotage.

Now make a list of the things you want to accomplish and how you will make yourself accountable.

Task	Time needed	Deadline	Whose help do I need? Who will hold me accountable for this?

If you've worked through this chapter with care, you will now be much clearer about when and how you sabotage yourself. And remember, these steps to self-awareness constitute a journey – not a destination – so revisit them regularly to avoid slipping back into old habits.

Notes:

ABOUT THE AUTHOR

Christine Sopa

Christine Sopa, founder of *Chris Sopa International, Inc.* and internationally renowned inspirational speaker and author in the field of self-improvement, is one of the emerging thought leaders in how changing your thoughts change your world. Her interactive facilitating style, humor and healthy dose of spirituality allow her workshops and keynotes to be a safe-haven for looking into your own soul to see where transformation can renew your love of life. Chris is known for her expertise in organizational change and behavior as well as performance enhancement and motivation in organizations throughout the globe. Chris possesses a Bachelors Degree in Biology, Pre-Medicine from Bowling Green State University and a Masters Degree in Industrial/Organizational Psychology form Capella University. After healing herself from a life-threatening, stress related illness; Chris made it her life purpose to help empower others to heal themselves by changing how they think and view the world around them.

Chris also guides individuals on journeys to sacred sites around the globe such as Machu Picchu and Greece to continue their personal development through challenging them in a "non-ordinary" environment to face their fears, behavior patterns and conditioning that has shaped their lives thus far.

Chris is the author of *"Choosing the Life You Were Born to Live: How Changing Your Thoughts Will Change Your Life"* published by Balboa Press.

Chris lives in Scottsdale, AZ and has two grown daughters. You can contact her by mail at PO Box 27871, Scottsdale, AZ 85255, through her website at www.chrissopa.com, or via email at chris@chrissopa.com.

SEVEN

Your Relationships Are Only As Healthy As YOU Are

Christine Sopa

Know that your true happiness is found not through someone outside of you, but with you alone.

We all seek them. We all cherish them. We all learn from them. The relationships we hold with the people in our lives are the very things that help define us, teach us and allow us the space to learn how to love ourselves. Relationships are the one area in our lives from which we learn our greatest lessons. Whether it is our relationship with our children, our significant other or a dear friend, all relationships serve as a mirror in which we are able to glimpse a view of the exact things we need to work on in our relationship with ourselves.

In every relationship you find yourself in right now, you are playing a role and so is the other person. People come in and out of our lives for a reason and always at the perfect time. We serve as teachers for each other and those who undoubtedly cause us the most pain are, by far, our greatest teachers. They teach us how to look within ourselves, as we try to overcome the pain we feel, so we can thrive, learn and move on to be that much better in our next go-round. Every relationship we are in gives us an opportunity to learn something new about ourselves. Ultimately, knowing ourselves is the key to having amazing relationships.

How Well Do You Know Yourself

"There is a circular relationship between our ability to know and love one another and our ability to know and love ourselves."
—Charlotte Kasl, "If the Buddha Dated"

I would like you to ask yourself the following questions but I want you to do it in a specific way. I want you to answer these questions twice: the first time after you have thought about your response for a minute and the second time, after a short break, answer with your immediate, intuitive response. Have two columns and place your answers next to each other.

- What do you most need right now?

- What do you most want right now?
- What is your deepest fear?
- What is your biggest dream?
- What do you need to be happy?
- What is your greatest strength?
- What is your biggest obstacle?
- In what area are you your own worst enemy?
- What is the most satisfying part of your life?
- What is missing in your life?
- Where would you like to see the most change in the next year?
- What is your life purpose as you see it right now?

Do you see any patterns in your answers? How easy or hard was it to answer these questions?

Many of us go about life on autopilot, allowing those around us to dictate what we do and what we think about ourselves. How aware are you of yourself? What are your beliefs about yourself and where did they come from?

The majority of our thoughts about ourselves are not ours but have come from other people in our lives; parents, friends, religious figures, society, you name it! This is called conditioning. Your conditioning spans to every area of your life, including how you feel about yourself. Your mind is a very powerful tool and dictates your thoughts which in turn dictate how you feel. It is helpful to understand exactly how your mind works and for the purposes of the discussion here, we will make it simple. Your mind is basically divided into two sections: the conscious and the subconscious. Your conscious mind is your filter. It is your center of choice. It is that part of your brain that has the ability to choose whether to accept or reject any bit of information that enters your awareness. The subconscious mind can only accept the information it gets from the conscious mind. It does not have the ability to choose. It assumes that what you choose in your conscious mind is what you want. Your subconscious mind cannot decipher between what you want or don't want, what is good or bad, right or wrong, happy or sad, positive or negative, etc. It assumes that what enters from your conscious mind is *the truth.* Even if what you are telling it is negative. The subconscious mind expresses itself mainly through your behaviors. Over 90 percent of your behaviors come directly from this part of the mind! Every thought that we have generates a feeling and everything in life, every choice, and everything we choose to do or not do is based on how we feel. This feeling then drives an action.

Ultimately, what drives the decisions we make regarding relationships is the how we feel about ourselves.

How Do You Really Feel About Yourself?

You wouldn't worry so much about what people really thought of you if you knew just how seldom they do. —Anonymous

One area of my life I personally have to really pay attention to in regards to how I feel about myself is in my romantic relationships. When those little heart strings start to stir because of someone special in our lives, we tend to forget that we are the ones in control. In the past, I always had a habit of adjusting "who I was" to fit the person I was with so they would like me. I would never do this to a drastic measure, of course, but enough that I was not truly being myself. These things would always be what I thought were little things, such as not speaking up if something was said with which I didn't agree, not mentioning a certain thing I liked or didn't like, or just simply holding back my enthusiasm for something we would experience so the person I was with didn't think I was "weird." We are meant to express and be who we are, so when we suppress any part of ourselves, we trigger a stress response within us. We start to become very critical of ourselves, which in turn causes us to be very critical of other people. How we feel about and treat others is always a reflection of how we feel and treat ourselves. Our minds start to race and we do not know what is right and what is wrong anymore. We lose who we are in the other person. When we allow this to happen, we lose our center. Our center is that place we can come back to when we are feeling "off" to re-group and get our head back together—or said differently, to remember who we are. You only have a "center" if you have self-esteem.

Having self-esteem, or said a different way, valuing yourself, allows you to know what you are worth having in any relationship and what you are worth *not* having. Self-esteem allows you to set the boundaries needed to show others how you want to be treated in the relationship.

Where Are Your Boundaries?

One of the most unique and beneficial gifts we can give ourselves is to know our own personal boundaries.

When we hear the word "boundaries" we immediately think about a boundary as something that keeps something or someone *out.* A boundary's purpose is never to keep a person or thing out necessarily, but to "draw a line in the sand," so to speak, as to how you want to be treated. It is a matter of what you will and will not tolerate. Boundaries are all about your personal space and the protection of that which you hold most sacred: You.

In life, we only ever get what we tolerate and settle for and when you honor yourself and hold yourself in esteem, there are new rules. There have to be "safeguards" in place in order to support and protect the space in which you now operate, keeping it pure for those things which you want to create in your life.

Your personal boundaries begin in your mind. You need to decide which behaviors from others support the new you and which do not. Some may come to mind immediately. Examples of healthy boundaries include not allowing a particular person to raise their voice to you anymore, not going to certain low vibration places, such as bars or pubs, not consuming certain foods or beverages, and so forth. Others may suddenly appear when you find yourself in a particular situation, and you realize: "This behavior is not working for me anymore." Through your feelings, learn to become aware of when you lose your power and to what or whom. The minute you start to feel "bad" (not in a state of joy) or "in your head," you know you have lost your power. Call it back by taking a deep breath and re-centering. Remember, no one thing or person can make you feel powerless; only you can do that.

The most important boundaries, however, aren't related to outside things and people, but instead are connected to our own thoughts and behaviors. You may want to call these "self-disciplines" rather than boundaries, but whatever you call them, you need them to keep yourself in check and on track. Decide which thoughts and behaviors support the "new you" and which do not.

In any relationship, ask yourself the following questions:

- Does this relationship empower me?
- Does this relationship make me want to be better than I am or less than I am?
- Are my decisions in this relationship being empowered by my higher self or by ego?
- What are my non-negotiables or "deal-breakers" in a relationship? (Example: honesty, loyalty, keeping your word, etc.)

Defining your boundaries develop the muscles of your soul. People with well-defined boundaries are the people who you can trust the most. They are the people who tell you how it is in a loving way and honor themselves. No one should ever be asked to compromise "who they are" for the sake of *any* relationship!

Be Your Own Parent

Relationships always come in the form of what you need, not necessarily what you want.

In any relationship, the only thing you are ever responsible for is your half of that relationship. You have control over how you communicate, how you respond to any given situation, who you are and what you do. Mistakes happen all the time in relationships, especially around communication. It is always better to make an honest mistake and learn from it than to follow the external cues from another and act in a way that is not in alignment with who you really are.

In raising children, part of the role of a parent is to guide, teach and lead by example. When our children make a mistake, we don't belittle them but we show them where they made a poor choice and teach them what would be a better choice the next time. We point out to them where the patterns are in their behavior that are not serving them and allow them to learn by experience. We can never take away another person's lesson. That is not our role. Our role is to serve as teachers for each other by how we act and what we say.

Learn to be your own parent. Allow yourself to be aware of your own behaviors. Look at your life from two points of view; from the participant and from the observer. The participant is the one actively making the choices and carrying them out. The observer is simply watching the choices made and questioning if they are the highest choices for that particular situation. The observer is objective and teaches the participant a possible better way to do it next time.

Observers can ask themselves the following questions and not be afraid of the answers or the change that needs to occur to move forward:

- Where do I get "hooked" in relationships? (In other words, where do I feel as if I lose control?)

- Can I call myself out on and identify my own mistakes and admit to the other person that I was "wrong?"

- Do I see any patterns in my relationships? Do I constantly attract the same type of person or situation and if so, why?

Be honest with yourself and take care of *you* the same way you would take care of those you love.

F.E.A.R.

Fear is simply False Evidence Appearing Real.

Sit down right now with a piece of paper and a pen and list all of the fears you have around relationships. Are you afraid of being alone the rest of your life? Are you afraid someone you care about won't approve of you if you do what you really want to do? Are you afraid of truly being yourself in any relationship for fear of rejection?

Now I want you to answer this question for every fear you listed: *Who would you be without that fear? How would you act if that fear did not exist?*

Fear is like the darkness. When you shine a light into the darkness, the darkness no longer exists. When you identify and face your fears, they no longer exist. Your awareness of them and your courage to face them takes the juice right out of the lemon! Remember that even if you get hurt in a relationship that hurt means you are at least feeling something…it means you are *alive!* Decide starting right now to live your life according to your dreams and not your fears. Be grateful for the life that you have, fears and all, and do something you fear every day. You will find that every day you are then one step closer to your dreams and a truly authentic relationship with not only yourself, but with others.

The Keys to Successful Relationships

"Real love is accepting other people the way they are without trying to change them."—Don Miguel Ruiz, "The Mastery of Love"

Some important things to remember in order to have fulfilling and authentic relationships:

- Remember that those things you see in others that bother you are the exact things you need to work on in yourself.
- When you judge others, you are truly only judging yourself.
- The Universe is a kind place and everything that happens does so for a reason and for the highest good of all involved.
- Be grateful for every experience in every relationship you have had – the "hurts" are what teach us our greatest lessons.
- Let others be who they are and where they are - they are learning their own lessons as well.
- No one will be without their own "stuff."
- Live from the present moment only. Be aware of what is and how you feel at every moment and live from that place.
- Don't concern yourself so much with the result or outcome of a relationship – but focus on how it feels in the *now.*
- Listen to and trust your intuition (your gut feelings). If it comes from inside you, it is never wrong, no matter what everyone else may think.
- Hold true to your boundaries and allow them to change as you change.
- Never take anything anyone does to you or says to you personally. Others actions never have anything to do with you – their actions come from where they are and their own perception of the situation.

- Be open to changing and challenging yourself - always be "on" and observe your patterns and where you may need some work to improve.
- Know you can never change another person but by your actions you *can* influence them. The only person you can ever change is you.
- Stay true to yourself. No one will ever love you as much as you love yourself. The less you love yourself, the less you can love others. You can only give what you have.
- When you have an unpleasant experience in a relationship, take the lesson and leave the experience behind. Every time you re-live a situation in your mind, you call that energy into your psyche and your mind believes it is happening all over again. You then act accordingly.
- You sometimes meet people you need in your life (teachers) that you will meet in un-expected ways. Be open to all relationships, no matter what form they may take.

I've heard it said that people come into our lives for a reason; always bringing something we must learn and we are led to those who help us most to grow, if we let them, and we help them in return. Lyrics from the song For Good from the Broadway musical "Wicked"

ABOUT THE AUTHOR

Dr. Claire Maguire

Dr. Claire Maguire is the creative program director at The Retreat at Split Farthing Hall, a place where women come to be inspired to take the next step towards living a fantastic life. As a well-being and food coach, Claire combines transformative life coaching techniques with the power of alkalising and energising food to bring about clarity, focus and momentum. Claire draws on her diverse background and experience to create truly comprehensive programs that address all aspects of our well-being - health, energy, fitness, passion and emotional strength. With a PhD in medical biochemistry followed by working in top universities as a researcher Claire uses her analytical mind to laser in and get results whilst her background as an independent music company director utilises her creative mind to evoke fun, laughter and out of the box thinking to create lasting change. Her own health challenges with breast cancer and overcoming the devastating results of treatment have reinforced in her the upmost importance of our own self-worth, health and positive body image. This is what drives her to inspire other women feel fantastic about themselves.

Claire was nominated as Start Business Woman 2012 by Forward Ladies in Business and APCTC Health Coach of the Year 2011 for her work with women; is involved in creating a community of entrepreneurial women to thrive and is a supercoach graduate.

Her passions include dancing; watching her children grow and having fun; travel and yoga.

Dr. Claire Maguire is available for seminars, workshops, keynote addresses and corporate and/or personal coaching.

Contact

Dr Claire Maguire
The Retreat
Split Farthing Hall
Bagby, Thirsk
North Yorkshire YO7 2AF
United Kingdom
Tel: +44 (0) 1845 597 041
Email: info@splitfarthinghall.co.uk
Web: www.splitfarthinghall.co.uk
www.clairemaguire.com

EIGHT

Stop with the Cruel Words: Release the Inner Critic Putting You Down

Dr. Claire Maguire

"You look awful today, dressed like that. Fat. Frumpy. No, you don't look great. I do wish you could be better, project more confidence, be more self-assured. Yet, you are just so incapable of it. No wonder you never get what you want. You're just not good enough."

Can you imagine somebody saying that to you? Or words which are worse - words of cruelty, hatred, belittlement and discouragement? How would they make you feel? Not so wonderful at a guess! And yet, thousands upon thousands of women say such words to themselves. Are you one of them?

Looking in the mirror and disliking what you see. Bringing your self-esteem plummeting to a depth defying low, which in turn affects your confidence, your belief in yourself and your abilities. Resulting in a perpetual cycle of thinking you cannot be nor do what you would really like. Allowing you to settle for well, whatever! Never really pushing and never really going for it.

Dreams remain just that, dreams trapped in your mind. For dreams only come true for other women. You know the smart ones, the slim ones, the beautiful ones - all that you believe you're not. Don't they?

However, those cruel words, the ones you speak with such negativity do not have to be considered as the truth. They are words spoken from within you, yes, but from a part of your psyche named the 'Inner Critic'. **And yes, you can be free of her.**

Yet if we can be free of her, why do we choose to hold onto her? For what purpose do we listen so vehemently to our inner critic? Why do we choose to listen and be directed by words of cruelty about ourselves rather than words of encouragement?

Firstly, know that you are not alone. This trait of listening to our negative chatter, our inner critic, is common amongst us all. When women are asked to write out fabulous, wonderful stuff about themselves it creates a fear. They stare at the blank paper unsure of what to write. It brings up all kinds of emotions and they feel they cannot write positive words about themselves. And yet.... if I was to ask you to write out all the horrible things about yourself, well it becomes easy, for that inner critic can and does appear to rule the mind.

It's as if, the inner critic is protecting you. Seriously, those cruel words are stopping you from being hurt by others, by situations, by the unknown. We will explore this further below.

For now though, let's go and confront that inner critic. Although I know this is an unpleasant thing to do!

Yet, the more we can start to acknowledge who she is, her purpose, her needs (for yes, she has those too) then the more we can come to recognise her role and in doing so successfully overcome it, and break free.

So, grab a journal and let's start exploring your inner critic.

I want you to take a deep breath and get in touch with that part of you. The part of you that calls you names, puts you down, doesn't truly believe in the innate wonder of you.

- Can you feel her?
- Hear her?

Let's continue with the breathing and start to expand into the feelings of the inner critic, allow them to wash over you, really allow her to take charge.

- What sensations occur in your body when you let the inner critic take over?
- Where can you feel them?
- Make a note of them.

Next, start to listen to what she is saying.

- What words or phrases come up?

- What does your inner critic say?
- How does she say them?
- Is she mean, angry, judging, sarcastic and so on?

Write in your journal all the words and sayings of your inner critic.

Ok! Now take a deep breath and release. We are still going to stay with your inner critic. I want you to close your eyes and start to visualise her. Start to see her as a separate identity in your mind.

- What does she look like?
- Really go into to detail describing her. Her features, her style, her way of being.

Again, write all this out in your journal.

Now you have felt her, heard her and seen her. You are getting familiar with this part of you.

- I want you to start to identify when does she pop up, in what situations?
- Is it when you look in the mirror at yourself, when you are in new company, when you think of doing something different, bringing a dream of yours to life?
- When does your inner critic come into play?

Write out these situations.

Excellent.

Let's get creative. Then immediately follow with go find a picture....

Go find a picture, or draw a picture that represents your inner critic.

Stick this picture in your journal. If you wish you can put around this picture speech bubbles with the words she says, how she makes you feel, where in your body you feel her and when she is likely to show up.

You may not be feeling your best after confronting your inner critic so take a deep breath and let's move onto the next part:

Understand Her.

Why, exactly, do we have this part of us? As I see it, our inner critic can serve us very well. In that she protects us. Yes, as hard as it might be to believe, our inner critic can keep us safe. For our dreams and desires may be wild, difficult, and confrontational which take us out of our comfort zone. This leads to you confronting fears, making decisions and perhaps hard work. And this could result in failure. Not so good. Our inner critic, therefore, stops us in our tracks before we commit to making change, following our dreams and in doing so prevents us from rocking our status quo. Everything carries on as it is and all is well. Right?! Well, yes and no. For staying the same means we won't fail, confront fears, make decisions and work hard but.... you still know you want more and dreams don't just go away. We want them to become true.

As much as our inner critic is protecting us from any heart-ache we need to find out what our fears are regarding breaking free.

In your journal, write out all these fears regarding breaking free that you hold:

- About what your dream would entail and how you feel about chasing your dream; be this getting your body or health in better shape, improving your relationship, starting a business, transitioning to a new phase in your life, finding a creative pursuit and so on.

In your journal, write out what happens to you when you listen to these inner critic fears:

- What happens when you listen to those fears which are put forward by your inner critic?
- Do you overeat, sabotage your best laid intentions, argue, stop planning, react to life, not take any action?
- What is it you do?

As strange as it may seem, let's think of your inner critic having needs. Start to see her as a hurt person that only knows how to be noticed by saying these cruel words. Why do you think she has to say these words to be acknowledged? What do you think she would be getting out of it?

In your journal, write out a statement that, yes, you acknowledge your inner circle:

Congratulations, you have just seen why you have an inner critic and recognised that she has a purpose. A purpose to protect you from change, from moving out of your comfort zone and into the unknown - a place where you could fail and show yourself up.

You know though that this is your time to break free, to let that inner critic go. However, will she really go? No, she will always turn up when you take the next step but you are now aware of why, you are aware of what she will say, how she appears, what she feels like in your body so let's forgive her. Forgive her weakness and acknowledge that she is in her own sweet way caring for you.

Forgiveness towards yourself is a powerful tool. For it immediately takes you out of the cycle of listening and acting on your cruel words. For where do they come from? You!

Take a piece of paper and start to write…

This can be in the form of a letter, a poem or just a jumble of words. What you are doing is writing out how all the things your inner critic says and does affect you and then forgive. Write this out as a way to blast away all the negativity, acknowledge all that she has done for you, how she has protected you, kept you safe. Understand that the words you say to yourself, those cruel words are to be seen as a way to stop you failing. Forgive them. Forgive yourself. Keep writing until you have it all out of you.

Read it back and see if you can take some lessons from it.

- What is a positive spin you could give to those cruel words, to the inner critic putting you down?

For, you have the power within you to choose how you see yourself, to choose what you want to hear and feel.

Let's take this one step further. What could you say to yourself when your inner critic decides to rear her head? For if we acknowledge that negative chatter will constantly come up we need to have a way of effectively dealing with it. We know the power of words, how they affect us and make us feel. So isn't it time then to consciously create words that empower you?

In your journal, write out words to charm your inner critic.

- Words to flatter her, tell her how amazing she is, how gorgeous, how fantastic, comment on what an amazing ability she has, what a great job she is doing and so on. What would you say? Write them all out.

What you are doing is allowing yourself to change the direction of the stream of negativity that your inner critic creates. You are slowly beginning to release her. You are stopping her from putting you down. For the words that you just wrote in your journal, those words of positivity are words you are going to say to yourself - you are charming yourself, flattering yourself, complimenting your ability.

Every time your inner critic rears up, smile, breathe and say thank you. Know that there is only one of you and that you are special and worthy. You are here to make a difference to your life. To have the life you wish for. It's not only for other women, it's for you too.

Acknowledge yourself every day, every hour.

And when your inner critic triggers you into a depressing monologue of how awful you are, when you hear those cruel words, decide to do something else.

In your journal, create a list of 10 things that you love to do.

It could be music, dancing, reading, walking, sex, eating something nourishing, taking a bath, lighting a candle, meditating. What is it that is something simple yet rewarding, nourishing and nurturing, something which takes you out of listening to your inner critic? Something that brings you up and delights in the person you are. Make your list and when you feel your inner critic taking over, do one or more of those things from your list and see how you feel afterwards.

- Does it take your mind off the cruel words?
- Do you believe in yourself more?
- Do you see yourself in a different light?
- Do you feel at peace?
- Start to note how doing something from your list changes your self-esteem and confidence.
- If you find there is no change, ask yourself why?
- Is it because you need something more, something different?
- Keep exploring until you find your release.

Why is this so important?

For the more you believe in yourself and hear great words about who you are then you can truly break free from the self-sabotage of your inner critic. You no longer make comparisons to others. It really does start from within, when you take care of your inner critic and release her. Then your life becomes one of confidence as you believe in your abilities, you see a wonderful person, you appreciate your body and who you are. You can start to attract into your life that which you desire, that which you want. You can create a life where you are at peace, happy, joyful.

You surround yourself with beauty. The beauty that is you...

Notes:

ABOUT THE AUTHOR

Di McLanachan BA

Di McLanachan is an international personal development trainer, Life & Executive Master Coach, Master Practitioner of NLP and Managing Director of Learning Curves Personal Development Ltd.

She is the best-selling author of 'NLP for Business Excellence', and has also written 'Successful Customer Care in a Week' and 'Persuasion and Influence in a Week'. Di is often featured in newspapers and magazines, and has appeared on BBC prime time Television. In addition, she was the pioneer of live, phone-in coaching on BBC Radio and is in much demand as a motivational and after-dinner speaker.

Di is passionate about helping others to be the very best that they can be. Her ethos is that everyone has an inner potential for excellence and she delights in being able to play a part in others' personal transformations. She works with groups as well as with individuals, and specialises in one-to-one VIP days where life-changing breakthroughs are often achieved.

Di first became interested in Self Sabotage as a result of being married to a man who developed a severe personality disorder. She likens the experience to living with someone who was possessed by unpredictable, destructive demons. The marriage became intolerable and eventually ended in divorce in 2001. In 2009, the demons finally won and took Ian from self sabotage to self destruct with his suicide in September of that year.

Di's mission now is to increase people's awareness of their own self sabotage patterns, and in so doing, empower them to make positive changes, 'get out of their own way' and avoid self destruct. Her innovative 'inner pendulum' principles and techniques are highly effective, light-hearted and transformational.

Di is based in Havant, Hampshire (UK) and can be contacted on +44(0)2392 473699. Her e-mail address is di@learningcurves.co.uk and her two websites are www.learningcurves.co.uk and www.stop-self-sabotage.com.

NINE

Your 'Inner Pendulum'

Di McLanachan

Perhaps you, like me, are fascinated by "what makes people tick?" Why do some people seem to effortlessly attain great success in life while others never seem to get off the starting blocks? Perhaps you have experienced times when, on reflection, you feel you may have "got in your own way" and you wondered how on earth that happened, especially if things seemed to be going well for you at the time.

Many years ago, I developed an interest in how and why people sabotage themselves. I started to research this extraordinary phenomenon and after extensive study, concluded that this is not a 'black and white' topic, that is, it's not a matter of you either do it or you don't. I discovered that there are numerous ways to sabotage yourself, in fact at the time of writing this, I have so far identified 26. So you could say that rather than seeing Self Sabotage in monochrome, I'm seeing it in a huge rainbow of colours, and I believe that *everyone* dips into some of these from time to time.

So let's start by exploring what makes people tick. Imagine that you have an 'inner pendulum', gently swinging from side to side like a clock. When life is "normal", this is how your pendulum behaves. This is how you 'tick'.

> I'd like you also to imagine that you have a 'neck-top computer', in other words, your mind. This is similar to a laptop in that it runs, on demand, various software programs that you have installed. You may not consciously realise you have installed them but they *are* there.
>
> Now imagine that something happens to you or around you. Some kind of stimulus that you react to and it upsets the balance of your inner pendulum, which swings violently to one side and triggers one of your software programs to fire up. If this is your Diva (or Drama Queen) program, you may well find yourself throwing a tantrum, shouting, generally losing the plot and not caring at all about what people might be thinking of you. You could be doing this in a crowded street and it wouldn't make the slightest difference to you.

Conversely, the very same stimulus could happen to someone else who has different software loaded into their neck-top computer. Instead of going into Diva, their pendulum swings to the other extreme and they become a Dormouse. They shrink back from dealing with the situation, look for somewhere to hide and would worry about what people might think of them. They would probably feel very upset about the whole episode and wish that they'd been able to deal with it differently.

These are two extreme swings of the pendulum. They are a pair – polar opposites, one is high energy (Diva) and the other is low energy (Dormouse). And both of them can be forms of self sabotage if they develop into habitual behaviours. However, just as with a laptop computer, you can uninstall a program that you no longer want and replace it with one that serves you better.

You *do* have this choice, and your power is in your decisions.

In the space of this chapter, it is not possible to describe all 26 sabotage routines in a way that does them justice. However, it *is* possible to share with you the five principles that underpin self sabotage, how a Cycle of Self Sabotage is formed and how you can break out of it and move instead into a Cycle of Personal Excellence.

Five Facts about Self Sabotage:

1. **There are many different ways to self sabotage, with different energy levels.**

   For example, the Diva is high energy whereas the Dormouse is low energy. We mentally store these self sabotage routines as software programs in our neck-top computer.

   Here's how you create one of these software programs. Imagine that you are taking a walk in the countryside and you come to a meadow that nobody has walked across before. As there is no well-worn path to follow, you create a route of your own and in treading down the grass on that route, you start to create a path. The next time you find yourself at that same meadow, you see the route you took last time and take the easy option of following it again. After a few repetitions of this activity, you have a well-worn path which you will follow automatically, without thinking, every time you find yourself at this particular place. The path, or program that you have created has now been firmly installed in your neck-top computer.

Now let's say that this is your Diva routine. The first time you arrived at this particular 'meadow' was when you were at school and another kid made fun of you. You felt hurt and humiliated and you reacted by throwing a tantrum. Your reaction might have been vocal or it might even have been physical but in some way, it dealt with the situation at hand; it was your coping mechanism. You just crossed your meadow for the first time.

The next time somebody made fun of you, you remembered your route across the meadow and took it again. And this may have happened over and over until now, you only need to detect the slightest sense of somebody laughing at you and your Diva program will fire up, sending you on to that well-worn route of self sabotage.

2. **People always make what they believe to be the best choice available to them at the time.**

This means that even if you find yourself between a rock and a hard place, you will still take whatever seems to be the 'least worst' option. To others, your behaviour may seem inexplicable, pointless, negative even. But to you, at that time and in that situation, you took what you felt was the only course of action open to you. Later on, you may have found yourself thinking,

"If I'd known then what I know now, I would have dealt with that differently."

If this particular situation triggered one of your self sabotage routines, then you would have felt that it was the only option available to you.

3. **Underlying every behaviour is a positive purpose, which may at times seem to manifest in a negative way.**

Often, a 'secondary gain' is involved. In other words, your unconscious mind perceives a benefit from the behaviour. For example, the tantrum-throwing Diva loves attention and will be delighted to 'perform' in front of an audience.

I once ran a workshop where amongst the delegates was a young woman in her early twenties, single, who weighed around 20 stone (280lbs). She talked openly and emotionally about how much she hated being so overweight but, she said, if she were walking down the street at night, she felt safe because nobody would attack a woman of her size. This is a secondary gain talking out loud.

At some time in the past, possibly when she was still a child, somebody criticised her for being overweight. Her response was this 'safety justification' and it is a really good example of how a secondary gain can sound very plausible. This was now holding her in a self sabotage routine of over-eating. I remember that in the coffee break, she was the only one who headed straight for the confectionary vending machine and bought two chocolate bars to have with her coffee.

4. **We behave the way we expect ourselves to behave, based on past experiences and personal beliefs (empowering or limiting).**

   If you have a Cycle of Self Sabotage operating, then in order to break out of it, new experiences and changed beliefs need to be introduced. This is how you can uninstall unwanted software programs.

   The diagram that follows illustrates the Cycle of Self Sabotage and explains how you created and installed the 'software programs' that may now be undermining you.

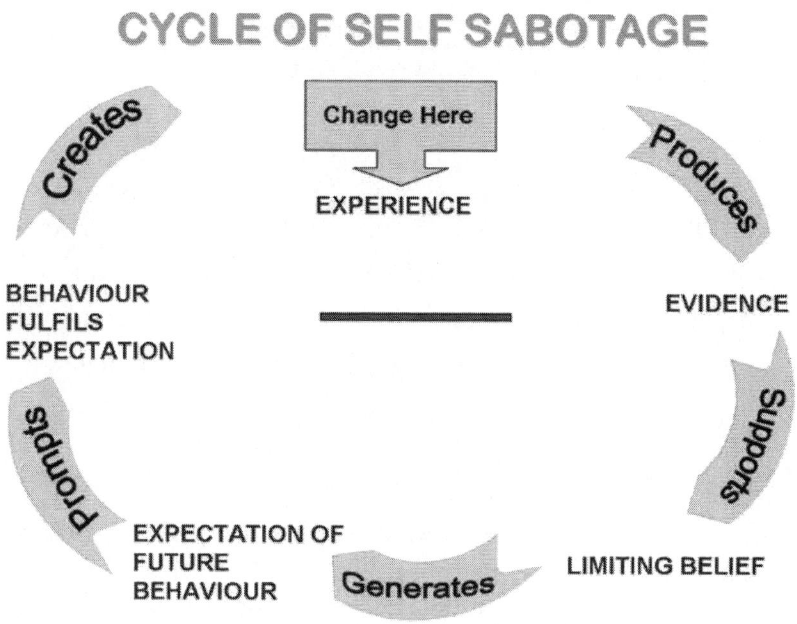

   It begins with you having an experience – something happens to you or around you that produces 'evidence' to support a limiting belief you have. This fires up one of your self sabotage software programs, which instructs you how to react. You then behave exactly the way you expect yourself to behave because that particular program is running. You are walking your well-worn path across the meadow. Not surprisingly, the 'output' from your self sabotage behaviour is another negative experience, which can send you straight round the cycle again. No wonder this cycle has a big fat minus sign in the middle of it! It is a self-perpetuating route to nowhere, or as Albert Einstein put it:

"Insanity is doing the same thing over and over again and expecting different results."

There are two points at which the cycle can be broken and transformed into a Cycle of Excellence. These are the 'Experience' point and the 'Limiting Belief' point. We're going to focus here on changing it at the 'Experience' point because the process is very quick, achieves lasting results and can even be fun to do. The process is detailed in fact number 5.

5. You always have choice and you can choose to positively respond rather than negatively react to self sabotage 'triggers'.

Whatever the event is that has generated a negative experience for you, it is actually your interpretation of it that has made it feel negative. The event itself is just an event. It is the way you have made sense of it that has given it a negative meaning. To quote a line written by William Shakespeare:

"There is nothing either good or bad but thinking makes it so." —Hamlet

So the reality is that you create your own reality, and you decide whether your experiences are positive or negative.

Let's examine the Diva program again. The 'event' is that somebody glances at you and laughs. You interpret this to mean that they are making fun of you and this is now a negative experience, complete with 'compelling evidence'. The limiting belief you hold, perhaps around the idea of not being good enough, just got reinforced. The way you have always reacted in the past (your well-worn path) is to shout, "What are you looking at? Who do you think you are?" And so you do that again. It produces an unpleasant result, probably some kind of angry interaction with the other person, which is in itself another negative experience and holds you in the Cycle of Self Sabotage.

Here's how you break out of it. Somebody glances at you and laughs. This could mean many different things, such as:

a) That this is an unpleasant person, perhaps known to be a bit of a bully, who is trying to feel superior by making you appear inferior. Bullies are known to suffer from a low self esteem and they compensate for it with intimidating, at times aggressive, behaviour. In doing this, they are trying to feel admiration and respect for themselves, which is really quite a sad way to go through life. This is their stuff, not yours. You do not need to get sucked into their Cycle of Self Sabotage. You could instead choose to smile back at them and get on with your day.

b) You really have no idea why this person just laughed. They might have just remembered the punch line of a good joke (maybe it was one of yours) or perhaps they're just having a good day and feel comfortable enough in your company to smile and even laugh out loud. Whatever the cause, laughing is great, it makes you feel good and there should be more of it in life.

You choose the reality you would like to experience. Choose a positive one and at the moment of making this decision, you will propel yourself out of the Cycle of Self Sabotage and into the Cycle of Excellence. It's that simple. It's that quick.

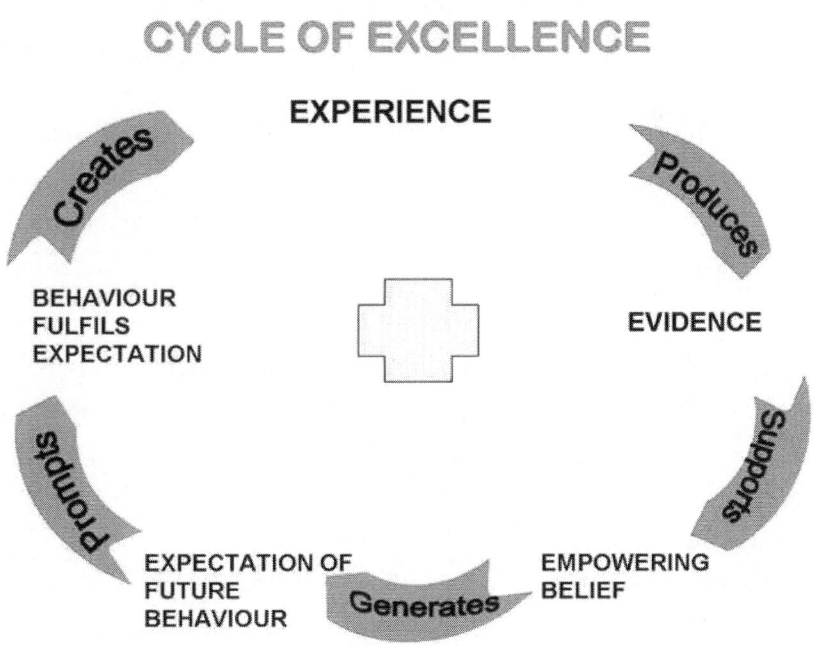

Now the new positive experience that you have chosen for yourself will support and reinforce an empowering belief, perhaps around self esteem, confidence and personal capabilities and you will behave accordingly. The more you do this, the more you are creating a new well-worn path, which will become automatic and thereby prevent you from going back to the old self sabotage routine.

There is a famous quotation by Eleanor Roosevelt, which is:

"No-one can make you feel inferior without your consent."

This is how you take back your power, by choosing to respond rather than react. This is how you step into your personal excellence and regain control of your 'inner pendulum'. This is how you become, and remain, the very best that you can be.

The following are two examples of famous self saboteurs, both of whom seemed to very publicly 'shoot themselves in the foot' and yet both have bounced back from these disastrous incidents.

Gerald Ratner

In the early 1990s, Ratners jewellery stores featured on almost every High Street in the UK. Gerald Ratner was the Richard Branson of his day and it certainly seemed that he had the Midas touch. That is, until one day in 1991 when he was guest speaker at the Royal Albert Hall in London, addressing 9500 members of the Institute of Directors.

Ratner's speech was going well, until he said that people often asked him how he could possibly sell a cut-glass sherry decanter with six glasses on a silver-plated tray for £4.95. The reason, he said, was because it's "total crap."

The audience gasped, many laughed nervously – they couldn't quite believe what he'd said. However, Ratner was on a roll and he continued by saying that his stores also sold gold earrings for just 99p – cheaper than a Marks & Spencer prawn sandwich, but that the sandwich would probably last longer!

Needless to say, his speech was reported widely in the media and it can still be seen on YouTube today. Virtually overnight, £500 million was wiped from the value of Ratners jewellers. The business crashed and the phrase "doing a crapner" became a slang term for serious self sabotage.

And what happened to Gerald? He built up and then sold a successful Health Club business, and he is now the biggest online retailer of jewellery in the UK. He prefers to maintain a lower public profile these days although he is available as an after-dinner speaker!

Hugh Grant

Star of the 1994 highly successful British romantic comedy film, 'Four Weddings and a Funeral', Hugh Grant made international front page headlines in June 1995 when he was caught with prostitute, Divine Brown in a rental car parked in Sunset Boulevard, Los Angeles.

Under different circumstances, the identities of the celebrity who "sounded like the Prince of Wales" and the hooker who was performing a $60 "trick" for him might never have been revealed. However, two police officers on a routine patrol were drawn to check out the parked car because the brake lights kept flashing on and off. It seems that Mr Grant kept pumping his foot up and down on the brake pedal during his illicit tryst! Divine Brown later said, "I guess he was having a really good time."

By rights, this should have been the end of Hugh Grant's acting career. The official identity photograph that subsequently appeared of him looking very sheepish, holding up a police serial number gave a whole new dimension to his public profile. Up until then, his acting roles had defined him as a slightly unadventurous, bumbling, foppish Brit with a well-educated accent. But now, a new, racy side to him had been exposed.

Ultimately, the only real casualty of this incident was Grant's romantic relationship with Liz Hurley, although they have remained very good friends.

Interestingly, Divine Brown referred to her liaison with Grant as a "blessing", mischievously adding that before that night, he was not very well known in the USA but all that changed, literally overnight. She also said that it had made her famous overseas, and the subsequent fortune she made from newspapers and TV companies enabled her to put her two daughters through private school.

Hugh Grant's acting career has remained buoyant and at the opening ceremony of the 2012 London Olympics, which showcased the 'Best of British', a short clip of Four Weddings, featuring Grant, was shown. Although this was of course eclipsed by the arrival of Her Majesty the Queen and James Bond 'parachuting' into the stadium, nevertheless, it demonstrated that Hugh Grant has suffered no lasting damage from the 'Divine incident'.

Summary

In this chapter, we have explored your 'inner pendulum'. To date, 13 swings of the pendulum have been discovered, resulting in 26 different self sabotage routines. *Everybody* dips into some of these from time to time, even celebrities. However, self sabotage does not necessarily lead to self destruct. You *can* bounce back from even the most devastating incidents.

We have also checked out the essential five facts that underpin self sabotage, and these hold the formula for breaking out of a Cycle of Self Sabotage and moving into a Cycle of Excellence.

What now?

To get the real learning from this chapter, you now need to apply the principles to yourself. Here's how:

- Think about any areas of your life in which you may be sabotaging yourself.
- What is the 'trigger experience' that fires up your sabotage program?
- What limiting belief has been holding you in this cycle so far?
- What is the supporting evidence for this belief and how can you challenge it?
- How could you create a different reality for yourself by positively changing your perception of the 'trigger experience?
- What is the new belief you would like to have, that would empower you in a Cycle of Excellence?
- How can you generate 'evidence' to support this new, empowering belief?
- Practise, practise, practise. Every time you work through these steps, you are walking a new route across your meadow. The better defined your path becomes, the more natural it will be for you to take it.

And finally ....

To keep up to date with the latest research, developments and resources for overcoming self sabotage, check out my website at www.stop-self-sabotage.com.

Notes:

ABOUT THE AUTHOR

Karen Donald

"Everyday is a second chance at life!" This is the personal testimony and mantra that is so often and eloquently spoken by Karen L. Donald. As a result, Karen stands boldly today as a beacon of triumph and victory. However, the road that this powerful woman has traveled to get to this point would make the average person cringe as if viewing a horror movie.

She endured rape, molestation, and mental oppression from community leaders and members of clergy. This, in turn, caused her to internalize the pain associated with the theft of her innocence. Karen's personal battles led to drug and alcohol abuse, depression, abandonment, and the carousel ride of one toxic and destructive relationship after another.

Today, Karen is an Minster, Speaker, Author and Business leader. With meetings throughout the United States and Africa and Central America already under her belt. Karen has set her sights on further delivering the word of hope inside her to the world. She is expanding into different forms of media via radio, TV, internet, and producing countless edifying products to heal the total man.

As an established entrepreneur, Karen founded Donald and Associates in 2000. As CEO, with over 20 years of multi media experience, sales training, coaching, marketing, and advertising, Karen has formed a team of specialist across the Globe to not only handle the needs of clients in the United States but Internationally.

Karen L. Donald is truly a woman of personal victory. This awesome woman, global business leader, dynamic life-coach, wonderful mother, and restored person is truly taking advantage of her victory and is sharing it with the world!

For more information regarding Karen L. Donald visit her web site at: www.karenldonald.com. Twitter and Facebook: Karen L. Donald.

TEN

Second Chance Living

Karen Donald

Second chance Living, what is it, what does it mean for your life? When I have had to answer the question asked of me, I can best describe it as an opportunity for daily walk to experience that what we may try over and over again. Second chance living allows you to wake up and try again what you could not do yesterday; no matter how many times you try. It is not living for one day or one time, it is having a chance to accomplish goals, see new things and even experience something lost again.

The concept of Second Chance Living was very personal and more so, very inspirational. There was a time in my life that I spent feeling that I had "blown" many great opportunities and I would never have a chance to go back again. I lived more in my past than for the moment always thinking of what I did not do. I became very miserable with life and found myself living in a make believe world, pretending that I had made great strides in my life. As a young child, I learned to love God and the worship and communication with Him. One day while in prayer God showed me that if I was still alive, there was still a chance to fulfill my destiny and that I did not have to live in regret and in rewind and so what I started really feeling is that since I am alive I have another chance. I realized at that moment that there were a lot of things that I did survive. Those things were harder and made me stronger than I realized. Being hard on myself and feeling that I did not deserve the better things and ways of life made me move on without revisiting my hearts desires, feeling that the time was up. Your time is never up, there is always another chance. It may not look the same as it did the first time. The players may be different, but the game will always be the same. If it is for you, it is for you and no one can take that away.

My experiences from a child made me feel that I could not believe or even dream. My feelings of regret, anger and depression soon took the place of childhood desires. Children come into the world learning to dream and desire for special things. My dreams were stolen from me through molestation, disappointment, and feelings of rejection. I had to comfortably learn how to go back and deal with issues that would never really come again, but had to be settled in my heart. I felt that the innocence of my childhood was stolen and I began envying people who spoke about their childhood. I started even feeling left out while watching children as an adult. As a teenager, I have a lot of great memories, but a lot of my teen life was spent as an alcoholic and drug abuser. I was great at sports, loved basketball and volleyball. What I could have done with my talents was lost because I had an addiction. Realizing that my opportunity to try out for an Olympic team was lost really depressed me. I did have a chance to help someone else, and chose not to. I was asked to help train a volleyball team some years later. I felt that I did not want to be called the looser. The exact reason why so many won't go back and give it another opportunity is because that word or other negative nouns and adjectives might come out of someone's mouth when you try. When in essence, they are the losers for not rooting you on. Going into my life of having two or three bad relationships, when I did not listen to what others were telling me about my self-worth, I could not see it or believe it. After the time I had my children that I realized that I was better than what others said about me and defiantly what I felt about myself. My children became my priority, which really became my hope for life. There was no one who could take that chance from me. The love I lost, the chance to lead and help someone else to survive was placed in my belly, two children, twins. It became my lifelong job though to make sure that my children did not have any regrets. After I raised my children, I saw that I never really allowed myself to have my own happiness. I took every day making sure that my children were happy. I am not saying that I should have not felt that way, but I saw I stopped my life and never picked it back up. After my children became adults, I was able to see that I became complacent and there was still that regret that caused me to feel like I did not want to live anymore. Some of those signs were depression, self-pity and extreme loneliness. I soon starting seeking a better life for Karen, the one of joy and peace by simply looking myself in the mirror every day and realizing that I don't have to be unhappy and that I can look back now on happiness and find me in it. There is a first step for everyone in this process. You don't want to lie down and die inside never seeking or making peace with yourself regarding your past. In the midst of all the bad that has happened, there is something good that was the intent. That will have to be your choice to seek. There is a place of sanctuary for everyone. My hiding place my grandmother's house.

Going to my grandmother's house is often a place that I visited in my mind that reminded me of happiness. It was a place where my family gathered, it was the place that my cousins and I came together to spend weekends and evenings. No pressure of rejection, whether we did it wrong or right, no pressure of school age problems. Just pure love. It was always the same because it was just what our grandmother gave us. I have conversations with family members who wonder why our grandmother had to leave us and still suffer great hurt behind it. I too had a great healing that needed to take place after she passed, because I could not imagine that place being taken from me. Even though we bugged her to no end, there was the place that only God could create for us. It was a place of escape where we were free to scream, run and be us. Not that our homes were so horrible, but there were challenges that were taking place there at a young age, our parents probably never even considered would impact us. The freedom of not being connected to the problems of life, love allowed me to be a child. Playing games, looking into our favorite jewelry box, eating treats, just having fun. As an only child, I always sought after the attention of others. I learned how to imagine who I wanted to be and who my friends were. At a young age, I learned to mask who I really was on the inside, hiding my true personality for fear of rejection. At my grandmother's house, I could be me.

At your adult age is when you begin to be reminded that there were issues and moments in time that are undeniably gone for good. You will see this either through your own memories or through the words of others that will always seek to remind you that you did not step up to the plate. This is the time you have the," I wish I could turn back the hands of time" syndrome. I started seeing things on TV, in the movies and at the mall that reminded me that I failed and the worse feeling of all is that it was my fault. It would be different if there were not enough money, or if I just could not get the clothes or popularity, whatever it may be. Going to back to what I failed at, like the professional athlete status in my life, I had a feeling that I blew it because of the addiction and abuse. Perhaps there was a chance for me to try again in the next 4 years. When you get to a point of only feeling that time has passed you by without you taking advantage of it, you never can see your second chance or time of reconciliation. I went through most of my life like many of us do feeling that opportunities to fulfill our goals and dreams only comes once.

Being able to see and take advantage of second chances in your life is directly tied to your life's purpose. Striving to fulfill your goals, understating who you are, and being able to fulfill your destiny will require you to go back and do quite a few things over again. When you are able to see and believe that it is your destiny, you begin to feel better about the entire circumstance. Your comfort is in knowing that although you did not finish on a particular day, it is ok to start again tomorrow because it is your destiny. The moment may be gone, but the assignment is well alive. Destiny living and second chance living is parallel in that you may have fallen or tripped along the way and really felt as if there was no turning back for capturing the positive or destined things in your life. Actually, the falls and trips are a part of your destiny. They make you stronger for what is to come and give you the courage to go back and try again. That is something like an adult going back to school to get a high school diploma or an older adult learning how to drive. I, like many, stopped to raise my children. What I did not do is realize that they too were a part of my destiny, so the stopping to help them grow was right in line with my life. My children are the precious gems of my life that actually made me care about someone else and more so, care about me again. I knew that I only I could carry them, nurture them and have the "Mommy" title officially! When I started over or went back to unfinished assignments, I launched wiser and a family support system that I did not have before. We can learn how through second chance living how to kill regret and the resentment of the past and recognizing those things that we are greater because of those things. Killing your past and letting go of the feelings of hate and always feeling like you have to be avenged and finding out how to get revenge. Most times, those people and things that are most in the forefront of our minds have gone so far away that they are only personal memories that other parties will never even consider again. You have to learn not be your past, but create the power from it to succeed. So you no longer are your testimony but you share your testimony, you are growing and learning how to feel good about who you are. You have to become at peace in your spirit and have to understand that you are important to someone and most of all yourself. I went through life believing that there was a population of people that were created to be rich, be poor, be happy and be unhappy. I mentally believed that I was in the unhappy population. I even told others that my destiny was to be unhappy. So of course, I never expected good things to happen; self-sabotage. My parents and those around me thought I was having a breakdown and in reality, I was. What you believe about life, about yourself and about your tomorrow is exactly what will come. Words, thoughts and imaginations have a lot of power over your life. Your expectations in life come directly from your character; your soul.

I am often asked what advice I can give a person who seems to be stuck in their hurtful past and need the power of moving forward. My story, for me, has changed faces many times. First, it was a story of no hope, no expectations of love and no desire to live after my childhood pain of being molested, bullied and then moving into a life of addictive behavior. I had been a young lady who wanted to have love, not knowing where to find it and turning to a spiritual leader who in turn took his power and his past and used it against me, raping me in my own home. And then I went in and out of very abusive relationships, raising two children in poverty. Those moments and more molded me into a very unhappy person with no expectation for change or blessings. When I was able to look at myself differently and stop making excuses for myself , there was a part of me that I liked. I began to believe in the part of me that was a survivor and listen to those who said they never could have made it through the same battles. Although many stories were not as drastic or tragic, they were hurtful and someone needed to have hope. My first experiences speaking to women and women in homeless shelters, drug abuse clinics and prisons, seeing the tears flow down their faces when they felt that I was an open book and an example of where they were going. Then my story changed into the first phase of a new career from media to education. I worked within the school districts working with at risk families and children. I was able to take my life and turn it into hope for others. Knowing the emotions of children who felt discouraged, I was able to see the signs of abuse and neglect a mile away. Although I achieved much over 13 years, awards and accolades from local and national agencies and authorities, they never really knew that every day I worked in the system; I gave myself a second chance through those families. I remember the day that I stood in front of major corporations to share motivation on how to become better team members and build up business ethics that not only improve others, but impact their own personal lives. Being called by organizations to speak to employees and workers on the proper and most effective way to work with families in need, it was my second chance to fix what I could not get before through helping others along the way. To know me and now know that I am a writer, author and coach helping others heal from past hurts and pain is to know that I am a survivor living in my second chance. I could have taken the road of escape. Many times, I sat and wondered that when people look at me do they see a drug addict, a person that had to have sex with men to save my family's life, a person that ate from trash cans, stole from grocery stores or wore two pairs of stockings at a time to cover the runs and holes. I would run from opportunity not really looking deep into the now, but living in my past, destroying everything coming my way for fear of rejection.

Second Chance living is just as simple as taking a step in the direction of believing and realizing first that you are a survivor. You made it maybe with a few war scars and wounds, but still you are alive. Those first simple steps, looking at yourself in the mirror when you go into the bathroom to wash your face and brush your teeth, start making a positive confession to yourself. I started saying I am alive, I have a second chance. Yesterday I was very disappointed, maybe I did not excel, maybe I did not pass the test in school, run the race fast enough. The power in looking at yourself is that you are alive, breathing and that means you have a second chance to do it again. Grab hold to those thoughts, those confessions, not worrying about what did not happen, because yesterday is long gone. Waking and being thankful that a new day with new opportunists are here for change. The confession is the same for everyone. There are foods that I would not cook again because I destroyed the recipe. When I took the second chance again, maybe 4 times again, it came out right. The words of hope and encouragement to one's self is the same for those who may have had a drug addiction, alcohol abuse, smoking habit, walking away from an abusive relationship. Fear of failure, in my opinion is worse than all of these because it causes you not to try. If you get up every day making a confession and placing a command upon your life, it will get easier every day. Depending on what others feel, say and do for you will not and cannot be your rock of dependency. Remember, everyone has a life to live and you will not get from them what you need for yourself all of the time. If I get up and see myself, I can determine what I see. For me, I choose to see what my creator saw, a woman with much to offer the world. My life has been a boot camp for empowerment and teaching others that their life beyond what appears to be failure.

When I stepped out to make the decision to be a part of this project, I was in the middle of an experience that could have changed my life forever and potentially caused me to go backwards in my thinking and my ability to cope. Changing your life into a success story often means that you have to step out during fear, depression and even in the midst of a negative environment. I saw the offer to write for this powerful project in the midst of my sister battling breast cancer. Two weeks later I interviewed was the same week I took her from a nursing home into a hospital with phenomena. I knew in my heart that I would never see her again after seven long years of being strong for her. She passed one week later after a hard fight in and out of consciousness. Throughout my years of being with her, she always appreciated what she saw as my strength and my courage. She often sat late at night and listened to what I taught her about herself, our power as women and what life has for us. I worked her to push her into a different life. I saw her settle and compromise before the cancer was detected in her body. After she became ill and started to slow down, I still saw her work hard to pretend that she was someone else; healthy and soon able to see her life change. She never lost hope in what would happen the next day. She against all of our wishes and the odds of life tried to go up and down three flights of starts every day to her home, go shopping and have a desire to enjoy life. In her last months in the nursing home, I watched her begin to work with others, pray and encourage others that they were going to be better and life was ok. For her, this was her second chance. The person she always wanted to be, a teacher and encourager. She found herself in a moment where she realized that destiny was calling her. Not because she felt she was passing, but because she started seeing that others around her wanted to listen and appreciated who she was. There was no one to tell her she was dumb, insignificant and worthless. She was suddenly put in a place that challenged her to either wait to die or get up living. She chose life and decided to help others along the way. Her determination to be a big sister to others would bother the nursing staff many days and her family. We would hear her all the time asking someone else if they were ok and we are wanting her to be ok. Like her, we all have to decide how we will see ourselves in the mirror. Are we ready for the challenges that may face us knowing that the biggest challenge could really be ourselves. Are we determined that we will win and work daily on our own lives and we are important to someone who is waiting for us to walk into their lives.

The week my friend, my sister passed away, she asked me to help her get out of bed and get ready to go home. She had not walked in several months, but her mind was taking her back to the day that she did. I told the nurses to let her try, because this is what was important to her. That same day, she whispered to me to remember our life together through a set of bracelets that I wore for her; one for me and one for her. I handled the night of her death well, but soon after feel into an emotional slump and many days of guilt and sadness. I started to feel that what I accomplished could never mean anything again because my strength could not bring her back. So this and other projects were in jeopardy of not happening for me, my mind no longer could focus on what I needed to do for myself. I had her as an audience for so long.

One day I woke up and looked at myself in the mirror again. I saw the tears of my heartbreak and loneliness for my friend. I started to think about all the other special people that were in my life, my parents, my children, my family and those who begin to depend on what I had to say and do. When I decided to look at myself deeper, I realized that failing would be letting my sister down. It would not be a perfect example of what I teach or what I represent. I remembered a conversation she had with me one day when I visited her in the nursing home. She told me she was depressed and needed to figure out something to do until she came home. I told her not to lie down in the pool of pity and regret, but to get up and begin to use what was given to her at her birth. That there were words inside of her that meant something to someone else. I told her to never stop saying good morning to the staff that said everyday they could not wait to see her. I reminded her that she was ready to teach a class at church a month prior to her fall that placed her in the nursing home. So I suggested she take the surroundings to practice and share what she knows. She did just that and did it every day until she really could not remember or talk anymore. With that same strength, I got up and decided that I would take a second chance to accomplish a goal and live for those who need me the most. There is a destiny inside of me that is waiting to come out. There was a man I met over 13 years ago that told me there was power in my life and strength for the soul in my testimony. His desire was that when he saw me the next time, I would be doing something different than nothing. There is a destiny inside of you that is waiting just for you. Have your mind made up that you will see yourself differently tomorrow and that you will see a person that is needed for the world; a world that is waiting for you. Our lives are like puzzles, we all fit somewhere to make the world what it is. Your family needs you, your babies need you and we need you. The feeling that your life has had no meaning is just a smokescreen to keep you from moving forward in life. The time is over for worrying about yesterday's failures and move into the success of today! It is your time and day to look at yourself in the mirror and begin to fall in love with who you are. If you don't see what you expected when looking in the mirror, keep looking. If you cry when you look in the mirror, be healed. Thank God every day you look in the mirror that you have been given another day to present a gift to the world; you and everything about you. As you are reading this, take a deep breath. As your lungs fill with air and you realize that you lived through your personal war, remember that since you are alive, so is your dream! Take a leap into the unthinkable and snatch your second chance.

Every day you Live Is a Second Chance at Life!

Notes:

ABOUT THE AUTHOR

Janet Christensen

Janet Christensen is President & CIO - Chief Inspiration Officer - of Dynamic Awareness Inc. As a facilitator, speaker, coach and author, she focuses on giving people practical and easy-to-implement tools and strategies to create shifts in perception to transform lives. Janet is an expert in connecting people with their authentic wisdom, intelligence and energy through her unique blend of expertise as a Master Passion Map™ Practitioner, Power Coach®, Performance Management Coach and pre-retirement coach. Her book Own Your Shift was published in 2012. Janet has also authored several published articles and co-authored the books *Leaders In Pearls* and *Expert Women Who Speak, Speak Out, Volumes 2 and 5.*

Prior to starting her own business, Janet had over 25 years of success in the corporate world in senior management, sales and personnel. In her role as sales manager for a national real estate company, she twice received the Manager of the Year award for Ontario. In her last corporate position, Janet lead two business operations from impending closure to viability and high profitability in a matter of months through employee engagement and strategic initiatives. Janet has received official recognition for her performance and contribution from The Canadian Diabetes Association, REALTY WORLD-Canada, and Kelly Services. In 2011 she was a co-recipient of the Canadian Association of Professional Speakers President's Award.

Janet now works with clients from around the world, sharing her expertise through leadership training, customized programs, keynote presentations and coaching. She is passionate about helping individuals and organizations create permanent positive change and achieve the results they desire.

Contact:
Janet Christensen
E-mail: janet@dynamicawareness.com
Web site: www.dynamicawareness.com
Dynamic Awareness Inc.
97 Devonshire Ave., London, Ontario N6C 2H6 Canada
Phone: 519-434-5397 Fax: 519-434-8344

ELEVEN

Standing In Your Personal Power

Janet Christensen

Life is a journey of self-discovery. You discover, define and develop the unique individual that is you through your experiences, the people in your life, what you are taught and learn, and the choices that you make. In the words of Helen Keller, *"Life is either a daring adventure or nothing."* When you feel that life is a daring adventure, you are empowered and enjoying the journey. However, there may be times when you feel disempowered, frustrated or stuck. These challenging times may be triggered by external circumstances or by self-sabotage. What follows are some concepts, examples, tools and techniques to help you break free and stand in your personal power, no matter what circumstances you face.

Awareness

The first step in making any change is awareness. You must be aware of your present situation and choices you are making to be able to evaluate what is and is not working for you. However, this is not an invitation to find fault and let loose the inner critic to beat up on you. Resist the temptation to judge and instead approach as an objective observer of your life. When you are able to evaluate your current situation from a neutral, objective viewpoint you empower yourself.

It is important to be aware of the filters through which you see things. You, like everyone, have stories that you tell yourself and these form your beliefs and frame your perspective. Have you ever noticed that two or three people can experience the same event, yet have completely different versions of what happened? For example, an athlete competes at an event a year and a half before the Olympics and finishes in 15th place. The sportscaster reports that the athlete is out of contention and the performance is a disappointment. On the other hand, the coach is delighted with the results as the athlete is on track with the training schedule that will have her in peak performance for the Olympics. The same situation, yet differing viewpoints.

Sometimes, our version of events can change overnight. My sister-in-law, a consultant, had a meeting with her client cancelled at the last minute. Her initial reaction was disappointment and anger as this meant loss of income. However, the next morning, September 11, 2001, at the time and location where the meeting was to have taken place - The World Trade Centre in New York - the planes hit. My sister-in-law's feelings changed dramatically as she was now feeling very fortunate that the meeting had been cancelled and that she was not there. Several people she knew were killed that morning, and the person with whom she was to meet narrowly escaped with serious injuries.

Your stories and filters begin to form at an early age. As a young child you may have been told not to talk to strangers, do as you are told, not to take reckless chances. These are all messages intended to help you stay safe when you are young. However, if these remain your stories and the filters as an adult, they can sabotage your ability to stand in your power and create the success you desire. If you learned as a child that pleasing others meant being accepted and loved, or in extreme cases staying safe, this may cause you to place everyone else's needs ahead of your own and try to please everybody, which is a disempowering impossibility.

The following are some helpful questions to explore as the objective observer to become aware of what is working well for you, what gets in your way, and how you self-sabotage. Resist the temptation to judge and consciously choose to be the empowered neutral observer.

Discovering what is working well and when you feel empowered:

- What am I doing when I feel empowered and joyful?
- What are my strengths, gifts and talents?
- What are 25 (or more) professional and personal accomplishments that I have achieved?
- What am I grateful for in my life?
- What are five key things that I have learned along the way?
- Who are five people that I have positively impacted and how?

Discovering how you self-sabotage and what gets in your way, disempowering you:

- What are my stories/filters that negatively influence my perception of people and things?
- Do I have competing commitments? (eg. balancing career and family; financial obligations keeping me in a job I dislike; my wants vs expectations of others)
- Do I put others ahead of myself? (pleasing others to be liked; expectations of others; 'shoulds'/obligations in life, etc.)
- Do I have limiting beliefs and, if so, what are they?
- What are my fears?
- Am I a perfectionist? If so, how does this sabotage me?
- If I procrastinate, how is this self-sabotage?

Use the insights and awareness you gain by answering these questions to consciously make different choices and stand in your power.

Being Free To Be Uniquely You

As you activate your neutral objective observer, become increasingly aware, and make proactive choices to stand in your power, it is also vital that you know who and how you want to be in your life. Only then will you be intentional about the life that you create for yourself. You are free to be uniquely you by defining who you are, how you want to be, and how you are going to live your life. Only you can do this. You may have some help, input and support from a coach, mentor or friends, however, ultimately, you choose to live your life by design, rather than by default. It is also important to accept that life is an unfolding journey where ideas and ideals may morph and change as you grow along the way. Ongoing awareness is vital.

The following are some suggestions and exercises to help you design the Unique You.

1.) Identify your top 10 values. This short list of some commonly held values will help you get started: family, health, honesty, spirituality, compassion, peace, courage, humour, joy, growth, self-reliance, truth, independence, education, respect, adventure, responsibility, creativity, balance. Add values that are important to you, then pick your top 10.

2.) Identify your strengths, gifts and talents. You may want to ask trusted friends, family and co-workers to give you feedback on what they see as your strengths, gifts and talents. A good resource is the book Now, Discover Your Strengths by Marcus Buckingham and Donald O. Clifton. By purchasing this book you get a link to an online assessment to determine your key strengths. Another resource is the *Inventory of Strengths Survey* on the VIA Institute of Character web site: http://www.viacharacter.org/SURVEYS.aspx.

3.) Knowing your values, strengths, gifts and talents gives you valuable information to help you with the next step, which is determining your *Why, Be, Do.*

Why are you here? What is your purpose or mission for your life?

Who do you want to **Be**? What is your vision; what impact do you want to have?

How are you going to **Do** this? How will you bring your Why and Be to life?

It is optimal to express each of these in a concise, easy-to-remember declaration:

Why: To help create a peaceful and compassionate planet

Be: To inspire others to love themselves and live to their potential

Do: To lead and inspire through my writing, speaking and coaching

Your *Why, Be, Do* declarations provide clarity, acting as a guidepost for your life and your choices.

4) Define what success means to you. The dictionary definition of success is: Favourable end or result; attainment of wealth or fame; accomplishment. These definitions are all external measures of success, dependent on something outside of you happening. This external focus causes many people to become materialistic, seeking better cars, houses, jobs, more money and so on. While material success is wonderful, the more a person becomes conditioned by outside factors, the more cut off from their own spirit they become. Many people get caught up chasing success rather than paying attention to what really matters to them most, such as family, health, spirit. You likely know some people who have achieved a great deal of material success, but at the expense of people, the environment, or other things that got in their way. When you

measure your self-worth and success by external measures, you hand over your power and self-esteem.

The key to inner success is to know what makes you happy and brings you joy and to bring this into your daily life. There is a way for you to feel successful that you control yourself and that is not dependent on what other people do or do not do. It is measurable on a personal level – you are either doing it or you are not. You find your truth, what resonates for you as an individual. You define your success based on the quality of life that you desire, using a subjective definition of success based on self-assessment and evaluation, rather than external results. It is a physical assessment, a gut feeling, based on how it feels and resonates for you. It is a measure of standing in your power.

To create this definition of success, you work with a specific phrase using this formula:

I know I am successful by how (quality/quantity) I am (verb) (object of verb).

For example:

I know I am successful by how much inner peace I am feeling in the moment.

I know I am successful by how much joyful abundance I am experiencing in my business.

I know I am successful by how naturally I am adding value for my clients.

Using this formula forces individuality and makes this about you, not the actions or judgements of others. The statement cannot be dependent on external results. If you find the word 'should' coming up for you, pay close attention as this is an indicator that you are experiencing an obligation that is imposed on you and it is not your truth. This success statement only needs to be meaningful to you. It is measurable on a personal level – you are either doing it or you are not.

Once you have your definition(s) of success, there are two aspects to be aware of as you implement this. The first is personal development – relying on yourself to do the work. Only you can make this happen. The second is personal evolution. This involves identifying and making the necessary changes to your surrounding environment to support the changes you want to make. A blend of both personal development and personal evolution are required, and you must be prepared to make personal and environmental adjustments to align with your definition of success. It is also important to connect with the feeling of your success, 'being' this way even before it shows up in your physical reality. Remember, this is a discovery process of connecting with your truth. When your choices are based on your definition of success, you can be confident that, no matter what life brings, you will handle it well, standing in your personal power.

"If your success is not on your own terms, if it looks good to the world but does not feel good in your heart, then it is not success at all."
—Anna Quindlen

Taking Personal Responsibility

The foundation for standing in your personal power is taking responsibility for everything in your life. Understand and accept that the choices that you have made until now have created the results you see today. This can be a challenging concept to accept, let alone to embrace. For one thing, taking personal responsibility removes the option of blaming others for your current circumstances. Yes, there are life events that occur, such as economic downturns, job losses, the loss of a loved one, a natural disaster or a serious illness. While you are not in control of other people, circumstances and events, you completely control how you choose to respond and your attitude about them. You can choose to react as a victim, or choose to respond with empowerment. When you can let go of resistance to and denial of the situations and circumstances you are faced with, you are able to work with the reality of what is. When you are able to evaluate your current situation from a neutral, objective viewpoint and without judgement, you empower yourself. Instead of reacting to circumstances, you consciously choose how to respond, making powerful decisions based on your values, strengths, Why, Be Do, and your definition of success. This allows you to grow and develop through the challenges and experiences that life presents. It allows you to draw on your strengths and to trust that you will find the people, resources and solutions to move forward. It harnesses your mental, physical and spiritual energies in a positive, pro-active way.

Taking personal responsibility also means being clear about whose version of your life you are living. Everyone is in many relationships of various kinds – family, romantic, friendships, professional, educational, social, to name a few. In most relationships, people have expectations of each other, and in some cases, they may have specific agendas for you. The first step to avoid or change the practice of unconsciously defaulting to others' expectations and agendas for you is being aware of what you are doing. Take a look at all of your choices. Where you are making choices and decisions based on other people's expectations of you, instead of your truth? Realize that you are choosing to do this, either consciously or unconsciously. It is no one's fault and no one is to be blamed. Our relationships are important - choose to have ones that are mutually respectful and win/win. There will be times when you compromise, or do things that may not be your optimal choice. Realize that these too are your choices and own them. Then choose your attitude to follow. Will you do it grudgingly with resistance, or proactively and joyfully? Where would you like to put your energy?

Ask yourself: "When I am in my power and truth, would this be my choice?" Taking personal responsibility allows you to stand in your personal power. It gives you choice and free will as you create your life by design - choice by choice, moment by moment, and day by day.

Personal Power Vocabulary

The words that you use have a significant impact on the quality of your life. Be aware of the words you are using and shift from destructive and disempowering words to powerful words.

Disempowering words	*Powerful words*
I can't (weak/no control)	I won't (choice)
I should (implies no choice/guilt)	I could (more powerful)
It's not my fault (helpless/victim)	I am totally responsible (ownership)
It's a problem (negativity)	It's an opportunity (open to growth)
Life's a struggle	Life's an adventure
I hope (victim/worry)	I know (confidence/power)

If only (whining)	Next time (learn from situation/choice)
What will I do? (whining/helpless)	I know I will handle it

Responding In Your Personal Power

People commonly react to situations and issues in 4 ways by choosing to:

- Fight – the best defence is offence
- Flight – removing themselves from the situation instead of facing it
- Freeze – shutting down and not communicating
- Facade – pretending everything is okay. "I'm fine. Nothing is the matter."

Instead of reacting, you can choose to respond, stand in your personal power and create win/win situations.

- Instead of fighting, choose to respond with **courtesy**.
- Instead of taking flight, have **integrity** and face the issue.
- Instead of freezing, choose to be **open** and communicate.
- Instead of putting on a facade, be **honest** about your thoughts and feelings.

All four aspects – courtesy, integrity, openness and honesty – must be present. When you choose to respond this way, you are empowered and able to overcome your fears and insecurity. If the person does not like what you have to say, the world will not end. It is better to speak your truth than sell yourself out. Commit to speak your truth on your terms, with courtesy, integrity, openness and honesty.

Techniques To Support Standing In Your Personal Power

Consider this selection of tools and techniques, pick one or two and start with those. Add others as you want to. Remember, this is a journey, not an overnight fix.

- Take time to 'be': Life can be busy and filled with activity. Allow yourself quiet time. Taking 15 minutes a day to 'be' is only 1% of your day! You are worth that. Is watching the nightly news or sitcom getting you where you want to be? Invest that time in yourself. You deserve it.

- Meditation: Learn to meditate if you don't yet know how. If you do know how, do it consistently. Meditation connects you with your inner voice, personal power and truth. Try different meditations until you find one that resonates for you. Meditation is a learned art. It takes time to learn to quiet your mind and allow your inner self to emerge.

- Keep a Journal: Writing is a wonderful way to work through things and express yourself. Spelling, grammar and neatness are not important. If you are not sure what to write about, answer the question "What did I learn today?"

- List what you are grateful for: Before you go to sleep, list at least 5 things you are grateful for. This helps you focus on the positives in your life and end your day with gratitude and optimism.

- Take time in nature: Being in nature is grounding, relaxing and healing.
- Read and listen to motivational material: There is an abundance of material available. Choose what you are drawn to naturally and what resonates for you as these will give you insight to your truth.
- Workshops/Courses/Seminars: Go with an open mind. If you learn one thing of value from a course that you can, and do, implement into your life, it is worthwhile.
- Find the gifts in every situation: These are sometimes disguised as adversities or difficult people. If the gift is not immediately apparent, explore these questions: "How does what irritates you about that person relate to you?" What can I learn from this?" "What is the opportunity in this situation?"
- Listen to and trust your inner voice: Your inner voice, or intuition, is wise and has only your best interests at heart. Pay attention. You will connect with your inner voice through quiet time, 'being', and meditation.
- Give your gift: Wherever you are, whatever you are doing, give your gift. This will bring you joy and express your personal power.

Break free! Give yourself permission to let go of the chaos and the energy drains in your life. Let go of trying to be everything to everybody. Embrace your journey of self-discovery and give yourself permission to be who you long to be. Discover, define and develop the Unique You and every day ask yourself "What can I put my whole soul into today?"

Stand in your personal power and let your light shine.

Recommended Reading:

The Four Agreements by Don Miguel Ruiz

Leveraging the UNIVERSE by Mike Dooley

Infinite Possibilities by Mike Dooley

Notes:

ABOUT THE AUTHOR

Barbara J Cormack MNMC, AFC(IIC), CIAC

Barbara is a Spiritual Life Coach, Mentor, Facilitator, Trainer, and Speaker. Born in Southern Rhodesian (now Zimbabwe), Barbara commenced her training as an Accountant in Malaŵi. After moving to the UK, Barbara soon reached her goal to work, as a Financial Analyst, in the City of London. Her third career-choice gave Barbara the opportunity to travel extensively (Africa, UK, Europe, USA and Canada); where she spent many years living and working as an IT financial software specialist and project/programme manager. At the beginning of this century, another career change saw Barbara qualifying as a Master Coach, becoming an Accredited Fellow Coach (IIC), and starting her own business. This now allows her to combine her extensive background and experience with a keen insight into the demands of balancing the personal with the professional.

Coaching is a wonderful journey of self-discovery and achievement.

From an early age, Barbara was very intuitive; selecting only to demonstrate the use of her intuition after training as a coach. Although her career choices were always based on her intuition or 'gut feel'; she now uses her intuition actively in her everyday life, with her clients, colleagues, and friends.

After many years of transition, Barbara now has the ultimate 'virtual working life'. This allowed her to move to her dream destination (her little piece of Africa in Europe; Madeira, Portugal). After her divorce she found herself on the move, and now lives in rural France.

Stop Dreaming, Start Achieving.

Author of Creating Sustainable Change, and a columnist for Magna Intuitum (Cormack's Capers); Barbara is available to coach, train students, carry out IT projects, facilitate or mentor from anywhere in the world; and travel to attend speaking opportunities.

Contact:
P.O. Box 582
Chatham
Kent
ME4 9BY
www.nyasa.biz
barbara@nyasa.biz
+44 (0)20 8144 2067

TWELVE

Unconscious Awareness

Barbara Cormack

Everyone is entitled to happiness, health, wealth, love, friendship, true expression, and peace of mind; but many don't achieve the things they dream they'd like in their life.

'Really?' I hear you ask. Absolutely! – something I have not only experienced, but also truly believe. 'But how?'

Without realising it we are all great at self-sabotage. We are programmed and conditioned from birth; and unconsciously as we think, feel, and believe, we condition our own minds. We'll continue with our self-sabotage, that is until we become *unconsciously aware*.

Coaching is a journey of self-discovery and achievement!
—Barbara J. Cormack

As a coach, one of the things that I am aware of is that until you want to work through your own self-sabotage; those dreams you have, you may not achieve. Yes, there are a vast number of self-development books, features, facilities, skills, products, that you can buy to help you move yourself from where you are today to where you want to be. Sounds easy? Well today you've picked up this book to help you stop yourself sabotaging your own dreams; so through this chapter, let's explore your Unconscious Awareness.

Unconscious Awareness is simply all about how you use your mind! There are a number of definitions of what your mind is; but really it is the 'totality of conscious and unconscious mental processes and activities'; in other words that element or part of you that reasons, thinks, feels, wills, perceives, judges, etc. So let's explore ...! Let's reveal the wonderful world of power within yourself; of your possibilities and promise.

Your Conscious Mind is the part of you that thinks and reasons; it selects or rejects ideas; it selects or rejects thoughts; it chooses what you want to think about; it chooses what you want to make decisions about; and it makes your decisions. In other words, your conscious mind will often determine the path that your life will take.

'You become what you think about.'
—Earl Nightingale (1921 – 1989)

All your successes, your pain, your pleasure, or your limitations, come from what you are thinking about in your conscious mind. Your five senses (hear, see, smell, taste, and touch) are experiences in your conscious mind; which in turn are processed as thoughts.

Everything begins with a thought, but where do these thoughts come from? Sometimes from a conversation with others! Sometimes, from research that you are doing. Sometimes, from books you've been reading, a film you've been watching, or a website you've seen. Sometimes, they just appear!

Your Unconscious Mind is known as your power centre; and it functions at every level of your being and within every cell of your body. Your unconscious mind has no ability to reject your conscious thoughts – it has to accept them. Your unconscious mind stores all your thoughts in an orderly manner and in just the same way that your computer stores your computer files – it stores exactly what your conscious mind is thinking. More importantly though, your thoughts are expressed through everything that you do (in your actions), in everything you express (in your words) and in everything that you feel (in your emotions and feelings).

So how does this affect your Unconscious Awareness? What you *consciously* choose to think gets stored in your *unconscious* mind exactly as you thought it. So if you think 'I can't do this', this thought becomes fixed in your unconscious mind. Over time the thoughts that you store in your unconscious mind become habits. Habits you continue to express in your actions and through your words, without any conscious assistance.

'If you think you can do a thing or think you can't do a thing, you're right'.
—Henry Ford (1863 – 1947)

Your unconscious mind knows no limits. In the same way that a computer stores and uses the files that are stored, your unconscious mind stores exactly what you consciously think; and uses what you've stored in how you act (your actions), in everything you express (your words) and in everything that you feel (your emotions and feelings).

'We tend to live up to our expectations'
—Earl Nightingale (1921 – 1989)

Earl is right. In what you think with your conscious mind and store in your unconscious mind, you are setting your own expectations. If you were asked to climb to the summit of Kilimanjaro tomorrow, according to research and my experience of working as a coach, your immediate thought would be 'I can't do that!' Your conscious mind is hearing what your unconscious mind is telling it. Unknowingly you have conditioned yourself, set your own expectations based on what you have experienced or know around you. What would happen if you were to think 'OK, although I'm not in Tanzania and very unfit, I can do this; just maybe not tomorrow'?

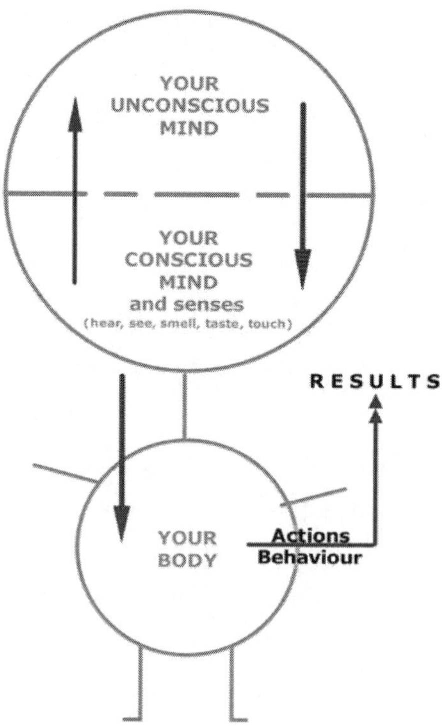

Your Body is the part of you that you are more consciously aware of and is merely an instrument of your mind. Your body is moved into action through the thoughts that you are thinking, or the habits that you've created, or through the thoughts stored in your unconscious mind. Actions taken by your body could either be physical or verbal or emotional. One important point to remember is that the actions you *select* to take, determine your results.

One way to think about this is to think about the way in which you experience things through your senses – you store in your unconscious mind, the smells that you like, the tastes that you enjoy, the textures that you like to touch; as well as those smells, tastes and textures that you don't like, enjoy or want to touch. These are experiences, which were converted into thoughts in your *conscious* mind, and stored in your *unconscious* mind. Your unconscious mind cannot determine whether you liked or disliked the smell, taste, or touch; but when someone offers you something that you have previously experienced you will know, from the information that you've stored in your unconscious mind, whether you have previously enjoyed it or not. It is for this reason you will say 'yes' or 'no' to what you are being offered. In the same way, when you are offered something you haven't experienced before or when you are in a restaurant and ordering your meal, without being aware of it, you will be drawn to those smells and tastes that you've stored in your unconscious mind as those you 'like'. What happens is that your unconscious mind answers without giving you (through your conscious mind) the opportunity to think about the response.

The phrase '**Mind, Body, Spirit**' is one that relates to your Unconscious Awareness; in that your mind relates to your conscious mind, your spirit to your unconscious mind; and your body to your body. One of the secrets of achieving happiness, health, wealth, love, friendship, true expression, peace of mind, and everything else that you dream of in your life, is that these three elements of YOU must be working together and working in harmony.

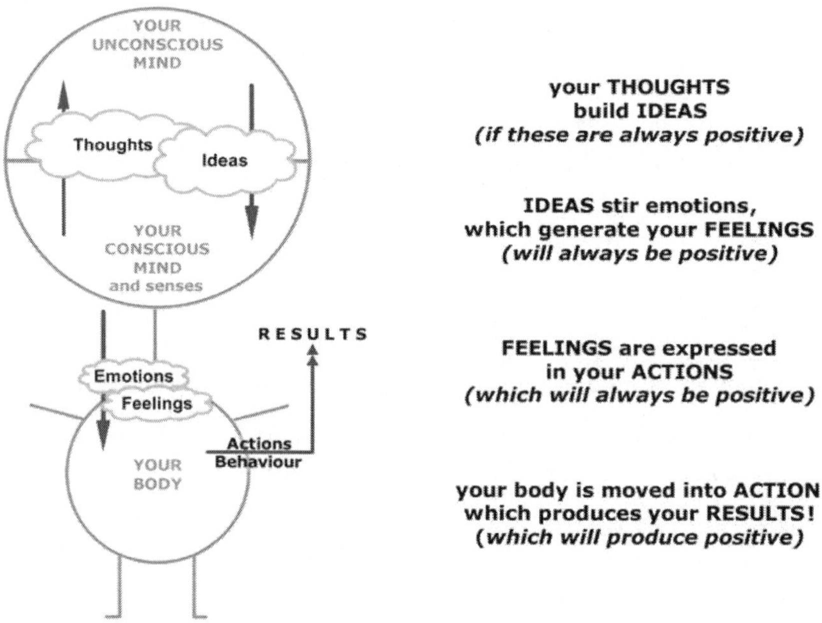

'The mind moves in the direction of our currently dominant thoughts'.
—Earl Nightingale (1921 – 1989)

Your dominant thoughts are those that come from the 'information' that you've stored in your unconscious mind.

Wallace D. Wattles (1860-1911) said '*A person's right to live means his right to have the free unrestricted use of all the things which may be necessary to his fullest mental, spiritual, and physical unfolding – in other words, his right to be rich.*' It is interesting how many years ago authors like Wallace D. Wattles brought the spiritual into his writing. Often the one area of your self-sabotage comes from not understanding how the **Universal Thought Process** works with your Mind, Body, and Spirit.

The Universal Thought Process is a major component of the Law of Attraction; and although there are many definitions of the Law of Attraction, it really means that you get what you focus your thoughts onto and into. In other words, The Law of Attraction means that you are a living magnet; which some have described as 'like attracts like'. In the film 'The Secret', Bob Proctor (1934 -) says that 'you will attract everything that you require. If its money you need, you will attract it. If its people you need, you'll attract them. If it's a certain book you need, you'll attract it.' The Law of Attraction is neutral; it cannot differentiate between those things that you want and those things that you don't want. Bob Proctor (1934 -) goes onto say 'You've got to pay attention to what you're attracted to, because as you hold images of what you want, you're going to be attracted to things and they are going to be attracted to you.'

It is important to remember though, that the Law of Attraction does not work in isolation. Your Universal Thought Process is a combination of your communication with yourself and in turn with the universe. How you attract your dream life to you! How you stop your own self-sabotage!

It has been said that everything you want in your life will be given to you or achieved through your unconscious mind. As you've read in this chapter, your unconscious mind stores everything you think consciously – your thoughts, your ideas, your 'I can do', and your 'I can't do'.

If you are a living magnet, how can you bring towards yourself the things that you need/want (or even those that you don't need nor want?). I talked earlier of how thoughts come into your mind – sometimes you will know where they come from and at other times you won't. Those that just seem to pop into your mind are thoughts that are coming through your own Universal Thought Process, or in other words incoming thoughts from your own Intuition. Although in the dictionary, intuition is described as a direct perception of truth, fact, etc. which is independent of any reasoning process; it is in fact a sacred gift which each one of us has; but are you one of the few who use it? who trust it? or who question it? Our ancestors relied upon their intuition, sometimes described as instinct, by actually listening to and hearing the thoughts as they popped into their minds.

Think about a time when you walked away from a conversation or meeting and thought 'if only I had asked that question', or 'if only I had said …'. What stopped you from asking? What stopped you from make the statement you wanted to make? What about the time when you 'followed your gut instinct' when the logic in you, and everyone around you was telling you to do something else? What happened when you went with your 'gut instinct'? Whatever you want to call it – your gut instinct, your intuition – what happens when you do listen and follow it? What happens when you don't listen and follow it?

In the film, The Secret, one of the guys interviewed talked about driving into a shopping centre car park and asking for a car parking place close to the door he wanted to use to get into the shopping centre. A friend of mine does the same. I know that I always ask for a gap when I approach a roundabout/traffic island. Although it doesn't matter how you describe it, these are all a part of our Universal Thought Process, our conversations with the Universe.

If you have this conversation within your Universal Thought Process with a belief that you will get what you are asking for, the answer will

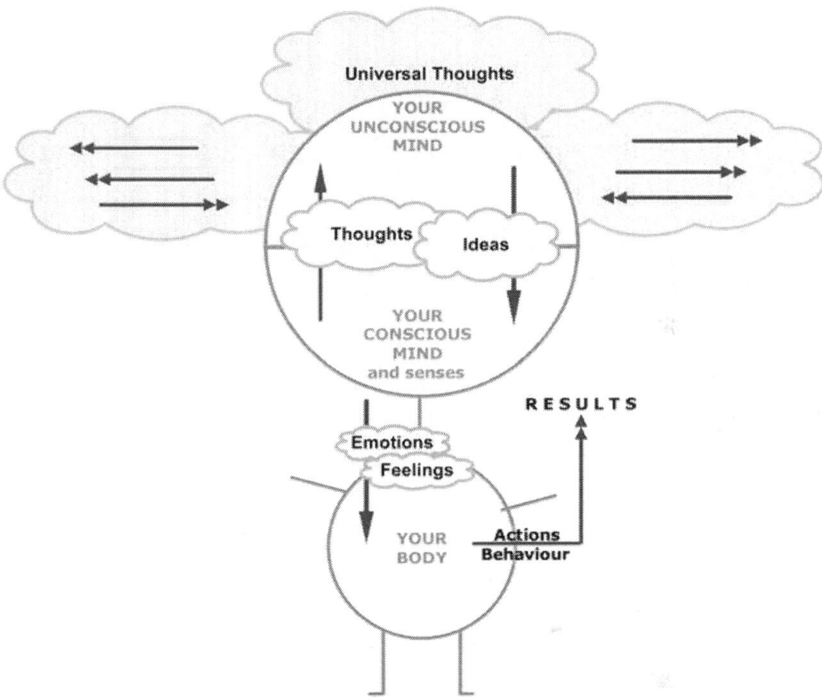

more often than not be positive; but if you have this conversation with a belief that it will not happen, then the answer will be a negative one. It's important to remember that the Law of Attraction is neutral – *you get what you ask for.*

Bob Proctor (1934 -) explains in The Secret that 'most people have a goal of getting out of debt.' which he goes on to explain that it will 'keep you in debt forever.' He says that '*whatever you're thinking about you will attract.*' If in your conversation you use the word 'debt', the Law of Attraction will attract debt. Bobs suggestion is that you 'Set up an automatic debt repayment program and then start to focus on prosperity.'

Unconscious Awareness comes from understanding how your mind (conscious), your body, and your spirit (unconscious mind including your Universal Thought Process) work together. It comes from becoming *aware* of how you are unconsciously communicating with the Universe, yourself and those around you. But how?

One of the things that you often don't give yourself is a time of **being still; creating space**. Creating the life that you dream about – happiness, health, wealth, love, friendship, true expression, and peace of mind – takes time. 'Time? in the busy life that I am living now', I hear you ask. It's no wonder that you feel 'busy' when you think that your mind has up to and 65,000+ thoughts a day. Think about it … your conscious mind is busy with the thoughts of the things that you want to focus on, while your sub-conscious mind is busy with everything else, including the assistance you require to achieve your goals, live your life, and many other things.

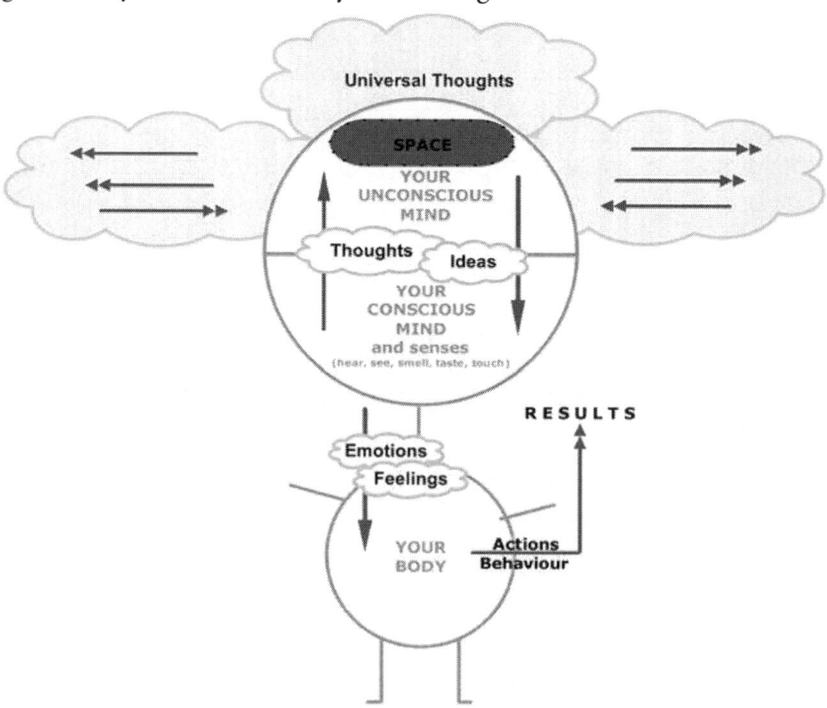

Creating space means finding a way to quieten your thoughts, calm your body, and allow yourself to 'be still'. It isn't always easy, but there are a number of ways in which you can create the space you need to calm your mind (conscious and unconscious) and body, to allow yourself the opportunity to develop your own dream life through your *Unconscious Awareness*.

Your **journal** is one way in which you can clear space. Although there are many definitions of your journal it is really your personal and private document, which allows you to capture your own thoughts, fears, concerns, dreams, aspirations, and unspoken goals. Finding somewhere quiet; where there are no disruptions, no interruptions, no phones, no-one wanting to talk to you; gives you the opportunity to capture exactly what is 'on your mind'. Often these are thoughts that your unconscious mind is trying to get your conscious mind to listen to and to hear. Capturing your thoughts exactly as you hear them, whether they make sense or not; releases them from your unconscious mind and gives your unconscious mind, together with the Universe, the opportunity to continue to work on the things that you want in your dream life. It is important that you capture them just as you hear them; don't try to analyse them, or to rationalise them, or to think about them – just write them down. Although this has a number of benefits – your conscious mind calms down, which in turn calms your unconscious mind, which in turn calms your body – the biggest benefit is that your unconscious mind now has the space it needs to continue working on your problems, requests, and/or dreams.

Meditation is a skill that allows you to get beyond the 'thinking' mind and move into a deeper state of relaxation or awareness. One purpose of meditation is to relax your body, calm your mind (conscious and unconscious) and quieten those many thoughts. Quietening your thoughts gives you the space (and time) to honestly focus on what you want from life. There are many ways and techniques which you can select to meditate and these encompass a wide range of spiritual or psychophysical practices. How ever you select to meditate, the way or technique more often involves turning your attention inwards to a single point of reference – focusing on your breathing, or waves breaking on the beach, or a candle flame, or a meditation CD/DVD, or a piece of music, or something similar. Whichever way, your meditation may take you from the achievement of a higher state of consciousness, to a greater focus, to a place of creativity, to becoming more self-aware, or simply to a more relaxed and peaceful frame of mind. Whether you practice meditation now or wish to learn how to meditate, the outcome of meditation is to move your mind, body, and spirit from the busy place it is in now, to a place of quiet and a deeper state of relaxation.

Meditation is a highly effective way in which you can create inner space to allow the thoughts, feelings and emotions of your dream life to come into you. You gain control of your thoughts you are thinking, the words you use, the actions you do, the emotions you feel, the experiences you have. You gain clarity of what you truly want from your life. You gain the peace and calmness that your dream life will bring to you. You develop a more relaxed frame of mind, enabling inner stillness, which allows you to truly focus on the life you choose.

This peace of mind will allow you to gain clarity of thinking, and the chance to develop your thoughts, your ideas, and your dream; while becoming clear about the words you are using in your conversations with yourself, the Universe and others, and in your thoughts.

"If you think you can do a thing or think you can't do a thing, you're right.
—Henry Ford (1863 – 1947)

You will have experienced those times when you've thought that it would be fabulous to have 'something'; and it appears! Sometimes what you've wanted has appeared immediately and other times it may take many days, weeks, months or even years. Sometimes what you've experienced was what you wanted and other times it wasn't.

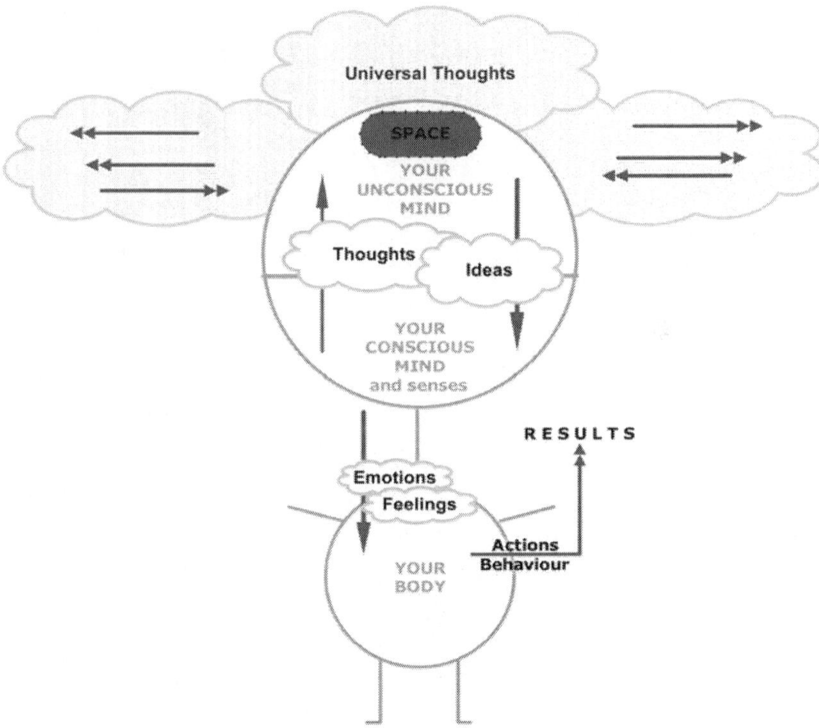

If you truly believe that you are entitled to a life of happiness, health, wealth, love, friendship, true expression, and peace of mind **Unconscious Awareness** is the first step. It's about becoming *consciously aware* of your own self-sabotage; in how you communicate with yourself and the Universe, through your *mind* (conscious mind, the words you use, the thoughts you think, the feelings and emotions you experience), your *body* (your actions and results), and your *spirit* (your unconscious mind and your power centre of belief and achievement).

Living your dream life is a journey of self-discovery and achievement!
—Barbara J. Cormack (Creating Sustainable Change)

Notes:

ABOUT THE AUTHOR

DENISE NORBERG-JOHNSON

Denise Norberg-Johnson, a Certified LifeLine Practitioner, Animal Communicator and Reiki Master, provides optimal living services to people and their animals as the CEO of Defyning Moments, LLC, a Chicago area corporation.

A former biology teacher, business trainer, and construction contractor, she holds undergraduate degrees in Biological Science and Architectural Interior Design, an M.B.A., and a Masters' degree in Secondary Education, as well as a Certified Construction Associate designation from the National Association of Women in Construction. She served as the president of two national associations and a non-profit education foundation, a scholarship administrator, and a director or trustee for more than twenty local and national organizations, including the Center for Scandinavian Studies at North Park University, the American Scandinavian Council, and the Small Business Committee of the U.S. Chamber of Commerce.

As a recognized speaker and trainer, Denise has given hundreds of presentations on subjects ranging from leadership and management to motivational and personal development. Her audiences have included association conventions such as the Construction Industry Institute, World of Concrete, The Business Roundtable, and the Construction Writers' Association, as well as multinational construction corporations.

She is a past national recipient of the ASA President's Award and the ASU/NAWIC National Outstanding Women in Construction Award, guest lecturer at colleges and universities, and has testified before governmental agencies and Senate subcommittees. For the past decade, Denise has written a monthly financial column for a national publication, and is currently completing a book on animal communication. She has been frequently interviewed as a subject matter expert on television, radio, and in print.

An avid reader, Denise has studied seven languages, including Esperanto, and enjoys movies, golf, singing, dancing, and playing the violin in family chamber groups, when she is not otherwise occupied annoying her husband of twenty years and five rescued cats.

THIRTEEN

Sabotage as a Defyning Moment - Reframing Our Concept of Success

Denise Norberg Johnson

"Character cannot be developed in ease and quiet. Only through experience of trial and suffering can the soul be strengthened, vision cleared, ambition inspired, and success achieved."
—Helen Keller

Self-sabotage has only recently become an issue for women in the workplace. Although we have always contributed to the economy, whether by working the family farm or holding jobs in the factories of the industrial age, our ability to achieve success in leadership was limited.

During my three decades in the construction industry, I learned to appreciate the degree to which women dropped everything and stepped up to build ships and airplanes during the Second World War, only to be bounced back to their kitchens when the men returned home. They were sabotaged by their society and its expectations.

Even in the 21st century, the potential of women in business is often unappreciated and underutilized. As we are more graciously accepted into non-traditional roles, we are often frustrated at the disparity between the career path we planned and the one we have actually been traveling. We complain of being undermined and unsupported.

Although we often blame others for our lack of progress, we must hold ourselves accountable, because we create at least a few of the obstacles in our way. Our internal self-talk tells us that we are unworthy of success, and we agree. We sabotage our own success and can't seem to break the cycle. Most of the time, we don't even realize that we have the power to break the cycle and understand the value of reframing our definition of success. Self-sabotage is actually a wakeup call. My own story is probably similar to yours.

HAVE WE FAILED TO REALIZE OUR OWN POTENTIAL?

How often have you rebuked yourself for failing to achieve what you were capable of?

Women are too often overly self-critical when analyzing past mistakes and failures. You may recognize portions of your own experience in my story.

I had every reason to be successful both personally and professionally. As the first-born child in a loving supportive family, I was blessed with innate intelligence and sufficient good looks to have a full social life. By all appearances, I had been successful during my first half century of life, and was happy, but as I approached my 50th birthday, I was painfully aware that I had fallen short of my own expectations. Anyone perusing my resume might see me as either a Renaissance woman or a dilettante, but it was clear that my career path was undefined. I had also begun a slow and steady decline in my earnings level with each career change, and began to joke that in my final job I would be earning nothing at all. What was wrong with me?

From the age of thirteen, when I pumped gas at a marina, I had held several dozen different jobs in a variety of companies and industries. I worked at the local theater in high school, for a podiatrist in the summer through college, on campus at the university, and afterward for a pharmaceutical company, several banks and restaurants, an accountant, an optometrist, a radio station, a Diet Center franchise, and in various teaching jobs. Confident that I would always be able to survive, I also recognized that I was clearly not on the traditional success track.

After settling into the family stair building business, I became involved in my industry, and believed I had finally found my niche. I was running a successful company and earning a healthy salary, with good benefits, a company car, and pride in my work. Surely this was the career path for which I was destined.

I took pride in my educational achievements – the B.A. in Biological Science, the M.B.A. at age 30, and an associates' degree in Architectural Interior Design to better understand my role in the family construction business. Eventually, I earned a second Master's and briefly taught science and business in a construction related charter school.

I grew up believing that I had the potential to do anything I wanted to – at least that's what my father had told me. As the first of four children, I was speaking in complete sentences at nine months of age, reading at three years, and scored impressively on standardized tests. I expected to earn a doctoral degree and use my God-given potential to have a stellar career and earn my Phi Beta Kappa key and perhaps even a Nobel Prize.

For me, self-sabotage began as procrastination. I crammed for tests and completed assignments at the last minute, and ensured that my grades would suffer by submitting work late and neglecting assigned reading. I failed a chemistry test and believed I would never understand that subject. I was still successful enough to graduate near the top of my class despite my lack of discipline, but Stanford University, my first choice college, rejected me.

I rebounded into Indiana University where I completed my freshman year with a 3.9 GPA. Then, I moved into a sorority and switched my major from foreign language (my favorite subject) to biological science. My GPA began to erode until I found myself studying for my last three final exams – all in science – at the Thursday bar night in a local tavern. That semester, I earned a 2.3. My Phi Beta Kappa key eluded me by a mere hundredth of a point. Had I known, I would have taken more hours in my final semester. Overall, I felt pretty proud. Not everyone graduated in 3 ½ years with twenty extra credit hours.

My personal life also lacked focus. I was good looking enough to get dates, but clumsy at sustaining or ending relationships. I dumped the nice guys and pursued the jerks, and my first marriage ended in divorce. It took a dozen years of floundering before I married a man who helped me understand what it takes to sustain a long-term marriage. Somehow, with all of our other interests, we forgot to have children, but have rescued several cats and created a family that works.

Like other women, I looked forward and was able to plow through the obstacles with some faith in my future purpose. Once I had established a place in the family business and the construction industry, and my personal life was in balance, it was easy to forget the past. People in my network had no idea of the mistakes I had made. They knew me as the owner of a very successful third generation family business, president of two national associations and a national education foundation, a fairly accomplished public speaker, and a strategic thinker who mentored other women and provided advice and support based on my own experience and desire to help others succeed.

But I felt like a hypocrite. I was not living my passion or maximizing my potential, so what right did I have to appear successful? When it became necessary to close the construction business, I felt tremendous relief. It was the right strategic and personal decision, but I was once again uncertain of my next step.

I got another job immediately, and barely a year later joined the staff of a national construction association as a trainer with a great deal of independence and a healthy compensation package. I ignored the obvious mismatch between my personal style and the culture of the organization, and tried to generate the requisite enthusiasm for teaching finance, my least favorite business topic.

Still, something wasn't right. I wondered how I had arrived at this point in my life without having any idea what I was meant to do, and was carrying the weight of this self-doubt as I checked into a hotel to teach a seminar the following day. I flipped on the television and saw Oprah interviewing Gary Zukav, the former Navy Seal and tough guy author of The Seat of The Soul. His career transition was intriguing, and I made a note to buy his book. Turning back to my unpacking, I was jolted by his next words – "You are exactly where you are meant to be at every moment of your life."

THE DEFYNING MOMENT

Something shifted inside of me at that moment, and the burden of guilt, frustration, and aimlessness evaporated. I began to see that every job change had meaning, every failure was a lesson, and I was already on the path I was supposed to travel. Maybe I hadn't actually been sabotaging myself, but my subconscious mind had been guiding me to the situations and places I needed to experience.

This was a "defyning moment" - an instant when the path you plan takes a turn that leads you to the next step in your true purpose. Self-sabotage carries a negative connotation that is largely undeserved. If we reframe the meaning of "self-sabotage" and remove the negative connotation attached to that concept, its true value becomes clear. Sabotaging our plans and goals actually takes us into a new path – one that is aligned with the purpose that has not yet appeared in our conscious awareness. Until we understand the meaning of each so-called failure, we cannot gain a clear perspective on how we define success for ourselves.

Why are we, as women, so ready to embrace self-doubt? Why are we so eager to let other people in our lives define success? The traditional straight line from birth through school to a career where every individual claws a path to the top of a pyramid hasn't worked for most people. Few reach the top of the corporate hierarchy. Many fail repeatedly to achieve goals they probably don't even care about, because someone told them that everyone should all wish for the same things in life.

Our decisions are made with the limited knowledge that is available at a specific time and place, combined with our own experiences. Each of us interprets the meaning of events in her own way. Each of us is also entitled to decide what she wants and allow herself to be guided along a crooked road that meanders through a wider variety of situations, without apologizing to anyone (including herself) for her lack of progress.

ACTION PLAN

You are fully capable of "defyning" the life plan you are on right now. Look around you at the women who are leading the largest corporations, at the pinnacle of the traditional career hierarchy. Do you see yourself in that role? If not, you will need to redefine your concept of success and make no apologies for living your own life, regardless of how convoluted your path might appear to the rest of the world.

Most of our inertia and confusion is driven by fear. Ask yourself what you would do if you awoke tomorrow morning and had no worries about financial security, physical safety, health, or relationships. Free of fear, you can redefine your path.

Take the time to find out what you want. Look at the women who are leading the largest corporations today. Do you see yourself in that kind of role? If not, decide right now to claim your own definition of success and make no apologies for living your own life, regardless of how convoluted your history might appear to the world.

Defy any plan you already have in place and redefine your path by asking yourself these questions and making written notes.

1. Redefining my personal success:

   - What gives me joy?
   - What kind of difference do I want to make in the world?
   - What are my core values?
   - What do I choose to do when I am free of other obligations?
   - What kinds of relationships do I most want to have?
   - What obstacles are preventing me from achieving what I wish in my personal life?

2. Redefining my career success:

   - What job would I most like to have right now?
   - What steps would I have to take to get into that job?
   - What financial support, contacts, or training would I need to make a change from my present position to the job I really want?
   - Do I plan to retire from work? If so, what will determine when?
   - What obstacles would have to be removed to allow me to have the job I desire?

This exercise can be stressful at first. You may not know what you want, because you have spent your whole life serving the needs of others. It may take awhile to get in touch with your own needs and desires if you have been trained to accept goals set for you by others, or been pressured or even influenced to make the "right" choices instead of following your heart.

You may have to reorder some of the relationships in your life to redefine your path. Be prepared to sever ties with people, even close friends or relatives, who want to define your path for you, and seek relationships with those who will support you in making these changes.

Make a list of people who support your choices and those who undermine them:

SUPPORTERS	SABOTEURS

Decide how you will create more time for your supporters and begin to distance yourself from the saboteurs in your life.

Most important, review your life and make a note of each incident of self-sabotage. When you created an obstacle or blocked your own path, consider what advantage or emotional release you gained from this "failure". How did each of these occurrences take you onto a different path? Looking back, did you actually benefit from making that turn and taking a new direction?

SABOTAGE	**NEW PATH/BENEFIT**

You will be free of self-sabotage if you understand the true meaning of it. Trust your subconscious mind to re-direct you and recognize when you are creating obstacles so that you understand the purpose of each one. When that happens, you will become aware of your choices and begin to focus on what you actually want, instead of the fears you want to escape.

You will live in the present moment, make your own choices, and attract the abundance you deserve. Your relationships will be based on mutual support and you will find yourself altering your routines, your environments, and your activities in ways that automatically improve your quality of life.

Self-sabotage is always a defyning moment. Defy the plan and redefine your path.

Notes:

ABOUT THE AUTHOR

Lisa Montalva

Lisa Montalva had to fall down in order to wake up.

As head of human resources for a corporate record label in New York City, her life consisted of working from early morning to 11 at night, living in a hotel six months a year.

Not long ago, Lisa found herself rushing through a nearly empty office at 6 a.m., setting up a staff meeting for later that morning. Then she slipped and took a header which resulted in a concussion.

By physically injuring herself, she came to the end of her rope.

"What am I doing?" Lisa Montalva, a 24-year veteran of the corporate world, remembered thinking as she woozily picked herself up.

With doctor's orders to cool out, she took two months off and never went back.

Instead, she opened her first company, an online job board called The Job Matchers, with an office in Hauppauge and a sales force of three in 2006 and then went on to her next venture, her first passion cooking and launched her next website; The Gourmet Mom. From this she had her first cookbook published. With all the hard work and knocks, she thought there had to be an easier way to get the word out about companies; especially women. Her struggle finding affordable marketing and promotional tools, ended in a lot of money lost and no gain. So she worked hard on what she thought was the best way to promote her businesses on the internet and is now using that model to promote other women in business. Her company is called the Women Owned Business Club. The WOBC promotes women daily to all the social networks for 18 cents per day.

Contact:
LMontalva@womenownedbusinessclub.com
www.womenownedbusinessclub.com
866-543-1608

FOURTEEN

Sabotage: The Consequence of Fear

Lisa Montalva

I am a big analyzer of my life and the actions of myself and others and I am thinking that we sabotage ourselves because our fear is really is the struggle of who we should be and who we really are. I have always felt different than everyone else. My beliefs, my thought process, what I wanted to do with my life as far as career and marriage. It was never cookie cutter, so to speak. So when you struggle with who you really are and what society, family and friends think you should be, how could you not sabotage everything around you that brings you to that part of your life that you truly want.

I realized about 9 years ago that something was wrong. My whole life I have been always making a mess for myself and I never knew why until I started analyzing myself. I am not sure why I felt more comfortable in pain, but I did. I grew up in a very happy home. I had 2 parents that adored me, a great sister and just basically I had the perfect childhood. I kind of always knew something was different about me from when I was much younger. I never thought I was worth anything and I was never told I wasn't. So how does this happen to someone? I married a man that I didn't want to because, I thought who will ever want me. I was 19 years old. I look back now and think how sad was that. I don't regret my marriage, I did love him very much and I have two of the most magnificent young women as daughters now to show for it.

Walking down the aisle I knew it was wrong, but I didn't want to break his heart. This unfortunately, began the cycle of self sabotage. We were already married for almost 10 years when the sabotage got worse and I was racking up thousands of dollars in credit card debt. I didn't buy anything of value. I would buy things and throw them away sometimes. I look back now and think how crazy was this. I was deliberately hurting myself and I wasn't sure why. For some reason I was more comfortable in pain that without it. As any young couple we were getting to a point where money and finances were easier and for so long they weren't I actually didn't know how to cope with that, so sabotage. I did eventually leave my husband and thought I was done with the sabotage, but no, it appeared again about 7 years later.

This all happened from 1983-1999. I was already into my self sabotage for 16 years. Sabotage comes in many different forms and did for me. I sabotaged myself from making money, relationships, business ideas, jobs, my health, and my weight.

Once 2000 came along and that last relationship ended, I felt back on my feet. I was in Manhattan working and successful. I was able to support my girls in a life style I wanted them to have. I had a very important job and I had many talks with myself, that I deserved this, I knew my job very well, I was excellent at it, people adored me, but still I had the urge to quit. Quit? Isn't that just ridiculous? I remember the line from Pretty Woman and it stuck with me. Julia Roberts said that it was easier to believe the bad stuff and not the good stuff. Those thoughts were in my head always. I was now divorced, 2nd failed relationship and I certainly got what I wanted if you were going be a failure or the illusion of being one, I was it. It's so funny how I was so good at faking it to everyone. I was so happy on the outside, but so sad on the inside and I really didn't and still do not know why I was that way. When I left my career in NYC in 2006, it was what I wanted, but it definitely was decision made on the fly. I was back in the cycle. I was in relationship with the most perfect man. He was the kind of man you dream your daughter marries. I remember one day driving and thinking something is terribly wrong and you know what was wrong? I had nothing to worry about, I had a great man who adored me, but it was so very uncomfortable for me as I always picked the men who would keep me in a state of misery. So what did I do, sabotage it. I had an affair with a married man. I don't have many regrets in my life, but I do regret this one. I had the perfect life, amazing kids, man, family and job. My life was like the one I saw my parents living, but it really wasn't truly what I wanted. I don't regret ending the relationship, but I do regret hurting him. That was a good lesson of ending the "Sabotage"... don't hurt anyone else is key or at least try not to.

The great things that came out of these events were the start of my first company called, "The Job Matchers"; which is a nationwide job board. This also had much sabotage during its process I am guessing for many reasons. First, my name began being searchable all over the internet. That terrified me actually. People could actually google my name and everything about me appeared. Ok, so do I really want to be successful?

Now let's sabotage it. I would do so much work to get it to a point of taking off like a rocket then bang, I would hit it with a club and take 10 steps back. The way I would do this, was start a new project. Bad move. When I look back, I think it was ok that I did put up these huge road blocks in front of me because I have learned so much about myself. I have learned so much about business and people. The Job Matchers is now thriving and very successful.

The Gourmet Mom started back in 1998. I had come up with the great idea of 30 minute meals, yes, me...although Rachael Ray is the queen of that now. I think she is magnificent and it was her turn and not mine, that's how I think about it now. A side not is, don't let the fear sabotage you or someone else will go to the bank with your idea. Back then I was naïve to all the business end of things and the person I was in a relationship with was incredibly abusive verbally and he certainly didn't want me to make anything for myself other than be his mate. Its funny I have some people ask me, did you sell our ideas to her and of course, I say no, but I do wish I did....I remember back then how I wanted this idea to work, it was easier than going to NYC to work and leave my kids in day care. My thoughts were, who would buy this, this is a dumb idea, who is going to listen to you Lisa, and the verbal and mental abuse I gave myself was really awful. I knew at some point I would pick up this venture again and so I did in 2008 when I met Joseph. A love interest that turned business partner. At the time of meeting him he was also a business man who was going to culinary school. He inspired me to give my recipes another chance. I put my first book together and after a few failures finding literary agents, I found a publisher who would publish the book called The Gourmet

Mom: Appetizers. Unfortunately, that publisher has been accused of stealing from their authors, but again another lesson learned. I have learned a great deal about publishing now and have found myself a great literary agent in New York City who is trust worthy and an expert in the cookbook genre. The relationship with Joseph was also toxic as he was involved with someone else at the time. I am not sure if that was my pattern or I attracted men who were attached to others or it was my insane way of keeping up the sabotage phenomenon in my life. I would say now looking back, its sabotage. Although he is for now greatest love of my life, the one person that I thought I could spend my life with and the only man that I felt the most comfortable with being me had to be semi-attached. I stayed in the relationship, but I sure did beat it to death as much as I could. My advice to my daughters and girl friends who if they were in this situation would be get the hell out quickly, but I stayed. Was it the love or was it the pain? I am thinking it was easier to sabotage everything I worked hard for and blame him then to blame me for being an idiot and staying in a relationship that was beneath me.

So I have picked myself up from that mess too and another lesson has been learned. I think by just being women and having morals we all do things that we do not want to so we don't hurt the people we love. I wouldn't call that sabotage, I would call that life.

Unfortunately, the life we don't want can cause the sabotage because of the fear that we are living the life we don't want. It is such a vicious circle. I always wonder why some people sabotage their lives and the others don't. My sister never does, same parents, raised the same way and she is normal, lol. I find myself to be eccentric in the fact that I think and live outside the box. By living this journey of self sabotage in life, love and business I wouldn't be here sharing it with you today.

My newest company is called the Women Owned Business Club and it was started solely out of need for women in business. I only realized when asked to be part of this book that others felt like me. I have so many members in my organization that I speak to weekly that have done many of the same things that I have done to sabotage my life, love and career. Now, I have the tools to guide them. Now I can maybe give them insight on why they do and why they should stop. I still battle it every day on a small level. Just finishing up this book I seriously thought of not doing it. I have to laugh, because why would I do that. I guess one reason would be that people would read why I wrote and say she's crazy, but kick the fear to the curb and continued on.

My advice to the women who will read this is that it really is ok to be fearful, but know when to let it go. What I do now is write down a list of things I am afraid of doing and take one of them off my list each week or month depending on how big the fear is. My last big one was my inventions and getting them off to the patent office. I coach other members and friends on getting their patents and the whole process and encourage fiercely on why and how they should do it, but sometimes the applications I drill into their heads misses and this the floor. So as of today I have two patents pending and working on having them manufactured and sold to the masses.

I believe that anything is possible; you just have to believe and follow through. If you are ok with the word no 99 times before you hear the word yes, that is key as well Hearing "no" was a huge fear of mine. Now, I can hear the word no many times in a day and it doesn't phase me because I know that there will be a yes out there.

Most people have dreams of granger in their hearts but the fear of failing, the fear of saying what they want to do out loud makes us/them bury it in a hole. Think of all the people who were not afraid. The Chia Pet, does anyone remember that crazy idea? They are multi-millionaires because why...they weren't afraid. Their fears didn't sabotage their actions. The next time you have an idea and really do not know what to do, send me an email and I will talk your right off that ledge.

Like me I am sure many of you who are going to read this book are creators of some sort and are up all night with new ideas. Maybe most of them will be silly ones, but if you don't try and see where it goes, how will you ever know. Isn't it worth giving your self a shot and wondering what if? Wouldn't it be a more pleasant thought to think back and know that you tried everything you wanted to and feared nothing. Who really cares at the end of the day if you they like your idea. Passion is key about any idea you have. Although, I can't work on every idea I have on my list at the moment, but I do have a list and I will eventually get it all done or maybe not as I could continue to add to the list. That's closer to reality.

In closing, all the fear of sabotage is what we think. I have in the past year and half changed my thought process. It's very interesting to see when you change your thoughts everything else in your life follows. Having negative thoughts gives you negative results, so I try hard to keep those thoughts out of my head. I am human and they do creep in daily, but I snap right back because what I think about immediately are my two beautiful daughters in which I do everything for. What I am creating and building is for them. They inspire me every day to be a better person, they inspire me to push the envelope a bit further and make them proud of their mother, they inspire me to show them that they can do anything they want, they inspire me to leave the legacy that I have in store for them and myself. They save my life everyday. So pick something or someone that you can focus on as your happy place. Just like in child birth, they say to pick something that you can focus on to keep your mind clear and focused. I pick my girls; Vanessa and Samantha Saunders. Their mom will be the next women billionaire on the cover of Entrepreneur and Forbes magazines, so sabotage has no place in my life.

Make sure it has no place in your life either as it is a useless emotion in my book and this is....

Notes:

ABOUT THE AUTHOR

Amaryllis Alexander

Amaryllis Alexander is a native of Birmingham, Alabama and currently resides in Atlanta, Georgia with her husband. Amaryllis is the Principal of A&A Project Solutions, a professional consulting company providing document consulting, project management and real estate title abstracting/due diligence. Amaryllis enjoys building relationships and engaging her customers through the project process. She helps clients manage their paper documents through workflow automation, increase floor space, create office organization and due diligence research. Prior to creating A&A Project Solutions, Amaryllis was a Dispute Resolution Project Manager for a commercial construction management consulting firm. Amaryllis Alexander holds a Bachelor of Science in Business Administration, Master of Science in Public Administration and PMP Certificate. She also serves on several civic and community organizations/associations. She is a former Board of Director for a Behavioral Health Foundation. Amaryllis has held several leadership capacities with non-profit associations to create awareness, implement policies, fundraising and co-chairing events.

Amaryllis has been an advocate for the "voiceless" through her years of volunteer efforts with at-risk-youth, women transitioning housing, community activism and public policy issues.

Amaryllis Alexander is available for speaking engagements both within the U.S. and abroad.

Associations/Affiliations

Atlanta Business League, Public Policy Committee (ABL)
American Imaging & Information Management (AIIM)
American Records Management Association (ARMA)
Project Management Institute (PMI)
Professional Women Network (PWN)
United States Women Chamber of Commerce (USWCC)
United Way Volunteer Improvement Program (VIP) Alumnus Program
Women Impacting Public Policy (WIPP)

Contact:

Amaryllis Alexander
4426 B Hugh Howell Rd. #304
Tucker, GA 30084
Telephone: 678-749-7878
info@de-clutteryourmind.com

FIFTEEN

De-Clutter Your Mind

Amaryllis Alexander

Have you ever had "uda" conversations with yourself – I should 'a, could 'a, would 'a, etc. You create internal conversations with yourself and self-doubt and criticism creeps in and takes over your mind? You have to wonder whose knocking? At the end of each topic is a list of my favorite affirmations. They are my guiding principles. I hope you are able to use them or create your own mantra or affirmations to help quiet your mind when you begin to feel the 'udas creeping in.

Knock, Knock. Who's there? Worry, Doubt, Fear, Judgment, Impatient, Disorder

Worry

When we worry, it takes a life of its own. We worry about lack, providing for our families, hurting others, being hurt by others, rejection, pain and the list goes on. How do we get here? I think it's because we feel rejected or failed at something long ago and never gave ourselves permission to say it's okay. What happens if I make a mistake, or if I fail? What happens if I succeed? What will I do when my dreams come to pass? Will I be able to handle it?

I consider myself a perfectionist which turns out to create anxiety when things don't go the way I plan. I try to create or manipulate the situation in hopes that it will happen on my timetable. I pray for certain rites to pass and when they don't happen on my timeframe, I begin to really worry that God did not hear me – How could he not hear me when I spoke to him? The harder I prayed, the farther away the dream seemed and the worst the worrying became increasingly loud. The more I tried to fix things on my own, the worst the situation looked to the naked eye.

I was drowning in my own need to feel I could control some outcome to avoid disappointment, pain or hurt. If I don't do this, then the disappointment won't be so bad, the news won't hurt as much! Have you ever gone to the doctor and waited on the doctor's report? They call you on the telephone and say, "Please call us." By the time you make the phone call, you have developed every conceivable illness on earth! When you hear the news, you are so relieved. And unfortunately, when you called and you got the answer you hope wasn't true. You just had a three-way conversation in your mind before you even pick up the phone. I am guilty of that. How silly of me to think that I am that clever, smart or brilliant to try to out-wit God? Imagine that. One day when things just kept sliding downhill in my life, it became apparent that I had no control. Yes, God did hear me but the answer was **"NO"** at the time. I didn't understand it. One day it hit me like a ton of bricks – Oh my God, I have to ask God for forgiveness and learn to Let Go and Let God if I want to live a life free of worry and control. It was on that day that I decided it was time. I had to De-Clutter my mind from worrying. That's no way to live. After picking up a few books and enlisting the help of several coaches, I learned to at least recognize when I am entering the two-way conversation of worry. I was advised to develop a few mantras or habits I could do on a regular basis – called mental sit-ups. I began to ascribe to this principle. Why don't you develop a few of your mental sit-ups when you find yourself entering into your two-way conversation of worry.

***Worry: My Guiding Principle*:** Take no thought for your life what ye shall eat or what 'ye shall drink, consider the lilies of the field, for they toll not. Matthew 6:25

Worry: Your Guiding Principle: ______________________________

Doubt – Worry's First Cousin

Have you ever wanted something so badly you begin to obsess about it. You know you are capable, you know you are well-equipped, well-abled, but you begin to hear this voice inside your head saying you're not good enough, you're going to fail, you will make a "fool out of yourself," " people will not understand my message" or "they just don't get it." You left the stage feeling the performance was not as good as it should have been, or the speech could have been more impactful? How is it that you got here, to arrive at this point in your career or life with these doubts and not really believe in yourself?

When I started my business in 2008, it was from scratch with $100.00 and the name of the company. I knew the economy was taking a dive, but I rationalized by saying it was time to make a move and this would allow me to have the necessary surgery that I needed to undergo, take the necessary business classes and meet with successful people who grew their own businesses from the basement to over $7 million dollars. I was successful at meeting those goals. As time marched on, I recovered from surgery, enrolled in business classes, attended every networking event I could attend, and met with successful business people to glean valuable information from them. However, the business did not grow at the pace I thought it should.

One day I attended a pre-bid conference and one of the purchasing managers was on site. I told her that I wanted to subcontract with a larger company so that I could get my feet wet as a business owner. I had at least owned up to the fact that I did not know what I was not doing nor could I do it alone.

She looked at me squarely in the eye and said, "Do you know what you are doing? Do you believe in yourself? Can you fulfill the bid? Is your company timely? Is your company financially sound? I answered yes to all of her questions. She said, "Well, submit your response and if you don't win, at least you will understand the process a little better. I wish you the best of luck!"

Hearing a perfect stranger express confidence in me was overwhelming. So, I went about preparing my bid and submitted my response. When I received the award letter approximately 90 days later, I jumped to the sky all the way to the moon on that beautiful August day! In fact, this person was already lined up for me to meet her.

From that day forward, I felt God had sent this special someone to breathe confidence into me which changed my perspective about ever doubting my abilities again. My doubting inner noise within had been in debilitating overdrive, but now the inner noise was subsiding into a quiet confidence. This person had believed in me when I doubted myself, even though I was going through the motions. I could not help but make the connection that the Divine Presence was speaking through this person to me. I was not alone and never had been. It was me who had allowed her mind to become cluttered with Doubt, Worry's First Cousin and it was up to me to DeClutter and move forward in renewed quiet confidence and self-assurance.

***Doubt: My Guiding Principle*:** He that is faithful in that which is least is faithful also in much! Luke 16:10

Doubt: Your Guiding Principle

Fear:

Some fear is good because it protects us by alerting us to a negative survival outcome such as fear of height and snakes. However, when taken out of the perspective of survival, fear can become debilitating. For example, fear of success, fear of failure, fear of dying, fear of judgment, fear of abandonment and fear of rejection. They are all unknown "***Falsehood Exhibiting As Real.***" And, they can become self-fulfilling prophecies if you let them. The fear is never as bad as the reality. For example, waking up from a bad dream.

What radio frequency do you listen to in your mind – Abandonment 38.1; Loneliness 90.3, Aging 30.5, Health 40.2; Lack - -1.1. All of these negative **attributes** create a degree of paralyzing fear if you let them. So, how do we overcome them? Where do we start? How do go about changing our radio frequency to a more positive and supportive channel?

My change started when I finally realized that my fears were simply that, unrealistic fears of not being good enough, of falling on my face. By owning the fact that yes, I felt afraid, and then by going further and answering the question of "what is the worst possible thing that can happen." I realized that ***I could survive no matter what***. After all, I've survived this far and life has been that box of chocolates – "you never know what you gonna' get."

What has comforted me in the past is that when I do the best I can, that is the reality that matters. When I know that I've run my race as best as I can, I've done well. When I know that I've given 110%, I could be at peace knowing that. When I show up at a meeting on time and prepared, I've done my best. When a friend needs an ear and I listen without judgment, I've done my best. When I honor my word, I've done my best. When my friends betray me, I can forgive and trust that I will make new friendships that are healthy and whole. When I feel that I can't jump the way I used to, I take comfort in the fact that at least I can still jump and that may be my new best. When I have a "not so good" doctor's report, I know that I can fight to the bitter end. When I recognize that the lack in my own mind is a fearful creation, then I more easily move into abundance. Love is the fulfillment of the law. It is your own critical thoughts and feelings of fear that will hold you back and keep you from fulfilling your destiny. ***(The Abundance Book, John R Price).***

Another big realization that finally occurred to me is that I had to stop thinking so much about what others thought of me. In other words, ***"What you think of me is none of my business"!*** While I'm still a work in progress, I know that I am headed in the right direction. I now take full responsibility and control of the frequency dial in my mental radio and while I might slip every now and then, I now hear very different possibilities that point me to living a much more liberating and fulfilling life.

What is your Mental Radio Frequency?

Fear: My Guiding Principle: He that dwelleth in his own heart is good, but whosoever walked wisely shall be delivered. Proverbs 28:36

***Fear: Your Guiding Principle*:**

Impatience:

Impatience used to be my middle name. We live in a society of "hurry up and wait" that makes it even harder for someone who is already feeling angst for having to wait an extra three minutes on that French Fry order at the drive-thru. I used to be restless, wanted to see the world and what it offered immediately, needed constant change and never satisfied with where I was planted for very long. No matter how much I twisted, tolled and cried, my internal state of discontent remained. This of course called for some misfortunes along the way. I call them life lessons now. ***This took approximately 20 plus years to finally understand what I was doing to myself was unnecessary.***

Many years ago when I first enrolled in college, I tried to short-cut the time it would take to finish my Bachelor's degree. Instead I got married and allowed other things to happen – good, bad and ugly. The actual completion of my degree took approximately ten years of off and on efforts -- Life got in the way, but I made it.

I lived a life of anger and 'victimities' and was always on the go. Always seeking something, but not sure what it was. I moved or was restless because it felt like I was not making progress soon enough. Now I've learned that some things just can't be rushed or circumvented. We want it now without the preparation or work involved to obtain it. I love this cliché: NO PAIN, NO GAIN.

What are you circumventing? Birthing your book, Completing your degree, Starting a business, Getting out of Debt, Settling down in a committed relationship, Learning to forgive?

Learning to Let Go -- learning to understand what caused the impatience:

Worry, Doubt, Fear, Immaturity

As I grew order, I came to respect a few things about life:

- ***Gratefulness*** – Grateful for what I already have in life. When I look at my life, I see so many blessings that I used to take for granted – a loving relationship, a comfortable home, loving family and friends.

- ***Peace*** – The sound of nothing -- not even my own breathing, just quiet time. Knowing that I have joy and contentment in my heart.

- ***Appreciative*** – The presence of the Divine Universe and all its infinite wisdom and resources showered upon me. I have many options and possibilities.

- ***Quality*** – Embracing and acknowledging the place where I am. I can prepare myself for success and victories.

- ***Meditation*** – Spending approximately 5 minutes every morning and evening thanking God and the Divine Universe for everything that is. Listening to the small still voice inside to guide me.

***Impatience - My Guiding Principle*:** The mustard seed "It looks so small and unimportant, but inside this little seed is the power to grow into a great, big plant. Matthew 13:31

Impatience - Your Guiding Principle:

____

Judgment/critical thoughts:

Do not Judge and you will not be Judged —Luke 6:37

We are constantly judged on every level, from socio-economics, neighborhoods, political affiliation, gender, race and even geographic regions (south v. north/east v. west). Now that social media is alive and kicking, it seems even easier to be judgmental. ***"Sticks & Stones may break my bone but words don't hurt"*** Whoever said that? We've all heard this childhood riddle! But darn it, the words do hurt. If they didn't hurt, we probably would not have the same critical thoughts and inner noise in our heads.

Critical thoughts of others and of ourselves are a detriment regardless how it's sliced or diced. Have you ever attended an event or meeting and did not know anyone in the room? Have you ever left home feeling on top of the world and got to the meeting and felt the presence of "eyeballs" descending on you like you were the last humanoid standing? You attempt to mingle and engage and everything seems off. All of sudden, you take to the back wall or nearest seat or door and hope no one else notices you. You become a wallflower. You say to yourself, I'm never going to that event again or I hate networking. So what inner frequency changed from the time you left home, got out of your car and went to the event? Your inner chatter! Your subconsious vibrations went into overdrive. I've read that our subconscious mind sends out emotional energy or vibrations, "***Think and Grow Rich, Napoleon Hill.***"

We now know that our subconscious mind sends out emotional energy or vibrations which are picked up by other people and vice versa. Much of the time, it's our own vibrations that attract the same frequency vibrations from others. **OMG!** If people can really hear my thoughts -- Oh, boy, I'm burnt toast! It wasn't until I read the book "Think and Grow Rich" and realized that I needed to shift my vibrations, shift my radio frequency. So now when I attend events, meetings or I'm just casually speaking with someone and begin to feel judged, I ask myself what vibrations am I sending out. Granted, it took me a few coaching sessions to learn and understand that there is no perfect person or thing. Coaching helped to shift my focus to see the good in people, to see the love and peace in everyone. Don't get me wrong, your inner intuition will also guide you to keep you out of danger or harm's way. But, try it sometimes. It actually does work. I had to De-Clutter my mind from judgmental and critical thinking in order to create healthier relationships with both myself and with others.

Judgment: My Guiding Principle: If we love one another, God dwelleth in us and his love is perfected in us. 1 John 4:12

Judgment: Your Guiding Principle

____

Disorder

As a young person, I was always very serious, trying to keep things in some type of order. I generally retreated to some corner of the house to read, write or organize "something" or "somebody." The reason for that was that I lived in a family of disorder. One way to overcome the disorder was through pulling myself away from their disorder and trying to maintain a rightful order for the things immediately around me. I could at least "control" that space.

As I grew older, this same pattern ensued trying to keep things organized and in order. That was not an entirely bad thing and it made me feel good to see things in "Order." But, what I learned later in life was that the pursuance of order was a result of my attempting to control the chaos that surrounded me. Even as an adult, failed relationships, domestic abuse, bankruptcies and attempted date rape, I needed something to "control." I reacted by finding something that I could control in order to bring some element of safety to my life. When things got out of order, it was simply too unsettling. I coped by trying to control the disorder. After several counseling sessions, it was then I realized that I did not have to own the pain of the chaos around me. I could simply recognize it and let it go. The "Order" began to look and feel different. It was then I also realized that I did not have to own other people's pain, agony, disappointment, anger, resentment, shame, guilt or pride. It was not mine to own, so I was able to ***let it go, too***.

What does disorder look like to you?

A dear friend once said to me, Girl, "your debt is paid in full." Let that "stuff" go. It wasn't your fault. You don't have to carry shame and guilt around anymore. You don't have to belittle yourself or minimize yourself to make others feel good about themselves. You don't have to live in the dark. ***Let your let shine.*** God has done a new thing in you. You are forgiven, now forgive yourself. I didn't realize that I was carrying those burdens of pride, ego, fear, shame, anger, doubt and worry all that time and it was keeping me shackled and from fulfilling my destiny. It's amazing what clarity does for your soul.

How do we clear the disorder? What's causing the "real clutter"
—Pride, Anger, Shame, Worry, Ego, Abandonment?

De-Clutter your mind then follow your heart and allow new things to happen. Set yourself free. Live a life of Openness, Boldness, Joy and Peace. You can overcome any challenge if you will D***e-clutter*** your mind.

You are a Winner!

Knock, Knock. Who's here?

Trust, Believe, Faith, Patience, Love, Perseverance

Perseverance: My Guiding Principle: The word is a lamp unto my feet and a light unto my path. Psalms 119:105

Perseverance: Your Guiding Principle:______________________

ABOUT THE AUTHOR

ANTON GAYTON

I started my spiritual journey in earnest in October 2005 when my marriage fell apart and I went through a bitter and achromous divorce. Since then I have been focused on turning my own life around and though this process I have found my true calling, which is to be a coach, author and speaker. For the previous 20 years I have been a salesman in the IT industry and whilst I was interested in self help I really was focused on my sales career. Over the last 7 years things have dramatically changed in so many areas I have become truly grateful for the all that has happened to me, even though some things were immensely painful and I found myself in some very dark places. I think these troubled and painful times have really shaped me and helped me to realise the true value and meaning of life. I have become more compassionate, loving and generous. I am able to feel more empathy with others and provide the support to them. I have also forged deeper and more meaningful relationships as well as enjoying more happiness, freedom and prosperity than ever before. I believe that there is no silver bullet to making changes in your life and personally strive on a daily basis to become a better person. I think this has brought about the a humility that allows me to truly see things as they are today and not how I would like to see them. With perspective and insight I am able to live a happier life.

Contact:
Fen Road
Bio Norton
Norfolk
IP22 2JH
United Kingdom
Tel: + 44 7810 202368
Email: anton.gayton@gmail.com

SIXTEEN

There is No Silver Bullet

Anton Gayton

Having read most of the world's self- help books over the last seven years, in this chapter I am going to distil all of this information down into some key points for you. These are the things which I have used personally to radically change my life and trust they may help change your own.

As the title suggests there is no silver bullet, but, if you work for it, you will achieve what your heart desires. I have done 100's of hours of therapy and coaching, attended workshops, self- help groups, homeopathy, and even done a stint in rehab, all of which was helpful, but I can't tell you which of these things did the most for me as they were all helpful to some degree. What I do know is that I tried every day to make a difference to my life, change the way I saw the world and the way I felt. I thought if I could have control over how I felt then I would be in a much better position to enjoy life. Instead of feeling anxious, fearful and uncomfortable, I could ensure that I felt happy, joyous and free, then life would be so much better, richer and satisfying. Even though I have some experienced some incredibly sad and painful events, today I live an amazing life. I have achieved a sense of peace and happiness that I previously never knew. As Viktor Frankl said "*Everything can be taken away from a man but one thing: the last of the human freedom - to choose one's attitude in any given set of circumstances, to choose one's own way.*"

I was a helpless, fearful, pessimistic victim, but today I am a strong, happy optimist.

From all the things I read and learned, I put together the following model which really does encapsulate the things that I suggest you need to do to change for personal growth.

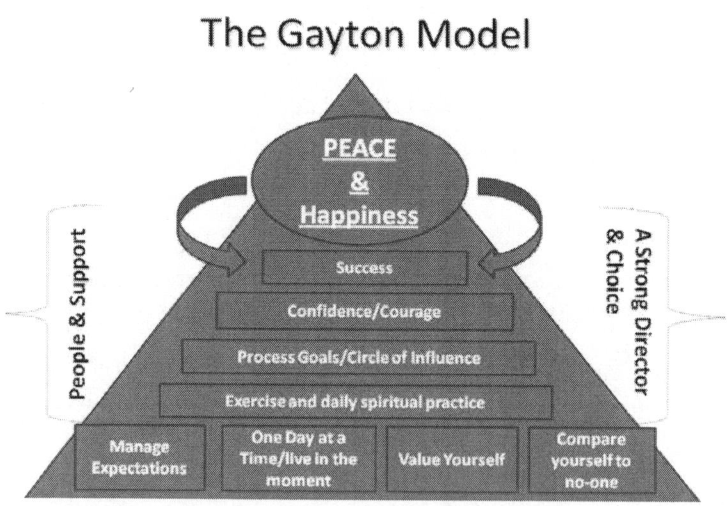

I am unable to cover everything on this model so here are the 6 keys that helped me to achieve this remarkable turnaround:

1. Focus on yourself
2. The curative nature of awareness
3. The power of support
4. The benefits of action
5. Feelings are just feelings
6. It takes time

In his book 'Happier' Tal Ben-Shahar talks about happiness being a currency, something that one accrues. It is about doing more of the things that increases your happiness and less of the things that drain it.

Focus on yourself

Start with wanting to change yourself, no one else is going to change. It's all about your reaction to life's events that determines how happy you are going to be. Ask yourself questions all the time; be curious about what is driving you, what are your motives, learn to change your thinking. Think about how you can change, what are you feeling, what makes me scared, ashamed, happy and above all be honest with yourself. If you can understand what's going on for you then you can change it. Look for patterns in behavior, are you eating or drinking more, reaching for the coffee, chocolate? Most of the time these actions are subconscious, but are you just trying to make yourself **feel** better? Most of the time I found it was my ability to deal with my feelings that was the most important thing. I just didn't want to feel anxious, sad or angry or uncomfortable. I just want to feel good all the time, which I do think is unrealistic. There are always going to be times when it's appropriate to be sad, angry or demoralized. It's about feeling the feelings and moving on, not staying stuck in the past and compounding the situation. Reinforcing positive thoughts and behavior is the goal. One word of caution, be careful of using the question Why, it can be quite negative and never really leads to a satisfactory conclusion, instead use questions with What and How.

Here are some things to try and ask yourself the following questions:

What am I feeling right now?

____

What 3 situations have I been in before where I have felt the same and how did I survive?

1. ______________________________

2. ______________________________

3. ______________________________

What 3 things do I fear most in this situation?

1. ______________________________

2. ______________________________

3. ______________________________

As fear drives most of our unwanted behavior it is important to understand what is real, fear is just our programming that says we can't cope with a given situation we are faced with but, 9 times out of 10 that's rubbish and we have to seek evidence to dispute the doubting voices in our head. We need to learn to argue with ourselves, dispute what you are saying to ourselves and amass evidence to support the positive aspects of life.

Ask yourself:

How helpful is this thinking?

What are the implications of this thinking?

Challenge your thinking, build new rituals and turn your life around.

It's what I call ABC - Always Be Changing.

If you focus on yourself and keep your side of the street clean, then you will be amazed at the way in which life changes for you.

The curative nature of awareness

I think the key to the changes I have achieved is awareness, which is curative in itself. Just by being aware of what we are doing; thinking and feeling will help you to come up with an answer. Or maybe sometimes there isn't an answer, because just being aware is enough. We have all heard that we only use a fraction of our brain and that there more power in the subconscious part. In my experience I believe this to be true, you can call it intuition, instinct, gut feel, it could be God or a higher power talking to you. Whatever **you** call it, listen to it. Of course, seek council, suggestions and advice from others, but always do what you think is best, listen to yourself, only you can make the best decisions for you. Learn to trust yourself; it will benefit you in the long run. You will need to live with the consequences of that decision and accept what happens, you may not always like the outcome and have to accept the unacceptable but you can always make another decision and use the ABC. It's important to take control of our own destiny, but don't do things to gain the approval of others or because you think that's what you should do, it will be difficult, other people may be upset with you, but if you don't then you will resent yourself and it's always better "to thine own self be true" as William Shakespeare said. But remember to be gentle with yourself too, you are a beginner, a learner and it takes time to undo the habits of a lifetime and learn new ones. Research supports the fact that it's better to create new habits than try to change old ones. Create new rituals that support what you are trying to achieve. Get up early, go for a run, meditate, take a yoga class, got to the gym and a big one for some people (myself included) say no. Above all, observe your behavior and reactions to situations. Look at yourself and see what you can do differently next time to change it, learn from what you notice. For me it's always been about seeing progress, that's not to say I don't fall back into old ways, I do, but if I can see what happened and realize the things that caused me to feel and act a certain way I can look out for the patterns and try to head them off when they next arise.

The Power of Support

Getting support is crucial to the process, and remember, it's a process. Changes don't happen overnight. Having a therapist, coach or close friend whom you trust or even writing in a journal can give you a completely different perspective on things and they can suggest things that might help. In my experience it is usually my thinking that's not very good. I can see things as a catastrophe, when really they are just an opportunity for growth. When I talk out loud to a friend I can listen to what I am saying and it helps me to think about what I am saying and if it's really the way to view things.

Taking care of yourself, emotionally, physically and spiritually is also vital, there is no one thing will help change your life. It is always a combination of things.

Be aware that thinking takes a lot of energy, it is draining and when we are tired things are more difficult to manage, so take care and be aware of yourself.

To help, answer the following questions.

What are the 3 things that drain your energy?

1. ________________________________

2. ________________________________

3. ________________________________

What can you do to change these things?

1. ______________________________

2. ______________________________

3. ______________________________

Also, look at the following lines and plot where you are on them right now, then ask yourself where do you want to be and what can you do to move myself towards that position?

Despair -- Hope
Anger --- Serenity
Lethargic -- Energetic
Pessimistic -------------------------------------- Optimistic
Depressed--Confident

We have been conditioned to think that asking for help is a sign of weakness or that we will be rejected by the person that we ask. But in my experience this has never been the case. On the whole people are more than happy to help if you ask. It may not be a good time and you may have to wait, but help will be given if you ask. Sometimes it's just being able to share with other people how you really feel and if you know the other person will understand you may feel less alone and isolated. Use your intuition on what you think is the best course of action. Do what's right for you not anyone else.

The Benefits of Action

So whatever you do, do something. Make a decision of some kind, if you don't like the decision, you've made, make another one. Inactivity, procrastination and indecision are killers. It's very easy to allow yourself to slip back into old habits and carry on the way you have for years. Action has the power to move things forward. It's also feeling empowered, doing things that are in your best interest as opposed to doing things that sabotage your life. Recognize you have a choice and that you can change, then take action. Action is about empowerment and energizing yourself, feeling useless and inadequate and sabotaging your one life is to resign yourself to being a victim.

It's about loving yourself, thinking and believing you are worthy of happiness, love and abundance.

Whatever you believe is true, what you think about yourself largely determines how your life will turn out, confront these beliefs that do not serve you well. Have the courage to really delve into what you think is your place in life, ask yourself:

Am I worthy of love, happiness, respect, wealth?

Do I deserve to be happy?

Do you deserve the job you have?

Reflect on your answers and it is superfluous

We can accumulate the evidence to support any belief we have. We can build great evidence that we are great at our job or we are just plain lazy. So we must have some perspective on it, granted we can't be great at everything, but we can be good enough at the things that are important and believe that we are wonderful human beings that deserve the best life has to offer.

The fear of the consequences is in my experience what holds us back. We have to overcome our fears and act with courage integrity and dignity. Courage is not the absence of fear; it is doing things despite our fears. We are normally afraid of what other people will think, we feel we are going to be judged and criticized, but again this is not necessarily true. Yes sometime we may have to say things that we are afraid of and we are concerned about the reaction of the other person, but we have to speak our truth. As I mentioned before being true to ourselves is a core tenant of living a wonderful life.

If you are afraid of going to a new yoga class, just try it, find someone to go with. We are all too quick to avoid doing the things we fear and we deem to be too difficult, yet it is usually those things which we need to do in order to move forward.

Feelings are just feelings

The one thing that a lot of people, including myself find difficult to deal with is their feelings. Feelings can dictate our lives and overwhelm us. I believe we all want to reduce are the so called negative feelings (fear, quilt and anxiety) and increase the good feelings. That's why there is such a massive drug and alcohol problem in the world. Most people want to escape their feelings and yet ironically allowing yourself to them and letting them go is the best thing we can do for ourselves. I set out to understand and embrace my feelings and bring them to a manageable level.

I was told that on a scale of 1 to 10 feelings of a 5 and above are old feelings triggered by past events. Feelings from 1 to 5 are feelings associated with present events and usually at an appropriate level.

I decided that I wanted to feel more happy and positive on a daily basis. So I read a lot on the subject to try and understand what I could do change the way I felt from the inside out. To have a core of self esteem and self belief that brought peace, serenity and happiness into my life. So I *decided* to feel my feelings in order to let them go and believed that they would pass. Through this process I tried to remember there is always a flip side to the feelings you have, like anger gives you energy, pain provides healing, and that feelings are natural. Use your feelings to propel you forward, use your feelings to be your guide. Feelings usually help us understand what we need to do, if something is troubling you then allow yourself to listen to them. Listen to what is causing the discontent. Learn to meditate, to live consciousnessly and with mindfulness and life will become more relaxed. If you find it hard to meditate them try some way to quiet your mind.

In his book the "The Inner Game of Tennis" by W. Timothy Gallwey he talks about Self 1 and Self 2. Self one being the voice in our head that is the constant critic and self 2 being your real and authentic self. This really resonated with me and I have focused a great deal of time and attention to on being able to clear my head of this critic and allow self 2 to really shine though. It has made a massive difference to all areas of my life.

Learn to feel and experience your feelings and try to understand what causes them. Learn to breathe into your feelings no matter how painful, you will be amazed at how life will change. Meditation was difficult for me, yet with persistence it became the most beneficial thing I did on a daily basis. You don't have to do it perfectly, just find time in your life to sit quietly and breathe, in and out and try to stay present to the moment. Listen to what self 2 is saying. Allow your body to regenerate itself. Even doing just 10 minutes is better than nothing. Try and get out of your head, quiet your mind, you will find this extremely powerful.

Thoughts and feelings are inextricably linked. If we can understand what we are thinking and feeling and realize that these feelings will pass then life will become more enjoyable.

Ask yourself the flowing questions:

What is making me feel nervous, angry or sad?

____

____

How can I think about this situation differently?

____

____

Allowing yourself to feel your feelings can open your heart, help you heal and experience life it new and exciting ways. Sharing your feelings also connects you to other people, with greater depth and intimacy. One of our deep desires as a race is to be known and understood and sharing our true feelings is key to this. Be generous with yourself, share your thoughts and feelings with others, and they will do the same, which ultimately bring you closer.

Open up your heart to love, come out from behind the façade. As I have said before, it's usually fear and doubt that keeps us hidden away, isolated and feeling alone. Its love and trust opens us to life. I know that we need to protect ourselves, to feel safe, but with time, patience and compassion, one can build a robust inner self that can allow you to feel all the goodness in life and shine your light on the world.

It takes time

Change of any kind takes time. Sometimes you will feel as though you are making great progress and at other times you will feel like you are sliding backwards. This is never truly the case, but it does feel like it. I know being patient is tough in today's world we want things instantly, we want a quick fix but it doesn't work like that. It takes consciousness, patience and perseverance on a daily basis to become aware of what thoughts we have and the associated feelings and change them. It takes hard work to change but the rewards are worth it. Study yourself, get to know yourself, truly understand what makes you tick and dedicate yourself tirelessly to change on a daily basis and this will bring about a life beyond your wildest dreams.

It's about progress not perfection, taking small steps and seeing the results will help build more confidence and momentum. As you see yourself changing and life becomes easier and more enjoyable, this fuels the ongoing process and provides the strength to carry on.

Decide to live a life of consciousness, awareness and action. Decide to dedicate yourself to change on a daily basis and as Winston Churchill said "Never, Never, Never give up" because there is no Silver Bullet.

Appendices – Recommended Reading

Learned Optimism by Martin Seligman

Quiet Leadership by David Rock

The Happiness Advantage by Shawn Achor

Mindset by Carol Dweck

Mindfulness by Jon Kabat-Zinn

The Six Pillars of Self Esteem by Nathaniel Branden

The Inner Game Series by W. Timothy Gallwey

Happier by Tal Ben-Shahar

Notes:

ABOUT THE AUTHOR

Lori Ruff

Lori Ruff, The LinkedIn Diva™, is among the Top 3 most-connected women on LinkedIn. A Microsoft Certified Master Instructor and internationally recognized Social Media Privacy authority, Lori writes, speaks and trains on Relationship-Driven Business Development via LinkedIn and Social Media.

Lori is a published author on the topics of LinkedIn, Social Media and Privacy: including *Rock the World™ with your Online Presence, #PrivacyTweet Book01*. She speaks on LinkedIn, Social Media, and Privacy at conferences and gatherings and is in high demand by executives working to establish best practices.

Inspire your audiences; hire Lori to tell her story. She is a survivor and passionate influencer. Even before a near fatal motorcycle wreck in 2005, Lori won Small Business of the Year and numerous awards because of her generous spirit and willingness to help, whether professional, community, or personal goals were at stake.

Today Lori is on Forbes list of the Top 50 Global Social Media Power Influencers and works tirelessly to bring quality education about the new world of Social to everyone. She and her partner created RockLinkedIn.com, a free high quality on demand training portal to serve everyone seeking to use LinkedIn to improve their lives, their career, or their results, whether they can afford the help or not.

Connect with Lori at http://LoriIsOnline.com or at a conference near you.

Contact:
Lori Ruff
The LinkedIn Diva™
Training@IntegratedAlliances.com
www.RockstarNetworking.com

SEVENTEEN

Breaking Free: Becoming a Passionate Social Influencer

Lori Ruff

Speak truth into the lives of those you love
and they will eventually hear you.

I love you. I truly do. And I am about to speak truth into your life. Please open your ears and your heart and hear me. Like me, you probably admire women who make a difference in the world and have often thought "I wish I could make an impact like she does!" The honest truth is that I too have said those very words. I was just going through the motions of life; aimless, just struggling to survive. Like you, I knew I wanted more; I wanted to be more. I wanted to change the world. But how?

> **Abuse:** according to a 2006 Harris Poll, 15% of all US adults admit to having been a victim of domestic violence and 39% of all adults admit they had experienced verbal, emotional or physical abuse by a close relative.

It doesn't really matter what your trap is: poverty, abuse, debilitating disease, even living someone else's idea of who you should be…

I was young. I was living in poverty. I was smart but had few marketable skills. I hadn't finished college and became a young mom in Birmingham Alabama. I was four states away from my family, and abused… literally.

With the violence directed just toward me and only when he was drunk, I felt trapped but could explain it away. I didn't have anywhere to go. I was afraid to try to escape. After my daughter was born, I knew I couldn't stay or she'd be trapped in that same life. I called my parents and asked if I could come home for Christmas. I packed the car with everything I thought I'd need (and could fit) and drove away for a two week visit home. We never returned.

It's not news. Growing up, girls are taught to be respectful and caring; to be a caretaker of the home. I wanted to climb trees and play soccer. Although my parents loved me, they fought to keep me clean

> **Poverty:** the U.S. Census Bureau released poverty statistics indicating that the 2010 poverty rate among women in the US had risen to 14.5%, the highest it had been for 17 years. That represents over 17 million women, just in the US!

and "appropriately dressed", a battle met with mixed success. The struggle could have been abated had my parents recognized that being a tomboy was not going to ruin my chances of success in life. Rather, allowing me to explore who I was and what I found interesting would increase the likelihood that I would remain curious and attentive to the things I loved.

Today girls are offered more options to explore and to succeed athletically and professionally, yet we are still treated differently than boys. I'm not saying this is bad; my point is that, as women, we are conditioned from birth to include others in our lives and to consider the needs of others before we consider our own needs.

As children, our parents introduce us to the things they love or the things they feel are important so we grow up to be "happy and productive adults." Those were the words my parents used. How about you? Did your parents ever use these phrases: "when you grow up and get married…" or, "when you finish college…" or even, "when you're a (fill in the blank of the appropriate profession)…"? We are all conditioned in subtle yet powerful ways our entire lives!

Then someone comes along and breaks the mold. Be it Angelina Jolie and her adventurous life or Tyra Banks and her exciting career as a top model turned entrepreneur giving other girls the chance to be discovered. Perhaps your hero is Katie Couric, an intelligent and polished news anchor, or Meg Whitman former eBay CEO now head of HP. Perhaps it's your mom or aunt; a friend or a female leader in your community. It doesn't matter who your role model is or what power or influence they wield, there is a woman out there for each of us; someone out there who inspires you.

Take a moment. Think about a woman who inspires you in each area listed below. Write down her name and note why she is attractive to you. Is it her courage; her accomplishments; her impact; her fame? If you can't remember a name, put what you can about whom she is and how she influences you. If you'd like to mention other areas of influence, write in the margin or a loose sheet but be sure to tuck it right here for reference later.

Area of Influence	Name		What inspires you about her?
Faith			
Relationship			
Economic Impact			
Charitable Impact			
Courage			
Morality			
Competitiveness			
Fame			
Accomplishment			

The exercise you just completed is incredibly important to discovering your own passion. Recognizing who and what characteristics inspire you will help you to realize a fulfilling life for yourself. I've talked to countless women over the last 20 years. I've listened and paid special attention when their eyes light up with excitement. Many call it living vicariously through others. Now you don't need to settle for secondhand living!

Of the women and attributes you listed above, put a star by those you'd like to mimic somehow. Perhaps you'd like to be courageous or famous or impact your community in some way. And who do you believe you cannot emulate? Tell me, and tell yourself on the lines below, why do you believe that?

Let me acknowledge that considering the needs of others is not bad. But allowing oneself to get completely lost in the lives of others will not provide you with a fulfilling life! Losing yourself in a soap opera will not make your life better. Considering your own needs and desires is not selfish, it is practical. If you choose to devote your life to the cause of someone less fortunate or to raising a family, or to chasing your dream, it is a choice. It will also make those you love happy that you are happy!

The problem comes when: a) we live the life others have chosen for us: our parents, our spouses, or our friends (women and men can feel unfulfilled and even trapped as if they are living a life meant for someone else); and, when b) we devote ourselves to the dreams of someone else so completely that we miss out on opportunities to fulfill our own desires as well.

In my late 20's I met Steve. We liked each other immediately. I thought he was quirky; he thought I was fun. He asked me to marry him and to adopt my daughter. We were happy. But over time, we made some very poor decisions that cost us dearly. Years later, Steve admitted he didn't think it was a good idea at the time but he wanted to make me happy. Steve was not confident in himself; he thought he might lose me if I wasn't happy. We had not joined in marriage as partners. We had fallen into the trap of assumed peer pressure. He assumed how I'd act if unhappy rather than taking a chance and talking things through.

Yet, to prove to you that you can make a difference in the world even when you are not in an ideal situation, it was Steve who supported my quest to start my own business. He encouraged me to start training:

> **Peer Pressure:** In 2006 Liz Claiborne, Inc. conducted a survey focused on Teen Relationship Abuse. 24% of teens (girls and boys) felt they were pressured into dating while 14% (inclusive) said they would do almost anything to keep a boyfriend or girlfriend.

a passion he helped me discover and one he shared. I have been training individuals, groups, and audiences since 1996 because Steve wanted to make me happy. And he did. Not everything turned out like we wanted, but I made a difference in my local community; I became a *Passionate Social Influencer*!

Perhaps you're not unhappy in the life you lead but you still feel there is something more for you to contribute. Let's begin to discover together what that something more is. For most people, it doesn't happen overnight but takes clear thought and direction.

Have you set clear, written goals for your future and made plans to accomplish them?

For the first five years of my marriage I fought to get diagnosed thyroid disease under control. As my health began to improve, in an effort to contribute to the family income, I started a business on July 10, 1996. In mid-1998, I was beginning to think my fledgling business might be successful. I registered for a small business course co-sponsored by the community college and business incubator. I decided it was time to get serious. We were taught to write a business plan and to document what we wanted our business to realistically look like in five years.

After the course was completed, I put the book on a shelf and had little time to refer back to it. In 2000, I moved from my home office to a retail location in downtown Concord, NC. Although I rarely pulled it out, having my business training course material on the shelf made me believe I could be successful because I had planned to be. In 2003 I was honored with my community's Small Business Person of the Year award. Nominees are scored based on the success of their business, the economic impact on the community in terms of job growth, and on community involvement. What made that happen was written goals. Although there are debates about the source of the original study, it has been proven that people who plan get more done than those who don't; and, people who work from a written plan are even more successful.

"Whether you think you can or you think you can't, you're right!"
—Henry Ford

All my life people said I was pretty. I always thought little girls were supposed to be pretty, but I thought they were saying it to get me into a dress! I was a dedicated tomboy but, as I approached my teens in the mid-70's I swooned over Teen Magazine. I remember the day I learned that I shared a birthday with David Cassidy. I ripped the page from the magazine to fill out and mail in the form and 50 cents to join the fan club. My sister and I loved to sing and, although I knew I'd never be like The Partridge Family, I wanted to try. So did my sister. So we sang every chance we got. We sang in church and at school and for family and friends. While it was fun and we made memories for a lifetime, we knew we would never be successful as singers, and we were right.

"Becoming a Passionate Social Influencer" creates a more fulfilling life!

I'm not suggesting that you exit the life you are in or become belligerent towards others in your quest to fulfill a dream. I am saying that now is the time for you to quietly and carefully consider what is missing in your life. What you love to do and who you love to be with? What inspires you? What do you do on the days that you end energized and grateful? What need might you work to fulfill in your family, in your community, in the world, or even in your own heart?

In the table, note 3-5 activities that energize you and 2-3 you wish you could avoid:

Activity		Tired or Fired Up?		What impact does this have?

In order to have a new beginning, something must end.

Sometimes, the only way to have a new beginning is to recognize what must end, to allow it to happen, and to mourn. Mourn? Yes! We often celebrate and recognize endings in our lives, even as we stand up to face the new beginnings. Consider high school graduation, a new job, getting married. In each of these scenarios, we happily move from one life to the next, but many of us feel sadness, even as we embark on new opportunities. Sometimes we fool ourselves into thinking that life won't be much different; until we are smacked in the face with reality. We all feel for the nervous bride about to walk down the aisle!

In 2003, I taught a 6 week small group course to nearly every one of about 500 hourly employees at the Charlotte, NC AT&T call center: "Creating a Vision". AT&T was preparing for possible layoffs and closings. The union had arranged for a pilot to determine if teaching a life course would help employees deal with the transition.

The most difficult module, without fail, was the first where we discovered what might be ending in our lives. The toll it took on people was harsh: crying, sleepless nights, internal conflict as they faced reality. Even though people knew the rest of the course would be invigorating and fun, that first week caused several to skip the remainder. Are you afraid to face what might end in your life to make room for something new?

Look back at the table on the previous page. What might end if you change your focus to do more of those things that energize you? What impact might it have on whom (positive or negative) if you move forward to find your passion?

Energizing Activity		What might be lost?		What impact might this have?

Another topic we tackled during those 6 weeks was Legacy. What will be written on your tombstone? What will be said at your eulogy? This is important. This will be your end game… your personal goal. Take some time to consider this question carefully and write it here:

Celebrate your genius; do something magical today!

My dad has long been an inspiration to me. I often wish I could be the daughter he always hoped for but I never seem to get it right. One thing my dad taught and shared with us was his passion for mercy. Dad learned to drive a bus so he could work Saturday School at church with my sister and I, busing kids in from the inner city to teach them about the Lord while their parents, often single moms, had some much needed time to focus on cleaning or shopping or even rest.

When I was a teen, Mom worked at a nursing home of about 125 beds. She and Dad would arrange to bring as many of the even somewhat mobile patients over to our split level ranch as they could for Thanksgiving dinner. I remember Elsie, a 47 year old woman with MS so severe she could hardly control her muscles. She was light as a feather for Dad as he carried her up the steps of our home and sat her in a real dining room chair for the feast.

As an adult, I'd ride with Dad as he picked up mentally handicapped people for Sunday school. As each one saw him pull up in the van, they'd rush as fast as they could with big smiles and hugs: "Bob is here!" they'd say. And their magic spread infectiously as everyone around them couldn't keep the smiles from appearing. It didn't matter what they were suffering, what they were going through, they were always happy to see Bob.

Dad taught me that being kind, serving the under privileged, and recognizing the genius in every person, even if others couldn't see it, was a priceless gift, not only for them but for those of us who recognize it in others.

Who might be positively impacted by the passion swelling in you? The people you serve; the people who watch you enjoy the fruits of your love? Keep in mind that there is joy in collaborating with those you care about. Sharing your experiences with your children or partner, while remaining open to what interests and passions they might develop will impact them their entire lives. Could it be too late? Don't worry. Everyone will notice (if not appreciate) the joy of following your passion. It's never too late to make a course correction and start a new journey.

July 2010, my left knee started to swell and soon sharpening pain set in. Without health insurance, I rented crutches yet within a week, my right knee started to hurt too. A couple more weeks brought unbearable pain. I borrowed a wheelchair. By September x-rays showed that, although they were inflamed and had a touch of arthritis from an old injury, my knees were "the picture of 47-year old health." Cortisone injections helped the pain but did nothing for the swelling. Soon other joints followed: my elbows, ankles, wrists and fingers... by the end of October I was in constant level 8 or 9 pain, ill with flu-like symptoms and exhausted. I was wholly dependent upon my partner Mike for most daily activities. By January, I was diagnosed with aggressive, wide-spread, debilitating Rheumatoid Arthritis, an excruciatingly painful disease that attacks the joints. This was never going to go away.

Chronic Illness: Centers for Disease Control and Prevention National Center for Chronic Disease Prevention and Health Promotion shares that 7 out of 10 deaths among Americans each year are from chronic disease and, in 2005 almost 1 in 2 adults had at least one chronic illness. About ¼ of those suffer from one or more daily activity limitation.

I thought the track we were on to change lives through the new world of social media, teaching people to use LinkedIn and social networking tools to find success was over. It was beyond difficult for us both in different ways, but Mike never left my side. As he cared for me, we continued to work toward our passion: changing the world for one person at a time and training others to do the same.

Now, I seem to be very successful and accomplished. Indeed, I was ranked number 21 on Forbes list of the Top 50 Social Media Power Influencers globally in Jan 2012. My journey isn't over; neither is yours. No matter where you are, no matter your age, you can make a difference by finding and following your dream to become a ***Passionate Social Influencer!***

Now, read back over your answers throughout the chapter:

- Who and what inspires you and starred those you'd like to mimic.
- You listed who and why you thought you could not emulate. (Do you still feel that way?)
- You listed activities that energize you and what you'd like to avoid when possible.
- You thought about what might end in your life in order to allow you a new beginning.
- You wrote what you hope will be your legacy.

Here are some final thoughts for you to help you reach success:

- Focus on what you love, what inspires you, what energizes you.
- Look for tools that will help you further the work of your passion.
- Talk about your passion to everyone who will listen. You'll find like-minded people who share your dreams.
- Don't hide your struggle. You don't need to highlight it, but people are more inspired when they know you overcame adversity to achieve what you do.
- Smile: it is easily shared and offers hope.
- Hug: hugs are always free and typically reciprocated.
- Show and share gratitude: there is always someone who has it harder than you.

- Use the new social media tools to develop your passion, find resources and supporters, and to learn and share best practices. Working together with others will ensure you are never alone and always mentoring while being mentored.
    - LinkedIn and a Blog – to display your professional credentials and educate people about your passion and work.
    - Twitter – either personal or for your persona to attract like-minded people and stir interest in your cause.
    - Facebook, Google+ and Pinterest – to tell your story, build a loyal following and showcase your successes.

Notes:

ABOUT THE AUTHOR

Felicia Shaw

Felicia has worked at State Farm for 17 years, with the past 10 years, as a Community Development Advisor. Felicia enjoys working to improve communities. When Felicia isn't doing community development through State Farm, she's developing people through her business, Simply In Your Purpose. As a Balance Expert, certified Life Coach and Motivational Speaker she empowers high-achieving individuals to gain a sense of their priorities and simply their lives.

Felicia is also a Best Selling Author of "Unbreakable Spirit", which is presented by International Speaker, Lisa Nichols. This book of inspiration is listed in four best-selling categories on Amazon. In late Fall of 2012, Felicia is releasing her newest book, "The Enemy Within", which teaches on caring for you in 15 minutes a day so you can give effectively to others!

She is the radio host of Minding My Business, which provides tips & resources for both aspiring and established entrepreneurs. This show is aired on WXRJ 94.9 FM every Wednesday at 6 pm CST. People can listen to the show on line at www.WXRJ.org.

Felicia received both her BBA and MBA from Western Michigan University. She received her coaching certification from Coach Training Alliance, a school accredited by the International Coach Federation (ICF). She also received her ATM & CL designations through Toastmasters International.

In addition to maintaining her personal coaching practice, Felicia is also a mentor to many, and sits on various boards and committees. She also enjoys inspiring people through action-oriented workshops & presentations.

Felicia believes if we help one another, we can all grow.

Contact:
Felicia Shaw
Balance Expert, High Achiever Life Coach, Motivational Speaker & Best Selling Author
Direct number: 309-706-9615
Direct email: Felicia@SimplyInYourPurpose.com
Website: www.SimplyInYourPurpose.com
Let's connect: Facebook Twitter

EIGHTEEN

I Am Enough

Felicia Shaw

Have you ever talked yourself out of something? So often we have the negative self-chatter in our subconscious mind, which stops us from achieving the greatness that's within us.

I still remember when Lisa Nichols asked me to be a part of her book. Lisa is a New York Times bestselling author, an International Speaker and Transformational Coach. She has a wonderful spirit and her presence is bright, but I was intimidated by her greatness. Instantly, my pulse started to race because I felt so inadequate and so small. My mind started to say "what will I write about that someone wants to hear", "you know you got a C in writing", "your boss even said that you needed to improve your writing skills and that's probably why you didn't get a promotion". My mind continued to build on this negativity by saying "I haven't accomplished as much as much as these other authors in the book", and "I'm not good enough".

My panic increased as I started thinking of an excuse to hide my shame and to make this awkward feeling go away. So I told her thanks for the wonderful opportunity and for thinking of me, but I couldn't afford it at the time. She then replied that I really couldn't afford not to and then she said "make me a radical offer that I can't refuse". Since I couldn't convince myself that I could do it, I said "let me think about it" and then I strategically let the deadline pass, so I didn't have to do it or better yet, say no. Notice that I said I strategically let the deadline pass. If I had spent more time strategizing on how to do it, I could have had earlier successes and less anxiety. I'm a motivational speaker, a mentor to many, and a High Achievers Life Coach. I have many experiences and stories to share. But that negative feeling or emotion of anxiety that flooded my body, caused me to crawl back into a shell and not put my best foot forward. I didn't feel that I was enough to be a part of this book. I was completely unaware that I self-sabotaged myself. My emotions got the worst of me. I let fear have complete control. Emotions are so powerful and are strong motivators of future actions.

What are emotions? Emotions are what drive us and often motivates us. They are described as consistent responses to events. Emotions control your mood, behavior and actions. They provide the signals of feelings, which cause us to react. So often, emotions, so to speak, get the best of you, due to an event that took place. As a result, you take either positive or negative actions. When it's a negative feeling, the response can be justification or repression of those unwanted emotions. If your emotion is attached to a positive event, you experience a positive emotion, which causes a positive action. Emotions affect our moods and that affects the decisions that we make, which causes certain behaviors or actions.

To change your behaviors, you must first understand where they are derived. Studies have shown that emotions are formed in the subconscious mind. Your subconscious mind stores and organizes your memories, and then it links common emotions to it. The type of emotion we feel, depends on the kind of experience we've had. Unfortunately, we tend to hold onto negative emotions long after the experience has taken place.

Your subconscious mind controls all of your perceptions and values. In the subconscious mind, habits are both stored and generated, and you're often completely unaware of it. Change happens in the subconscious mind, and you have to bring it up to your conscious mind; then your conscious mind needs to believe that the change is real.

As I've researched many articles, I came to the conclusion that the subconscious mind has difficulty processing negatives. For example, if I set a goal to "stop smoking", my subconscious mind first has to create "smoking", and then attempt to get rid of what has been created. Unfortunately, the word "smoking" is in my head. Well if that's in my mind constantly, it then becomes what I want to do.

In other words, when we try not to think of something, or when we develop a goal that involves "not doing" something, our subconscious mind doesn't understand that we want to eliminate what we are thinking about; not create it or solicit it. Once this thought is in your mind, it's difficult, but not impossible to change. Instead try saying "I choose to be nicotine free".

To begin to change your subconscious belief system, you need to be able to recognize your emotion.

Various experts have indicated that our primary emotions are: love, joy, sadness, fear, anger, surprise, disgust, and anticipation. Each of those emotions provides a subset of emotions that range from affection to rage. If you learn to recognize the emotion, then you can modify your response to it. We can't change our past or the way we feel about a particular situation. However, we can change how we respond to it. One way, is to journal your journey.

Step 1 – Journaling

Begin to keep a journal and update it every evening before bed. If you want to change your behaviors, then you need to have a better understanding of yourself. You can do this by looking at what triggers your emotions; this happens when you journal about what's taking place in your life.

On page one of the journal, write the statement "I Am Enough". This is the first thing that you will see every day. Let it become a part of your subconscious mind.

On page two of the journal, write down:

1. The date.
2. What was the emotion (it can be positive or negative)?
3. What were you thinking about, which caused the emotion?
4. Is there evidence to support or reject that thought?
5. What is the rational reason of why the situation happens?
6. What's another way to react to the situation?

Place these daily entries into your journal for a minimum of 21 days. The first reason is to create a healthy habit. The second reason is that this will enable you to see patterns of behavior. Remember, once you're aware of what's taking place, you can then make behavioral changes.

Step 2 – Awareness

Let's start by discussing self-limiting beliefs. When a poor experience happens in our life, we have a negative emotional response. To enable us to deal with that emotion, we create a belief. Many times we make assumptions to reinforce our belief without any evidence that it's real. For example, if you weren't selected to participate on a committee at work, you may create a subconscious belief that you weren't invited because you're not good enough. Then you shift that belief to other areas of your life. As a continuing example, you believe you weren't invited to lunch, because you're not good enough, and never considered that the person may have thought you were busy. We again shift this thought to other areas of our life and continue building upon it and making that belief stronger of I'm not good enough.

It's time to become aware of some of your beliefs about yourself. Once you become aware of some of your thought processes, then you can begin to change it. Please write down the first response that comes to mind in the current state (middle column) to the following statements:

	CURRENT STATE	WHY?	FUTURE STATE
I feel I am financially:			
I am motivated by:			
I feel I am:			
When the unexpected happens, I:			
My greatest strength is:			
I am weak when I:			
When around leaders I feel:			
When pressured I:			
My greatest fear is:			
I feel guilty about:			
I need to learn to:			
My biggest obstacle in life is:			
I get upset with myself because:			
What drives most of my behavior is:			
My most frequent emotion is:			
I keep trying to stop:			
I am most proud of:			
I am very dissatisfied with:			

It takes courage to be real with yourself. William Shakespeare quoted "This above all: to thine own self be true". Congratulations on beginning your journey. Do this awareness exercise every six months and be sure to journal where you are in this journey.

Step 3 – Reframing

Now that you are aware of some of your beliefs, it's time to go back to the above statements and now write how you would like to be. For example, CURRENT STATE: "When the unexpected happens, I: am frustrated". Why? Because when I was younger, surprises scared me. MY FUTURE STATE: I will think about it calmly and ask for help.

Use empowering statements, instead of saying "I can't", begin to say "I choose". Choices give you power. Also, lose the thought of being perfect. We're not expected to be perfect, but only to make progress.

Step 4 – Create New Habits

Begin to do new things to create new positives experiences that will encourage positive behavior, which can become habit forming. Below are a few ideas, but don't confine yourself to these only, think outside the box and find new things that work for you.

1. Disrupt the pattern – Anytime you start negative self-talk, you lose a privilege. For example, when you find yourself using "I can't" language, you lose an hour of TV/computer time at home.

2. Focus on pleasant memories – Think on times when you felt totally powerful, a time when you felt totally loved, a time when you fell down laughing, or a time when you felt totally confident, etc. This way you can begin to focus on the positive versus the negative.

3. The Law of Attraction – This is a theory which indicates that by focusing on positive thoughts and expecting the best outcomes, you will attract positive things into your life. Start your day by expecting great things to happen.

4. Anchoring – Close your eyes and think on a time when you were happy. As you focus on that memory, take your right hand and begin to squeeze one of your knuckles on your left hand. When this action is done repeatedly in conjunction with the positive memory, you find that in most situations, you can go back to that positive state of mind.

5. Have a full sensory experience - On a beautiful sunny day, I drove to Lake Michigan. When I got to the beach, I took off my shoes and I observed my footprints. At this moment, one of my favorite inspirations, called Footprints came into my memory. I then started walking out towards the water and I felt the waves washing upon my ankles, and my toes squishing in the sand. I felt the warmth of the sun on my face and the gentle wind blowing through my hair. I began listening to the sounds of nature all around me: the rush of the water, the birds singing, and the wind in the trees. I not only looked around, but I used all of my senses to experience the true beauty around me. I then picked up three rocks, and I closed my eyes while rubbing those rocks, to capture this into my memory. It was so peaceful there, and anytime my life gets slightly chaotic, I pick up my rock and I'm able to experience a tranquil moment. This relaxes me.

You, of course have to find what works for you. Where is a place that gives you peace or totally relaxes you? Take it in completely using most or all of your senses (sight, smell, taste, touch, and hearing), so you create a full visual experience in your mind.

6. Create your circle of support – Let your loved ones know what you aspire to do or be. Find a positive mentor or model of excellence. Look at joining professional or support groups. Begin to pray and meditate daily.

To summarize, begin journaling daily to have a better understanding of yourself. Become aware of your emotions. Continue to reframe self-limiting beliefs and use empowering statements. Whenever you have a negative emotion, proactively begin changing your behavior to create positive new habits.

These are a few suggestions that you can implement, which are intended to give you beginning steps to the change you desire. Your past doesn't define your future. You are more than enough to achieve your dreams and be who you were called to be.

What's your new I AM statement? For me, "I'm strong enough, I'm wise enough, and I'm good enough". My story has a happy ending, but it's truly not the end, it's just the beginning. The second time that I was offered an opportunity to be a co-author of Lisa's next book, I said yes. I'm now a co-author of the Amazon best seller, Unbreakable Spirit.

When I'm faced with a new challenge, the fear of the unknown and that negative self-chatter begins in my head. However, I remind myself that I only fail when I don't try, and I recall memories of success to encourage me. I pray and read scriptures daily, which empower me and strengthens my faith. Then I step out, in spite of the fear, and move toward my dreams. I employ positive behaviors and I don't have any regrets. I dare to continue to learn and grow.

I discovered that I Am Enough and you are too!

ABOUT THE AUTHOR

VANESSA SHAW

Vanessa Shaw has dedicated her career to helping people achieve greater success, happiness and fulfillment in their personal and business lives. As a leading Business and Marketing Mentor, she has a track record of helping many international clients to overcome business challenges and create lucrative businesses that positively impact the lives of others. She is passionate about helping entrepreneurs, business owners, coaches and consultants around the globe to step up powerfully into the world of business so that they can achieve the results and impact they truly desire and ultimately deserve.

Vanessa's aspiration for making a difference in people's lives is reflected in almost everything she pursues. In 2005, she herself made the leap from stay-at-home mother to successful entrepreneur. With no formal business training herself, Vanessa invested in learning the nuts and bolts of building a business from the ground up. Today, she helps others to replicate her own success through easy-to-implement programs like her *6 Figure Business Success System*™ and *How to Get 5 clients or more in the next 30 days and Generate immediate income*™.

Vanessa is highly sought after by clients around the globe for her coaching expertise and the rapid and tangible results she helps her clients obtain. She has coached entrepreneurs and business leaders from the United States, Canada, United Kingdom, Australia, France, Switzerland, Czech Republic and many other countries. Her clients have included International Law Firms, KPMG, World Economic Forum, Oracle, The Global Fund as well as numerous start-ups and smaller businesses. Vanessa has extensive international experience having grown up in the UK and then spent over 20 years in Switzerland where she worked for the United Nations and set up her own business.

Vanessa now lives in Scottsdale, Arizona with her husband Robert and their 2 children, William and Olivia. Outside of running the business she enjoys walking, practicing yoga, skiing, singing, reading, theatre, entertaining and world travel.

Contact:
www.simplyzest.com
email: Vanessa.shaw@simplyzest.com
Tel: + 1 480 284 6278 (USA)
Business address: Chemin Valmont 224, 1260 Nyon Switzerland

NINETEEN

7 Steps to Greater Business and Spiritual Success

Vanessa Shaw

7 ways that self sabotage is affecting your business and how to overcome them

Warning! read with caution – you may recognize yourself in one or more of the 7 points I'll be outlining below and this could naturally trigger your own *saboteur*. You'll recognize that he or she has been woken up if you find yourself saying, "I know this stuff" or "this doesn't apply to me" or, even worse, you read through it and still don't take any action. This feeds your saboteur's ego even more and then he is in for the kill with "see, you're not really up for this, you're not really good enough" or any of his other favorite ploys for keeping you playing small. You don't have to make every single change I discuss below but do commit to at least one or two of them so that you weaken your own saboteur.

For many women there is often a major disconnect between being successful in business AND being fulfilled spiritually. They often can't see that their business success can help them to grow spiritually, be of greater service to others *and* allow them to make a bigger contribution to the world around them.

Growing your own business can be a truly rewarding experience not only for you as a business owner but also for those who benefit from your products and services, collaborate with you and are employed by you. Having the right talents and skills to grow a successful business is only one part of the equation, as your journey has to also be a journey of personal growth. There will be many challenges along your path to success. Who you become on that journey can prove to be much more fulfilling that all the income that you'll be generating.

Women are naturally nurturers and caregivers, which typically means they take a different approach to business than men. Their skills of empathy, collaboration and care lend a refreshing balance to the more classic masculine style of competitive and action-oriented leadership. When women succeed in business this can translate into a much broader contribution to the world that has a powerful ripple effect of giving back by creating opportunities for others, supporting loved ones, donating to charities close to our hearts and teaching and inspiring others to also be successful.

Yet women also have an uncanny ability to get in their own way and self-sabotage themselves. In order to achieve greater business and spiritual success, let's take a look at 7 ways women self-sabotage.

1) **Mindset** – The results we achieve in business will be directly related to your own mindset as to what is possible and how you approach business. As Henry Ford is famously quoted as saying

"Whether you think you can, or you think you can't--you're right." Our inner thoughts influence the emotions we feel which then influence the actions we take which then influence the results we achieve externally. So it's important to have a clearer understanding of your own mindset so that you can build and grow your business on a solid internal foundation.

One key area of mindset that is directly related to business success is your perception of your own personal value and self-worth. In today's world of business there is so much being said about providing value for our customers and clients in order to attract and retain them and whilst this is true, the question of value starts a lot earlier than the client relationship. The question of value is especially relevant for service-based entrepreneurs who have the traditional business model of trading time (their services) for money. It's easy to undervalue the natural gifts you have and the value you provide to others which can lead to a fear of being found out, over-delivering and not charging the true value of your services. Women who are successful in business value themselves, the services they provide and the benefits their clients experience from their services.

Exercise: make an inventory of all of the experience, training, skills, knowledge that you possess. Consider the following areas:

- Qualifications
- Training
- Own mentoring
- Personal successes

- Life experiences
- Personal challenges you have overcome
- Work experience
- Previous client results
- Books you've read
- Seminars
- Self-knowledge, and
- Your own personal development

Create a list of at least 30 items to clarify your own personal value.

Once you've uncovered ALL that you bring to business from the different domains of your life, it's time to switch your attention to your clients.

Questions to ask yourself:

- What are the core results you help your clients achieve?
- How does achieving those results impact your clients physically, mentally, emotionally, spiritually and financially? Take the time to list all of the ripple effects across the different domains of their lives and you will quickly see how much value you are providing.
- Now imagine that the client doesn't work with you and doesn't achieve the results and improvements to their life that your work offers. How does that impact them

physically, mentally, emotionally, spiritually and financially? The gap between where they are now and the ultimate place they want to be *is* the value to them of working with you.

2) **Making comparisons** – The healthy side of comparison is that it can illuminate the path you want to follow, help you see just how far you've already come and inspire you into taking bigger steps for yourself. However many women frequently lose valuable time and energy with unhealthy comparisons and get caught up in feelings of envy, not thinking they're good enough and then finding fault with themselves that creates a negative downward spiral and keeps them playing small.

Take some time to do an inventory of where you compare yourself to others in an unhealthy way.

Who do you most compare yourself with? As you think about that person notice the automatic thoughts that pop up such as "she might be successful in business, but her home life is a disaster" as this will just feed the underlying mindset that it's not possible to be both fulfilled at work and at home.

Feelings of envy and feeling "less than" somebody else are normal. The secret is to transform them so that they work for you and not against you. What is it that you most admire about this person? How could you now emulate those qualities or skills in your own business and life? I'll share a little secret with you here – I have an amazing friend who is the "Queen of Organization". Everything she does is well organized, completed in a timely manner and beautifully executed so that she has plenty of free time to take care of her own needs, look after her family and be successful in her professional life. Before I had fully acknowledged my own feelings of envy and inadequacy, the little voice in my head would say things like "well it must be like the military living in her home or they can't possibly be having any fun" and then I would resist creating that level of organization in my own life. By taking a step back and recognizing that I was indeed feeling envious, I decided to ask her for her own tips on organization which she generously shared and in turn this dramatically improved the way I was approaching my own planning and organization, thus giving me more time for the things I enjoy.

3) **Going it alone** - trying to go it alone in business is a surefire way to limit your success and to create overwhelm and personal burnout. Support shows up in many guises from hiring somebody to take care of the home; administrative support for the business; outsourcing tasks (even when you can quickly do them yourself!); hiring a business coach who can hold you to your vision of success and achieving your business goals; to seeking joint ventures and other collaborative partnerships with professionals that could help to support you and grow your business at the same time.

Trying to do it all yourself is a form of self-sabotage that comes from thinking that in order to be successful you must demonstrate that you can do it all. The truth is though we all have the same 24 hours in any given day and your time and energy are valuable business resources to be used wisely. Here are 3 steps you can take to tackle going it alone.

- Step 1 - Start by defining the tasks that only you can do in your business. You may need to do this a few times so that you eliminate more and more tasks each round. Notice your own resistance to letting go!

- Step 2 – By letting go of these tasks, now write down how you will benefit from the extra time to grow your business and to spend more time in activities that are important to you in your personal life

- Step 3 – Identify the first step you can take to enlist more support for yourself and commit to making that happen.

4) **Procrastination** - procrastination is a convenient way of playing small and feeding your saboteur – you avoid doing the things that you know you should be doing and they then become very convenient excuses that prevent you from being more successful. Ironically, procrastination in business most often shows up in the areas that would most help you grow such as marketing, following up with potential clients, exploring a joint venture relationship, securing speaking engagements and so on.

Procrastination is ultimately an emotional problem and linked to avoiding activities that you associate with uncomfortable emotions. The most common are fear-based – fear of failure, fear of rejection and even fear of success!

Being successful in business though is just as much about a journey of personal growth as it is a journey of building necessary business skills. The biggest leaps in personal growth are made on the edge of your comfort zone (and that does not mean hiding out behind your computer screen!) – this is where the greatest learning and transformation takes place.

Exercise:

- What are you currently putting off in your business that would help you to make some big leaps forwards both personally and professionally?
- What are your biggest concerns about tackling this?
- If those concerns came to fruition, could you handle them? (Hint: most times these are not serious life or death situations and you WILL survive and be able to learn from them!)
- What could you do to now get started?

5) **Lack of clear boundaries** – personal boundaries are important to establishing healthy relationships, assertiveness and self-respect. Healthy boundaries set the stage for rewarding relationships based on respect and reciprocity, being the master of your own time and also open up more opportunities that will contribute to your overall success and well-being because you are able to say no to those things that will not serve your greater good and say yes to those that will.

You can tell if your internal saboteur is at work again if you are experiencing challenges in setting and maintaining boundaries.

What this will look like in practice is tolerating unhealthy relationships that undermine your self-confidence and drain your energy. It may be that you find it really difficult to say no and then find yourself later feeling resentful about what you've accepted to do. Others are constantly setting the agenda for you and determining your priorities and you simply can't master your time. This probably translates into little time to take good care of yourself too.

In order to be more successful in both life and business, it's crucial to surround yourself with friends, family, clients and team that will support you in being your best self.

Reflections:

- Where in your life can you see evidence of "sloppy" boundaries?
- Who are you afraid of hurting if you were to say no more often?
- Where could you start to say no right now?
- What "yeses" would then start to open up for you?

6) **Creating drama and chaos** – it's amazing how women can attract drama and chaos into their lives as a way of sabotaging their own success. They can feel like this is something that is happening to them and for sure we all have challenging moments when unexpected events occur in our lives. However if there seems to be a consistent amount of drama and chaos you may want to take a closer look at the common denominator - you! Drama and chaos can take on many different forms to constantly being late or pushing up against tight deadlines to attracting needy friends or clients who require your attention to being in a feast or famine cycle with your business.

Drama and chaos act as distractions (and plausible excuses) to take your focus away from your business goals. It's important to find out how this drama is serving you because it does have a purpose, even if it's not that healthy.

- Do you love the adrenaline rush of doing things last minute?
- Do you love to feel needed by others or love the attention that this drama creates for you?
- Or are these convenient ways of avoiding stepping outside of your comfort zone and being more successful?

If you love the excitement that momentarily surrounds the drama, consider new and healthier ways to create more excitement in your life or business that doesn't impact your bottom line. After all, drama and chaos consume valuable time and energy – take an inventory for yourself of how much time is lost each week and consider how you'd benefit from that free time.

7) **Money** – your own relationship with money also impacts the level of success you achieve in business. Ultimately the amount of money you generate through your business is an indicator of how successful you are and how big an impact you are making in the world. Women are very generous and nurturing by nature yet when their own financial needs are not being met it can quickly start to limit how they express themselves through their work and contribute more fully to the world around them.

Our relationship with money was unconsciously established in childhood, influenced primarily by parents, caregivers and other family members. Often something we don't talk about openly, this relationship with money can lay dormant for a long time but then starts to bubble up to the surface and show up in business and financial results. A woman's relationship with money is often tied to her own sense of self-worth which can prevent her from standing fully in her power when it comes to generating more income, keeping more income and effectively managing the financial aspects of her life and business.

The bottom line for all of us is that if we are suffering from financial stress and not getting our own financial needs met, it becomes considerably more difficult to show up powerfully, contribute fully to others and express our full potential.

Consider what your own relationship with money looks like. What are the automatic thoughts that pop into your mind? For example, are they "money's not important to me", "it's not about the money" or "you have to work really hard to earn money".

What are the thoughts and beliefs you have about money?

____

____

____

____

Once you've identified your predominant thoughts and beliefs you will then start to see how these are impacting your business. I love to help my clients at a very practical level clean up some of the money messes that are currently in their lives so that these money messes no longer drain them financially, emotionally and spiritually. Here are my top 3 questions to get you started:

Do you know each of these 5 crucial numbers in your business?

- Your business costs?
- your income or revenue?
- your profit?
- the salary you receive (or wish to receive)?
- the next bold money goal that you want to set for yourself?

What courageous money conversations are you avoiding having?

- With clients who owe you money?
- With suppliers who owe you money?
- Others who owe you money?

If you were truly standing fully in your power as a successful business woman, how would you handle these conversations?

Are the fees you are charging consistent with the value you deliver to your clients?

Many women undercharge for their services so ask yourself the question "What would need to be true for me to raise my fees?"

Stop playing small

Life is simply too short to be playing small and allowing the saboteur to determine the level of success and impact that you achieve.

It's time to get out of your own way, step up as the powerful and inspirational woman that you are meant to be and serve the world more fully with your amazing gifts. As a final gift to you I'd love to share the quote that continues to inspire me whenever my saboteur starts to speak to me too loudly.

"Our deepest fear is not that we are inadequate. Our deepest fear is that we are powerful beyond measure. It is our light, not our darkness, that most frightens us. We ask ourselves, who am I to be brilliant, gorgeous, talented, and fabulous? Actually, who are you not to be? You are a child of God. Your playing small doesn't serve the world. There's nothing enlightened about shrinking so that other people won't feel insecure around you. We are all meant to shine, as children do."

—Marianne Williamson

ABOUT THE AUTHOR

Mala Shah

Mala has grown up surrounded by the very positive, entrepreneurial spirit of the family firm – an import/export business specializing in food products from around the globe.

In 1990, Mala decided to go it alone, and started working as a secretary at the European Bank for Reconstruction and Development. Over the next 14 years she worked her way up to a Portfolio Analyst, where she was managing Multi-Million Dollar contracts in Russia, Georgia, Bulgaria as well as Ukraine.

Mala achieved her Degree in Psychology BSc from Birkbeck College, London, while working Full time at the European Bank for reconstruction and Development. Education did not stop here for Mala, she went to train as a Life Coach with Noble Manhattan. A Neuro-Linguistic Programming (NLP) Master Practitioner qualification from Paul McKenna and Richard Bandler's training school. Thought Field Therapy Practitioner with Dr. Roger Callahan's training centre.

In 2007, she decided once again to go it alone and set up her own Coaching and Mentoring business, under her own name, Mala Shah, with the mantra

"Nothing is impossible if you put your mind to it".

Mala has frequently volunteered her services, especially where Youth have been concerned. She has been very passionate about going to schools and talking about, amongst other things, how she "created" the Change she wanted to see for women in society!

Lately, over the past couple of years, Mala has embarked on another business venture, together with her own immediate family, and now offer their Managerial expertise at Seminars and Events, where attendance had been from the low 500s up to 42,000 people attending!

They have assisted at seminars by T. Harv Eker, Robert Kiyosaki Richard Branson and many others!

Contact:
Email: mala@malashah.com
Website: www.malashah.com
Cell phone: +44 7877 470 333 (United Kingdom)

TWENTY

Mission to Success

Mala Shah

"Attitude is a little thing that makes a big difference"
—Winston Churchill

Success comes in many forms. What may be a success to one may be a disappointment for another. For example person A, baking a cake for the first time and it turns out to be a bit dry yet for person A it was a successful mission. However, for Person B, who is an expert in baking cakes, this would be a disappointment or a catastrophe. But we must not forget that there are times when things are beyond our control where we cannot be solely responsible for the disappointment. Let us consider the following:

- What were your greatest accomplishments?
- What were your biggest disappointments?

Once you have listed your accomplishments and disappointments,

I would suggest that you identify several takes for each one: What did you learn from these? Bring self-defeating actions, if any, to the surface. There may be one or more (than one) lessons to be learnt from both our achievements and disappointments. There are a couple of lessons I learnt during one project I was managing. These lessons listed below helped to avoid self-sabotage and so to improve on my mission to success.

Learn from others: If the recipe works do not modify it. Robert Kiyosaki, author of "Rich Dad – Poor Dad" book, emphasizes about different attitudes to money and how his biological father who was poor and his friend's father who was rich, influenced the key decisions in Kiyosaki's life.

"Don't reinvent the wheel, just align it" —Anthony J. D' Angelo

Listen to yourself: Listen to your instinct: Follow your gut feeling. Usain Bolt an Olympian had mediocre events before the Olympics. Everyone had begun to doubt his ability to even win a medal. Bolt was unwavering; he never gave up on himself and did not accept any negativity. Even on the night before the heats, all he said was "I know how great I can be, just watch me". Bolt became the first man to successfully defend both 100m and 200m sprint titles in the 2012 Olympic Games, clocking 19.32 for 200 meters. Bolt listened and believed in himself.

"Listening is a magnetic and strange thing, a creative force. The friends who listen to us are the ones we move toward. When we are listened to, it creates us, makes us unfold and expand" —Karl A. Menniger.

Learn to be Patient: If you lack patience you will fail even before you have started.

If Thomas Edison had called himself a failure we would not have the privilege of the light bulb. As an inventor, Edison made 1,000 unsuccessful attempts at inventing the light bulb. When a reporter asked, "How did it feel to fail 1,000 times?" Edison replied, "I didn't fail 1,000 times. The light bulb was an invention with 1,000 steps". Thomas Edison **believed** in himself and his idea. Another person with lot of patience is Nick Vujicic, born without limbs due to the rare Tetra-amelia disorder. Throughout his childhood Nick had to live a life of difficulties and hardships. However, he managed to get over these with great patience and at seventeen, started his non-profit organisation: Life without Limbs.

"Patience, persistence and perspiration make an unbeatable combination of success" —Napoleon Hill.

Practically every individual resists analyzing their mistakes because they think they have failed in a big way. The trick here is to examine what preceded our success and disappointment and what we can do differently to improve. Remember the purpose of this exercise is not simply to know yourself better but actually to use what you learn from it and triumph.

Beliefs are so important to us because they allow us to create the life we desire. If you are filled with powerful and empowering Beliefs, you will attract the people and events you need to become successful. On the other hand, if you are filled with Limiting Beliefs you will attract failure, poverty and ill health. Therefore it is important to recognise how we interpret events in our life and take the opportunity to learn from these actions in a positive way. By taking the positive action we are allowing ourselves to progress forward and this positive action reinforces and empowers other positive beliefs you would already have.

Beliefs are often expressed in the following forms:

Positive Empowering (allows you to move forward)	Negative Disempowering (Limiting your choices)
I can	I can not
I should	I should not
I must	I must not
I have got enough	I have nothing

We must learn to re-program our **self-talk** and change the negative statements: “I will never achieve this” into “I will definitely achieve this!” A Belief is an idea, an assumed truth. It is a generalised opinion we have about the world around us, why we act as we do, what we are capable of achieving and who we are. Our unique beliefs start to develop during our childhood. After two years of age our beliefs are adopted from our parents, teachers and then friends and also from what we see and hear around us. Seeing is believing. Till then we believe that anything is possible. For example when I saw the following pictures for the first time I could see only one image and not more than one as I believe my awareness of how I saw the world around me at that time was restricted. What do you see in the following pictures?

Ambiguous Images **What do you SEE?**

Answers at the end of this chapter

1)

2)

3)

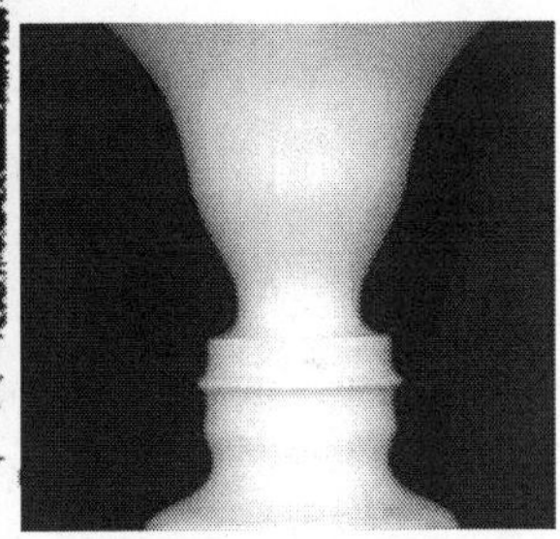

Beliefs and Awareness

We are all aware of our physical, emotional, social and intellect make-up. The value we place in these areas of your life will affect our attitude to how we react to achieving our goals. The table below shows an example of an individual who scored from scale 0 out of 10.

Belief and Awareness: How satisfied are you?

Belief and Awareness	
• **Physical Attributes** 6/10 Health, fitness and appearance	• **Emotional Make-up** 5/10 Are you happy, a loving person, caring and considerate, calm/secure
• **Intellect** 7/10 Your intelligence, skills and qualifications	• **Social Skills** 6/10 How comfortable you feel in social situations and what you believe others thing of you?
What is your Score (out of 10)	

What is your score? Take a moment to reflect on why you have given yourself these marks. What would you achieve if you had loads of confidence: One thing is for sure; "You are capable of far more than you think".

Sir Edmund Hilary failed to climb the mountain Everest the first time around. He could have given up like many others before him? What did he say "I will be back" - I am growing and you are not. So I will be back with better preparation because I know I will conquer you. On 29 May 1953, Edmund and Tenzing, a Nepalese Sherpa were the first mountaineers ever recorded to climb to the peak of Mt. Everest.

Positive ways to Boost your Confidence

Belief and Awareness	
Physical Attributes • Walk with confidence • Start Walking/ Join Gym • Treat yourself to a Makeover	**Emotional Make-up** • Reward yourself -Celebrate • Action one good deed a day • Forgive yourself
Intellect • Join evening classes • Request training at work • Develop Will Power	**Social Skills** • Start a conversation • Share your positive thoughts • Enjoy being complimented

We often become what we believe ourselves to be. If I believe I cannot do something, it makes me incapable of doing it. When I believe I can, I acquire the ability to do it even if I did not have it in the beginning.

—Mahatma Gandhi.

"Your Beliefs become your Thoughts; Your Thoughts become your Words, Your Words become your Actions; Your Actions become your Habits, Your Habits become your Values; Your Values become your Destiny."
—Mahatma Gandhi

Values:

Values are who we are! What we value determines what life means to us and what actions we take. When we respect our values regularly on a C**onsistent, Insistent and Persistent - CIP©,** basis we will gain clarity on the **mission to our success.**

Your values will change for example, when you start your career, you may measure your success by money and status and during this period this may be a top priority for you. But later on you get married and have a family, than work-life balance may become a top priority. As your definition of success changes, so do your values. Keeping in touch with your values is a lifetime exercise. The more you become aware of these values the better choice you can make in any situation.

To Identify your Values: Find an example from both your personal and career life.

- Identify when you were happiest, or fulfilled and satisfied.
- What were you doing? Who were you with? What contributed to the happiness? Did it feel really good and were you really confident that you were making the right choice.
- Based on your experience, decide what is important to you in your life? *Integrity, Love, Fairness, Peace, Security*

When you define your values, you discover what's truly important to you.

As Steve Jobs, the co-founder of Apple Computer, said, "The only thing that works is management by values. Find people who are competent and really bright, but more importantly, people who care exactly about the same things you care about."

Self Esteem and Confidence

Self Esteem and Confidence
Remember: **Whatever your mind can Conceive** **and Believe, You CAN Achieve.**

Who is responsible for your Confidence? **YOU!** If you don't start the process of building your confidence than nobody else will! How many times have you blamed others or circumstances for things that have gone wrong in your life? Start by surrounding yourselves with people who are willing to support you when you take up responsibility for whatever actions you take.

If you want to achieve something you can and you will. Where there is a will there is a way. We have to train our mind and let our sub-conscious do the work. If the mind is saying something and the body is doing something else there is no synchronisation, so no matter what you try you will not succeed fully. So let us look at training our mind to think more positive than negative. Turn Negative into a Positive.

Your Behaviour and its Impact

Your Behaviour and Impact		
TOPIC	Negative Response	Positive Response
Perfectionism	I did Ok, but	I am satisfied that I did my best
Age	I am too old to do that	I may be in my later years but I would like to try it
Comparison	I am not as good as	Where can I learn from?

Our Past and Forgiveness

We may learn to change the language from negative to positive but what if we are still holding on to **Our Past** then what happens. All of the above, our beliefs, values, awareness and confidence will not be in synchronisation with us and will not work. Our past is not the future, we cannot erase it but we can release it before we can move on to new goals. At the same time we must learn to forgive and move on. If you are unable to communicate directly with the other person then write down all your feelings and give it to the other person when both of you can read through it and discuss it. This may create a portal to understand where the other person is coming from. If this not practical then you may decide to throw the letter away. The purpose of writing down is to release and free yourself, from any unexpressed feelings. This exercise is vital for our future success. Some of you may have heard about the book called "The Secret" or seen the movie. It is about the Law of Attraction, for example if I hold the resentment and anger I will attract the same in my life. Then it does not matter how hard I try to accomplish the most achievable goal I may fail or take extraordinarily long to attain it and in the process may ruin my health, or have unnecessary arguments with family and friends.

As long as you don't forgive who and whatever it is will occupy rent-free space in your mind. —Isabelle Holland

It is very easy to draw tables and input the data but what happens when you are really down and don't know where to start? I would say: Be prepared, plan and set your goals. Use the SMART or GROW or ITIA models that you may already be familiar with, or even create your own.

Models and Formulae

Set S M A R T Goals	G R O W Model	I T I A Formulae
S pecific **M** easurable **A** chievable **R** ealistic **T** imely	**G**oal: **R**eality: **O**ptions: **W**hat/**W**ho/**W**hen:	**I**ntention: **T**hought: **I**magination: **A**ction:

"If you fail to plan you will plan to fail". For changes to be of any true value, they have got to be lasting and Consistent" —Anthony Robbins

As an NLP Practitioner I have come across many individuals who found it difficult to follow certain models/ formulae. Whilst listening to their comments I decided to investigate and came up with my own model which I have called "**C I P ©**". This model allows me to monitor the progress on own goals. I reviewed the goals which I have achieved in my life and what it was that kept me going. I wrote down phrases and words and noticed that few words came up again and again. I also observed similarity amongst famous individuals. The three key words were consistency, insistency and persistence.

C I P©: stands for Consistent, Insistent and Persistent.

C I P© Model

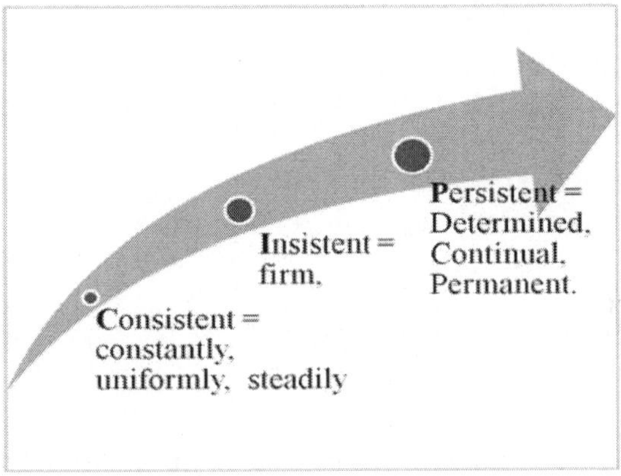

"When I thought I couldn't go on, I forced myself to keep going. My success is based on Persistence, not luck."—Estee Lauder

I must emphasise that the middle word "Insistent" in **C I P©** model may be too strong and not applicable to everyone, but certainly **C**onsistency and **P**ersistence are relevant in almost everything we aim to achieve.

We know that our beliefs and values, self-confidence and self-esteem and our behaviour have an immense impact in achieving our goals. Once we have achieved our highest goal and feel on top of this world we must have the tools to maintain the energy and keep the success at the top. There are several success tools out in the world, which I highly respect. I have created my own seven success tools.

1.	Know yourself:	Have faith in your beliefs and values.
2.	Identify your Goals:	It helps to discover our mission in life. Be Specific.
3.	Learn and Improve:	Accept Change and move on. Get organised.
4.	Conquer your fear	Turn weaknesses into strengths. Overcome any limits.
5.	Self Control:	Be disciplined. Honour commitments. Respect others.
6.	Exercise and Health:	Exercise at least 20 mins per day. Medical checkups.
7.	Master your Mind:	Power your mind with positive thoughts.

"Thoughts Becomes Things. Choose the Good Ones"
—(c) Mike Dooley, www.tut.com

Answers to Ambiguous Images What do you SEE?

1. An old and young lady
2. A red Indian and an Eskimo at his den
3. A vase and two faces

Resource:

Ambiguous images: from Google search engine

Recommended Reading:

Napoleon Hill, (1983) *Think and Grow Rich,* The random house publishing group.

Canfield J, and Switzer J, (2005) *The Success Principles,* London: Harper Collins

Anthony Robbins, (1989) *Unlimited Power,* Simon & Schuster ltd,

Rhonda Byrne, (2010) *The Secret The Power*, Simon & Schuster Inc

Recommended Video Clip to watch

Usain Bolt, (2012), "The Olympian": http://usainbolt.com/2012/08/bolt-leads-jamaicas-sweep-of-the-olympic-games-200-metres/.

Nicholas J. Vujicic (Born 4 December 1982) Life without Limbs: http://www.youtube.com/watch?v=DeTMVq6kQZI&feature=related.

Recommended Websites:

The Secret – The Power: http://thesecret.tv/thepower/.

ABOUT THE AUTHOR

Dr. Angela Roman Clack

Dr. Angela Roman Clack is CEO of Woman's Empowerment Group International, LLC, an international coaching organization created to empower women to achieve their personal and professional goals in business and in their personal lives. Dr. Clack is a Psychologist and Licensed Professional Counselor practicing in the state of New Jersey. Dr. Clack earned her doctorate in 2002 with a degree in Clinical Psychology from Argosy University, Washington, D.C.

Dr. Clack is known for her ability to teach, supervise, coach and provide training in various areas pertaining to children, youth, and their families. Along with her training and teaching abilities, she has also mastered the subject area and is making a massive impact in her community in reducing the stigma of people of color who seek mental health treatment.

Faceted in the profession of mental health for greater than 20 years, Dr. Clack has developed and maintained her specialty arena which has included training direct care counselors, social workers, and juvenile detention workers on topics such as suicide awareness and prevention, managing challenging youth with mental illness, sexuality and the sexualized child, social skills and effective communication.

Currently, Dr. Clack's private practice treats adults and youth suffering from depression, anxiety, grief/loss, as well as general emotional distress and relationship/interpersonal problems. Dr. Clack's passion has been to provide emotional support and to empower women who are experiencing emotional distress and feelings of low self- worth.

Dr. Clack's approach to providing clinical care consists of teaching individuals to recognize maladaptive patterns in their thinking and behaviors that have resulted in inefficient emotional and behavioral functioning. Through her work with her clients she seeks to empower individuals to live life to their fullest potential!

Books:

Co-Author of Breaking Free: Overcoming Self- Sabotage.
Chapter title: Learning to Love Yourself: "Healing from the Inside Out" (2013)
The Power of God Daily Devotional 2013

Expertise:

Intrapersonal Development, Empowerment Coach & Consultant
Self-Awareness, Self Esteem and Image Building

Seminars and Training Offered:

African American Women & Depression
Balancing Act - Empowering Individuals to Live a Balanced Life
What's Eating You? - Emotional Eating...Are Poor Eating Habits and Unhealthy Food Choices Reflective of Your Emotional Life
Self-Esteem & Self Image:

Certifications:

Certified International Women's Empowerment Coach

Additional Services:

Psychotherapy for Youth, Adults, Families, Couples
Christian Counseling
Associations:
The Professional Woman Network
Kingdom Chamber of Commerce
American Counseling Association
Employee Assistance Professional Association
South Jersey Psychological Association

Contact:
Company Name: Clack Associates, LLC
Mailing Address: 2005 Liberty Place, Sicklerville, NJ 08081
Telephone: 856.875.5335
Fax: 856.875.5336
Email: clackassociates@aol.com
Website: www.clackassociates.com
www.facebook.com/ClackAssociates

TWENTY-ONE

Learning to Love Yourself: Healing from the Inside Out

"If you refuse to settle for anything but less than the best, that's what life will give." —Oprah and Guest Author Sarah Ban Breathnach [Oprah Soul Series]

The Merriam-Webster dictionary defines sabotage in the following ways: destruction of an employer's property (as tools or materials) or the hindering of manufacturing by discontented workers; destructive or obstructive action carried on by a civilian or enemy agent to hinder a nation's war effort; an act or process tending to hamper or hurt; deliberate subversion. The word sabotage is often associated in the media (movies, news, etc.) with an act of war, a stealthy strategy to defeat an opponent, or a government conspiracy that often ends in disaster. Now imagine putting the word 'self' in front of the word sabotage. That means a self –inflicted, intentional, deliberate act to hurt oneself in some form or manner.

Let's take it a step further. Self-sabotage is about making bad choices consciously. However, the motivation and drive underlying the "why do I do this?" is less available to our immediate awareness. We all are guilty of operating this way to some degree. The difference becomes more apparent when we have to deal with the consequences of those bad, unhealthy choices. In other words, when a person knows something is not good for them and he/she makes a choice to do it anyway (while denying the cost), consequently ends in the person being hurt and then angry at themselves for making the choice KNOWING the undesirable outcome.

The key to recovery and overcoming self- sabotage is about increasing one's emotional awareness and emotional language and developing the ability and capacity to reflect sooner rather than later when making decisions. Shakespearian literature profoundly captured it best, "*This above all: to thine own self be true, And it must follow, as the night the day, Thou canst not then be false to any man." (Polonius in Hamlet).* Unless we can be true to ourselves first, we cannot be true to others.

Why do I do this?

As a psychotherapist, I often encounter women who have struggled with self-sabotage behaviors usually in the context of relationships. However, by the time the woman presents her issues in treatment she has endured years of emotional pain.

The initial work of therapy is to facilitate the client in uncovering the drive or motivation for why one engages in self-sabotage and then work towards a healthy resolution to end self- destructive behaviors. In my practice, it has been my experience that many women are victims of abusive and dysfunctional relationships since early childhood. That includes family and non-family. Some even before they knew language or could speak. Some adults are given up for adoption at birth, or left abandoned as infants and young children; are the victim of in utero exposure to drugs/alcohol and toxins taken in by the birthing mother; and others are the victims of sexual and physical abuse very early in their development. Trauma and tragedy (early in life) often result in the messages ("I am not wanted." "I am unlovable." "I am not worthy.") that are then internalized and believed by the victim to be true.

You see, our earliest memories of love, care and nurturance is from our parents. When babies cry, emotionally available and healthy parents attend to their babies' needs and with time can even predict what's wrong by the type of cry (hunger, anger, pain, tired, discomfort). In turn, the baby learns and is conditioned to the fact that when I cry, my parents take care of me and meets that need. Thus, the child learns to trust and feel protected and nurtured by their parents. When we are rejected, abandoned or unloved by our primary caregivers (our first real love), those who are supposed to love and protect us, we are left without the capacity to develop those same feelings; thus we must learn very early to self-soothe. If a healthy adult that cares, teaches, and models healthy behaviors does not enter our lives, we grow into adults who have unmet needs for love, care, security, belonging, self-worth or validation.

Consequently, we begin to seek those needs (consciously and unconsciously) in others and find ourselves engaged in a pattern of unhealthy, unsatisfying relationships that leave us feeling that we are unlovable and undesirable. Unfortunately, we love ourselves less and less. The negative, early messages begin to play again "I am *broken.*" "I am *damaged goods.*" Yes you are broken, *broken in your spirit and soul.* You are NOT damaged goods. But your emotional mind has been greatly impacted by the early negative messages you received about "who you are and who you are not" that became internalized as part of your identity. Your sensor is *broken.* "Huh?"

Newer cars are built with computer sensors that can detect a problem before it happens and give you a warning for you to get the car looked at by an expert. If we ignore the sensor "…that engine light is always on, I just think that's the dealer's way of making money, there's nothing wrong" we may pay a higher price than we would have if we had just paid attention. How many times have you said that or heard someone say that. I have!

Like a brand new car has a sophisticated warning system that something is happening to your car's engine, your emotional sensor is designed to operate in that same way to warn you when you are in a familiar and unhealthy situation, relationship, etc. When you have a fully functioning *emotional* sensor, you are more aware of the signals of danger. Such as exploitation, abuse, being taken advantage of, feeling devalued). When your *emotional* sensor in *broken* or missing pieces, you likely miss (overlook, avoid, block out) the warning signals because the signs and feelings are all too familiar.

What are the behaviors and thoughts of someone who engages in self-sabotage (*warning signs for a broken sensor)?* Take a moment to reflect on your past and present experiences in relationships.

<u>Think About It</u>

- Do you detect a pattern of unhealthy, unsatisfying relationships that leave you with low self- worth?
- Do you find yourself moving from one unhealthy relationship to another?
- Are you drawn to the same type of person in your relationships?
- Is there a pattern of emotionally or physically abusive interactions between you and your partner?
- Is there a strong desire to meet an unmet need through a partner or significant other?
- Do you make unhealthy compromises in your relationships in order to be loved, approved of, desired, accepted, or to not be alone?

While these are just a few of the warning signs of self-sabotage, a pattern in any area above is indicative of a person "*looking for love in all the wrong places.*"

How does self- sabotage manifest in relationships? What's Love Got to do with it?

The title of Tina Turner's movie "What's Love Got To Do With It?" is not just any old cliché. It rings true for many women who lack self- love. Healing yourself from the inside out means recognizing <u>first</u> that I am loveable and worthy of love; that I am capable of giving and receiving healthy love in an intimate relationship; that abuse and rejection are not acceptable; that I am not defined by others opinions of who they perceive me to be; that I am fearfully and wonderfully made by God's grand design; that I am not my past nor does my past define me.

Learning to love yourself is a journey of self-discovery. It may seem initially to be a painful experience but the end result will be rewarding. Those of us that gave of our ourselves extensively to others at the cost of losing who we are (our self-identity) in the process, will have a difficult time being true to ourselves because we really never believed we deserved better. Thus we never took a risk to try something new and different for fear of another perceived failure or rejection.

By allowing someone else to define who we are, we lose our ability to discover and grow inwardly. We retreat to what is familiar instead of re-defining who we want to be and who we believe we are. Replaying the negative childhood messages in our heads and critical and negative messages we tell ourselves about who we are make us no longer able to discern a truth from a lie. For many of us, we have accepted the opinions and perceptions of others about who we are or who we are not for such a long time, that finding out what is true about us and creating a healthy identity takes time and hard work.

The journey to self-discovery and learning to love ourselves will require determination, persistence, and accepting the truth about

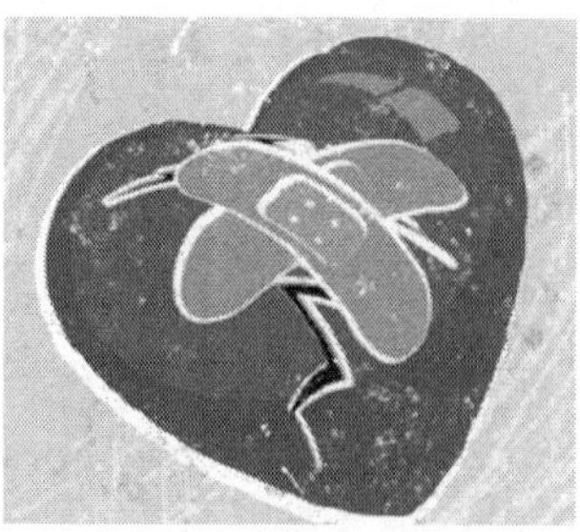

ourselves. You cannot accept truth without change. Accepting the truth about ourselves is difficult, especially to those who have been in abusive relationships or who have been exposed to exploitation. *Remember, the broken sensor?* Victims of abusive and dysfunctional

relationships develop distorted ideas about what true love is.
Take for instance female victims of domestic violence. Women often report staying in abusive relationships and tolerating mistreatment for years because they believed this was the way the abuser showed love and affection. Often the abuser made condition the woman to believe that she did not deserve better and was not worthy of receiving anyone better. Much the same way this "expression" of love (the act of abuse) was modeled by her parents. Thus, being exposed to helplessness and victimization early in her life.

But there is good news! The word of God (the bible) is true: The truth shall make you free. In this case, accepting the truth about yourself will set you free from abusive relationships, bondage, addiction, low self- worth, the need for self- approval from others, the need to be loved and accepted by others, and the need to seek validation from others about who we should be.

Healing and Recovery from Self- Sabotage: Learning to Love Myself from the Inside Out and The Journey of Self-Discovery

"A journey of a thousand miles begins with the first step."
—Chinese proverb

Learning to Love Yourself From the Inside Out will require a transformation in your thinking. If your thoughts about yourself, your future and the world is full of negative and anxiety-ridden thoughts, you will live your life as a negative person in a scary place. If you can think positively about yourself, your future, and the world, you will be able to live your life free from the old ideas and perceptions of others and to live a fulfilling and satisfying life.

Sounds easy doesn't it? But I know it isn't. The following are the lessons I learned from my own life experiences and countless stories and testimonies I've heard from my clients over the last several years. Each person I encountered along the way in my journey showed me new truths about myself. After forty years, believe it or not, I'm just now learning to accept the truths about myself and learning to love myself from the inside out! By being honest with ourselves, we are able to love ourselves and embrace our imperfections, knowing that we are a "work in progress" towards our highest, truest expression of self and therefore we no longer need the approval of others. For the first time in my adult life, changing the way I think, resulted in my shedding 50 pounds last year. My weight was an issue in my life that affected my self-worth. *What's your issue???*

Keys to the process of healing and recovery:

1. Self-love defeats self-sabotage.
2. Awareness of your emotional self: learning to be attuned to your feelings
3. Embracing your imperfections: accepting myself as I am created by my creator (recall the Serenity Prayer)
4. Personal responsibility and accountability for my actions: placing blame where it goes and "own my stuff"
5. Knowing God's purpose and plan for your life
6. Journaling

7. Prayer and Meditation
8. A healthy support system
9. Discover your strengths: focus on your strengths not your weaknesses
10. Learn what your spiritual gifts are and use them to fulfill your purpose and destiny
11. Balance: healthy balance between work, home, social life, etc.
12. Create and maintain healthy personal boundaries to achieve the relationships and purposes God intends for you
13. Read good books that fill your mind with positive thoughts; avoid media that glorifies dysfunction and exploitation
14. Asses and change your inner circle : TD Jakes, pastor and bestselling author once said "if you are the smartest person in your circle of influence, you need to change your group". In order to grow, you have to expand your social, spiritual and intellectual influences.

Power Thoughts and Emotional Affirmations

I am creating my destiny by every positive decision I make.
I choose my inner circle of associates and friends wisely and thoughtfully.
I live my life fully and authentically.
I have a positive self- image.

I am worthy of being loved and I deserve the best love.
I am attentive to the needs of those less fortunate than I am therefore I am blessed to be a blessing to others.
My worth is not determined by the opinions of others.
I value, love, and respect myself.
I will not allow any of these to be compromised.

The Bottom Line

Learning to love yourself from the inside out requires you to change the perception you have of yourself as well as the attention you give to the perceptions others may have of you. It is a process that requires intentional and deliberate thought and effort. It's all up to you! It's a choice.

If you want to have a more fulfilling and satisfying life, you have make hard choices, but in the end, the reward will be greater! You can have the relationships you want, the family connections you desire, the love you seek, and the success you desire in your life by learning to first love and accept yourself as the person you were created to be. For those who find it difficult to love themselves, you might find it easier when you walk in the truth about who you are and remembering whose you are (a child of God). The bible teaches that if we walk in truth, we walk in perfect love, and if we walk in perfect love, we do not walk in fear, because perfect love casts out fear (1 John 4:18). Be blessed. I wish each of you much success and happiness in your journey to self-discovery and embracing your truest expression of yourself.

Recommended Reading

Buckingham, M., and Clifton, D.O. 2001. *Now, discover your strengths.* New York, NY: The Free Press.

Robbins, M. 2011. *Stop Saying You're Fine: Discover a more powerful you.* New York, NY: Random House.

ABOUT THE AUTHOR

LINDA ROSE MONGELL

Linda Rose Mongell is President and CEO of Marketing Me Ltd., a professional consulting firm focused on enhancing image, brand and culture. She is an accomplished speaker, facilitator, trainer and consultant with more than 25 years in the corporate environment.

Linda Rose has extensive experience and a diverse background in the areas of marketing, executive management, strategic development, retail, public relations and communications, professional development, promotions, sponsorship management, event marketing, new business development, process management and project and event production. She has also designed and developed needs assessments, communication and marketing strategies and various training programs and systems.

Linda Rose holds a B.A. in Public Relations and Communications and is a certified trainer in the areas of diversity, women's issues, brand and image building, as well as a certified coach from the Professional Woman Network. She is an advisory board member of the International Professional Woman Network (PWN), a member of the PWN's Speaker's Bureau, as well as a member of the American Management Association (AMA), American Society for Training and Development (ASTD), and National Association for Female Executives (NAFE).

To add to her list of credentials, Linda Rose is a published author, a recently appointed radio show host, and is also a professional belly dancer and has taught belly dancing for beginners.

Contact:
Marketing Me Ltd.
2913 El Camino Real Suite 812
Tustin, Ca 92782
E-mail: lrmongell@marketingme.com
Website: www.marketingme.com
Office: 714.389.1728

TWENTY-TWO

Out with the Frumpy and in with the Fabulous

By Linda Rose Mongell

A girl should be two things: classy and fabulous. —Coco Chanel

Are you letting yourself go or have you just not noticed? As I become more consciously aware of the aging process, I can't help but notice women around me who are about my age but look significantly older. And what I have found so interesting is, it isn't as much the years starting to show from our sun goddess days, but it is the frumpy, relaxed, outdated look that I have a tough time comprehending. All through my growing up, I would look at a woman and try to guess her age. I can't say I was good at it but what scares me today is when I play the guessing game now, I look at some women around my age and guess them to be considerably older.

I will be the first to admit that I don't look or feel my age, most simply because I was blessed with amazing genes and frankly I don't want to feel my age, but truth be told, I am not sure what it should feel like. I guess I never thought that far ahead or ever even considered getting older. I had an idea in my head then when you reached a certain age you looked a certain way and now that I am in one of those age categories I don't want to look like what I may have thought was normal when I was younger. I want to maintain my youth and vibrancy as long as I can and I don't want frumpy to take over.

I think some women have done all of us a complete injustice. Women have aged before their time simply by taking a more laid back approach to how they look at a certain age. Of course I am not talking about everyone as this is a generalization but I challenge any of you to look around and see if you don't see what I am talking about. Everywhere I look I see "fabulous over 40," "fabulous over 50," "fabulous over 60," and I ask myself why is there an assumption that we would not be fabulous at any age? And then I remind myself of my observations from my childhood. Is that what 40, 50, 60 is supposed to look like because I don't want to look like that. I want to look fabulous. What I have come to realize is that we can choose to look any way we want and that our age doesn't drive that, our desires drive that.

Unfortunately, my observations of how old I thought a woman was when I growing up still resonate loud and clear for me when I look around I see baggy elastic waste pants and polyester blouses and hair that is un-coiffed or outdated and if there is make-up it is years out of date. Granted that is probably an exaggerated comment...or is it? I admire poised, well-dressed, have-it-all together women. And, for the record, there are some beautiful women in all shapes and sizes that have mastered the art of aging but what I continue to see is a whole lot of what I call frumperallas.

When was the last time you looked in the mirror – front AND back? I often wonder to myself if on some level we've just stopped caring, or if we have settled into the comfortable or even if our numerical age has somehow dictated how we should look. But then I ask myself, if it is our numerical age that dictates how we should look, then where did we get that information since the last time I was shopping I didn't notice clothing defined "by age" for adults. I honestly believe that for many women allowing any of those reasons to justify a lackadaisical appearance is a crime. They, for all intense purposes, have become excuses and those excuses have blindly sabotaged us. Sabotage to me is the unintentional intent to simply stop trying to look and be our best. For me, it isn't something that I consider an overnight occurrence yet rather a slow process whereby the comfortable and the familiar move in and take over. The issue with self-sabotage is that it is subconscious and it is so familiar that we don't even know we're doing it to ourselves.

I am the first one to understand as I get older how my desire to hide the extra pounds, to become fond of 3/4" sleeves and to no longer have aching feet probably require a different look at what I wear. The blouses no longer get tucked in and the shoes – well the heels get a little lower. And I also get that we have lazy days when we just want to stay in our jammies and lounge around. But I am not talking about the sensible changes we all make and the necessary lazy days. I am talking about why we stop trying so hard to look fabulous like we use to when we were younger and how do we combat that. I look around and I see women and I wonder if they have settled in to simply growing old or if they even realize it. We don't need to be older than we are. We need to be the youngest and best version of ourselves.

I also recognize that for many, the toll of life's struggles have taken over. The demands whatever those might be, heartache, depression, devastation can all lead us to a place where trying to look and be our best is no longer important. Life's trials have stepped in to rule and it's all we can do to get up in the morning. I am certainly not an authority on traumatic events and the roles those play in our lives, however what I do know is that as long as we are here on this planet we serve a purpose. And as we serve our purpose we have a right to do so looking and feeling our best. The challenges many of us face are temporary yet we can use them for a lifetime to not take care of ourselves if we choose. The decision to turn that around is only one you can make for yourself.

To see if you need a lift from the frumpy let me ask you a few questions: Do you feel and look your best? Or maybe should I ask – is it important for you to feel and look your best? And if you say yes, you might very well feel your best but how do you know you look your best? Remember, I am not the one you need to convince. It's you who you have to convince. Have you let yourself go? Have you settled in to the comfortable and familiar and stopped trying? Do you feel like your age has given you permission to settle?

If you are wondering if maybe you have but you aren't sure then you need to ask yourself a few more questions. You are the only one who can answer honestly. Are you limiting yourself in anyway? Do you find you come up with a lot of excuses for doing what you're doing or not doing? For example are you not doing things because you have nothing to wear or you're "too old"? Will you go shopping once you lose weight? When will that be? Have you hid behind the weight excuse much too often? What excuses are standing in your way? Is it someone else's fault for what you are or are not doing? Are you playing the blame game? Are you waiting for something or someone? Do you think maybe you are procrastinating? Are you ignoring reality? Do you refuse to face the facts and live in denial? Have you considered your true feelings or are you burying them so you don't have to face them? Have you put obstacles in your way so you don't have to make any changes? When was the last time you took a good long look at yourself in the mirror or do you simply not want to?

Let's get a little more specific. When was the last time you changed your hairstyle? Do you feel the need to have to wear it a particular way because of your age? Are you still wearing those glasses you bought 10 years ago? When was the last time you had your eyes checked? Is your bust sagging to your knees? Let's be honest now. Look around. Do you see anything that might resemble frumpy or saggy? Look a little closer. You can lift the girls without having to have surgery. Try a trip to the lingerie department. Bras aren't meant to last forever. Are your toting around the old lady handbag with the unstylish old lady shoes? If you aren't sure about the answer to that question look in a current fashion magazine.

Just because you can still fit in something that has been in your closet for 30 years doesn't necessarily mean it still looks good on you. How do you know the closet monster hasn't sabotaged you?

I can assure you that although I am in a position to share and educate, many of these thoughts and processes I too am familiar with. We simply change as we get older. We know more of what we like, we have more stuff, we sometimes just don't care what other people think (for me more times than I care to mention) and we get comfortable. Unlike when I was 20, it takes me less time to get ready in the morning (maybe I should rethink that and spend more time), I don't shop for all high heeled shoes anymore and I have been guilty of using last year's handbag. So I think one of the greatest gifts we can give to ourselves is to take inventory and pay more attention to what's around and how we're feeling and not simply just allow life to happen but take control as best as we can.

Steps to Take to Fabulous

If you feel like you're in a rut and feel like frumpy has caught up with you and you want to make an effort there are a few steps you can take to get moving in the right direction. Relax and take a deep breath. This is on your time and in your way.

Look in the Mirror

When you're ready you have to look at yourself in the mirror. Start in the front and then look at the rear view. What is the first thing that you see? Make some notes so you know what you need to work on.

Take a Closet Inventory

Do a careful review of what you have in the closet. Does Omar the tent maker live there?

Identify what you currently wear and what you don't. Those items you no longer wear, why don't you wear them? If they are too small and one day you are going to lose weight, put them to the side. Most people will tell you to get rid of them but I know how difficult that can be. For now, put them to the side and if you stay on the path to fabulous you will know when to part with them but I will remind you that there are a lot of women who can benefit from your unworn clothes taking up space in your closet.

Take a good look at the clothes you have. What are you are currently wearing? Do you have a closet full of baggy clothes? Remember, baggy clothes make you look even heavier than you really are. Even if you're overweight you can highlight your silhouette. I would recommend trying things on and if they need to be tailored then do so. If they won't work then get rid of them. Clothes shouldn't cling; they should hang nicely – not too loose and not too tight.

While you are in the closet, look at your shoes and handbags. Are your shoes old and outdated? Are they worn? Do the heels or soles need to be replaced? Do they still fit and do you or would you wear them? Do the same with your handbags? When was the last time you used it? Is it still fashionable? Is it in good shape?

Assess the Lingerie Drawer

When was the last time you refreshed your lingerie and I am not talking about the washing machine. Let's be real, most of us have worn the wrong bra size for years. I strongly recommend you have a fitting at a reputable store for the proper size. You can buy one at a time to begin to replace the old outdated bras and while you're at it, I'm sure new undies won't hurt. Feeling sexy underneath will work wonders and it can be our little secret.

Do Do the Hairdo

Why is it we get so comfortable with the same old hairstyle? What are we afraid of? Try something different be it the color, some highlights, or a trim. I know it is a little risky but you might be surprised with the results. Look through some magazines and bring in photos to your hairstylist.

Face the Face

Even though I've listed it last doesn't mean it is the least important. There are some things we just need to take care of as part of our regular maintenance.

Let's start with the eyes. When was the last time you had your vision checked? We should get our eyes checked once a year. In the event that you wear glasses or will need to wear glasses, bring a friend with you to pick out new frames. Glasses are a key accessory item and should be carefully selected.

How is your smile doing? I know most people despise a trip to the dentist but our dental health is crucial in our overall health. Whenever I go to the dentist (once every six months) my blood pressure goes up and I tense up in the chair but I still go to the dentist because the thought of not going and the repercussions of that are not an option. So add it to your list of must-dos.

One of my greatest surprises in life was that day when I looked in the mirror and I looked different. Yep, I had visible lines that appeared overnight. There are creams for those little pesky lines but nothing beats a trip to the dermatologist. Yearly check ups are recommended to not only help diagnose things you aren't aware of but it is a great way to keep your skin, hair and nails healthy. It also just makes you feel good knowing you are doing something for yourself like a lot of these necessary check ups.

Pamper the Pups

While we are talking about hair and nails, how about treating yourself to a mani-pedi. Manicured feet with painted toenails look so much better in sandals, which are my shoes of choice contrary to my podiatrist's recommendations not to mention that it feels so good when someone else does it. So as long as we are working our way to fabulous this is always a nice step.

Looking fabulous will most likely take some more time than the frumpy option but will be so worth it on so many more levels.

"You can be gorgeous at thirty, charming at forty, and irresistible for the rest of your life." —Coco Chanel

ABOUT THE AUTHOR

Dawn Campbell

You know how people always want more happiness and less discomfort in their lives. Well that's exactly what Dawn Campbell, Master Health Coach and Holistic Practitioner helps clients achieve.

Working together, self-sabotaging behaviour is identified and replaced with positive habits. Following which, clients experience the joys of inner-happiness, blooming confidence and sexier lives filled with vital health.

Freelance for 10 years following a 20 year successful corporate career, Dawn has created a thriving health practice around her home and lifestyle. Thereby offering fellow health seekers an oasis to rebuild, rejuvenate and revitalise their mind, body and spirit.

A lifelong vegetarian, Dawns experience includes being a high raw vegan chef following a natural hygiene lifestyle. By her own admission, her family live the 'good life'. Financially free, they continually strive to be self-sufficient which adds to their contentment. At 50 years old, she's happier, healthier and fitter than ever so must be doing something right!

Dawn's also a 'Heal your life' teacher; Callahan trained Thought Field Therapist and Mentor Coach for Noble Manhattan, Europe's leading coach training provider. She's currently studying Naturopathy and Life Science.

Dawn's ethos is no-one knows our body better than we do. Her mission is to educate, empower and encourage others to reclaim responsibility for their health and become their own health guru.

Dawn would be honoured to be included in your dream team supporting you achieve your goals, after all, if we don't look after our bodies, where else will we live?

Contact:
E: dawn@holistichealthcoach.eu
W: http://www.dawncampbellholistichealth.eu
T: +33 (0) 2 43 64 37 48
S: dawncampbell1
A: Pays de Loire, France

"BBC radio interviews, writing for national and local press, presentations, in-house company training and workshops with 1 -1 follow up sessions mean that hundreds of clients have benefited from Dawns result orientated supportive style".
Erica Connelly, Business Link, UK

GUEST AUTHOR

Food: Our Secret Relationship

Dawn Campbell

Why being too thin or too rich is irrelevant.

"Food is the most widely abused anti-anxiety drug."—Bill Phillips

What do the Crown Princess Victoria of Sweden, Elton John, Joan Rivers, Sharon Osbourne, Oprah Winfrey and The Spice Girls (to name but a few) have in common? If you guessed they've all had a secret relationship with food, you've guessed right!

If I'd been writing this chapter a decade ago, I'd have had to include myself in that list too. For more years than I dare admit, I was bound by my secret obsession with food.

Unfortunately, for some sufferers their preoccupation with food became a fatal attraction. Compulsive eaters have been known to dig their own graves with their teeth. While anorexics, literally starve themselves to death.

So if you like me have, or are currently involved in a secret relationship with food, then take heart. You're in esteemed company! More importantly, when you *do* finally commit to breaking free from this toxic relationship (and you will when you're ready), you'll be free to make healthier choices. Then you'll fully experience your birth right to live a life filled with the vitality you deserve.

Chances are that's exactly why you're reading this book! Perhaps you're exhausted living a double life? Maybe you've reached rock bottom? Or else you've surrendered to your internal voice crying *enough!* Whatever your reasons, well done for being proactive and deciding today is the day you'll swap your destructive relationship with food for a nurturing one.

Q. What's your inner voice crying out?

A.

What constitutes disordered eating?

"Unhealthy dietary habits top the list as the worst and most common."
—Natural Hygiene Society

Historically, disordered eating habits have existed as long as food has. People overeat during times of abundance; they've 'purged' using enemas, diuretics, laxatives, or vomiting, or else abstained from eating for reasons of culture, religion or ritual. Done to extreme, these habits sabotage vital health.

People who think of people suffering with food addictions as weak-willed rather than ill are mistaken. Eating disorders are medical illnesses with complex psychological and biological causes. Modern day disordered eating typically manifests as:

1. *Anorexia nervosa someone deliberately maintaining body weight approx. 15% below the norm through starvation and or excessive exercising.*

2. *Bulimia nervosa someone who tries to control body weight by binging and purging.*

3. *Binge eating compulsive non-stop over eating.*

4. *Abnormal attitudes towards food that causes changes to eating habits / behaviours to the extent someone is totally preoccupied with food and weight.*

5. *A missuse of food to resolve emotional problems whereby a person will over-eat (reward), or refuse to eat (punish) to satisfy a psychological feeling rather than a physical need for food.*

Disordered eating is a coping mechanism due to being starved of something. Physical triggers are due to chemical imbalances owing to poor quality nutrition which leads to malnutrition. Emotional triggers include frustration; unhappinessimpatience; routine; security and fatigue to name but a few.

Q. What is the name of your hunger?

A.

How many people are suffering?

"Addicts look in the wrong places for pleasure."—Deepak Chopra

Secret relationships with food are one of the last taboos. Consequently, there are no qualified world-wide statistics about how many people are suffering with unhealthy eating habits.

Not least because there are varying degrees of secretive eating from simply being in denial to night eating syndrome to full blown eating disorders. Also, 'guestimates' by definition only include people who've disclosed their secretive habits.

Statistics vary wildly depending on the poll. Seemingly, 1 in 3 women and 1 in 5 men are reported to have suffered with disordered eating. Apparently, 90+% of the population are at some point worried or unhappy about weight or body image. This dissatisfaction acts as a precursor to future disordered eating and determines the severity and duration of the condition.

What we *do* know is that overeating is more prevalent than under eating. Disordered eating traditionally afflicted young women (including body-image distortion where they perceive themselves fatter than they are). Today, it's not uncommon for either mature or professional people to also suffer because we often measure success by appearances (i.e. in the world of entertainment, media, sport etc.) Additionally, it's become equally distressing to young men who may also suffer with dysmorphia (where they view themselves as too thin). Worryingly, ever younger groups of children are now being supported for weight and image issues too.

Q. Whose support do you need to save you from yourself?

A.

Why it's *not* your fault?

"Eating disorders are responsible for more loss of life than any other type of psychiatric condition, one in five sufferers die." —Lancet 2001

- Eating disorders know no bounds. Nor do they adhere to class, age, race, wealth, status, religion or gender. Whether you're rich, famous, royal or ordinary like me, the misery of disordered eating doesn't discriminate.
- Research provides no single cause; it arises due to a mixture of biological, social and psychological issues.
- The origins of disordered eating typically stem from puberty; not fitting in; trauma; abuse; over-protection; stress; negative weight / image related comments; culture and pressure at university, careers or relationships.

The rise in disordered eating is often blamed on the media perpetuating the social ideal to conform and be thin. Unmistakably, subliminal marketing is partly responsibility, but it's not the whole story.

Contributory factors over the last 40 years include but are not limited to:

- Portion Control: our ancestors ate from plates 2-4 inches smaller than our current standard 12-14 inch plates. Subsequently, we eat 20-40% more. The bigger our portion, the more we eat, the more we want (despite the fact that our stomach is only the size of a clenched fist).

- Natural appetite: has been over-ridden to fit school and work timetables. Now we eat three meals a day on autopilot regardless of hunger.

- Sizing: has been manipulated to accommodate our growing figures. Boutiques offer bigger cubicles with flattering lights and mirrors so we buy clothes with modified dress sizing because no-one wants to buy bigger sizes! The result is we've developed unrealistic perceptions of what represents a healthy body shape and size.

- Advertising: impacts our food choices, not least because we're exposed to 50+ TV adverts during an average 4 hour daily viewing.

- Fast food: campaigns have changed the social norm about 'eating on the go'. It's given us permission to eat anything, anytime, anywhere. We eat at our desk, on public transport, even while shopping. In fact, anywhere except the family dining table. This declining tradition has compounded our unhealthy eating habits and accounts for over 50% of meals now being eaten outside the home.

- Cravings: If all that wasn't enough to contribute to our on-going struggle with food, we're biologically programmed to seek and store foods high in sugar and fat. These nutritionally deficient foods result in cravings and feelings of lethargy.

- Exercise: is then highly unlikely. Consequently, a vicious cycle of self-sabotage begins.

Q. Which factors contribute to your disordered eating?

A.

Who benefits, them or us?

"The food industry polices itself, that's like letting Dracula police the blood banks." —Jorge Alday

In the 60's we experienced supersized popcorn tubs and soda cartons, the brainchild of David Wallerstein. The scheme was so successful; he was head-hunted by the McDonalds brothers.

During the 70's corn production become the focus of industrialised farming. The result was a reservoir of inexpensive corn that shaped the cheaper end of the food market. Excess corn then went into mass production as HFCS (high fructose corn syrup).

By the 80's HFCS infiltrated the soft drinks market as an artificial sweetener because it's cheaper than sugar cane. Despite the fact we don't fully understand how HFCS are metabolised by our body, we still consume vast amounts of HFCS. Furthermore, HFCS mostly comes from genetically modified sources.

The 80's also saw McDonalds offering us 'extra value combo' meal deals and counter service. Their up-sell assumption '*is that the large size*' saves us the indignity of asking for more.

In the 90's despite a controversial history, commercially sold genetically modified (GM) foods were introduced. Starting initially with tomatoes, GM crops and products are now wide spread.

Alarm bells were also ringing concerning obesity as we noticed people become 'supersized'.

Then there's the health issue of 3,000+ chemicals, additives, colourings, flavourings, preservatives added to food and water. This isn't a new practice, but the scale is. Consequently, food is uniformly produced, packaged and transported to a wider audience than ever before.

All of these processes are supposed to improve the colour, texture, flavour and look of food, but how can natural food be improved? Accepting not all industrial changes are bad for health (one positive reformulation is the phasing out of Trans fat); the key driver is fundamentally profit.

Combine these few developments with the public's naivety, growing apathy and willingness to relinquish responsibility for its own health. Then it's easier to understand how we're in the unhealthy situation we're in today.

Q. Where could you find out more about how food impacts your health?

A.

Who's fooling who?

"We don't have a health care system, we have a disease management system and the majority of disease that we're trying to manage is lifestyle related, therefore, preventable." —Dr. Andrew Weil

During the 1990s The United Nations public health arm WHO reported on how our health was deteriorating in relation to the food we ate. In 2003 they challenged the food industry to review its marketing policies. Consequently, every food was re-categorised and its potential profit and loss was calculated.

This calculation enabled manufacturers to diversify and increase profits by 'tweaking' their recipes. Reformulating, repackaging and rebranding thousands of products as 'healthier' created a misconception of what is essentially the same foods as now being healthier. The gap between profit margins and less nutritionally accurate information continues to grow.

Government is reluctant to regulate the food industry whose only real accountability lies with their shareholders. Therefore, it's no surprise that 'profit' rules. Manufacturers state their case as simply meeting consumers insatiable demands (who they also say should exercise more responsibility for their food choices). However, the practice of reformulation is actually about increasing profits through dictating market trends.

Trends such as the 'duo' and 're-sealable' bags; 'family packs'; 'multi-buys' and '3 for 2' deals. These offers give a false perception of 'better value for money' while encouraging consumers to continually snack *despite* still eating the same size / number of meals.

Q. Which 'value for money' habits will you swap for healthier ones?

A.

How to recognise ☺ food from ☹ food?

"Eating for pleasure has replaced the concept of eating for nourishment."
—Paul Nison

Apparently food isn't the enemy (though that depends on the interpretation of food). Some people believe its how and why food is used that causes the problem. Others believe *everything in moderation*'. However, anyone with a secret relationship with food knows they *cannot* practice moderation and all foods are not equal.

My definition of bad food is the calorie dense, non-real food items that unfortunately fill the majority of every supermarket. They are what I call the 5 P's: pre-prepared, processed, preserved and packaged for profit items.

These items need labels without which consumers wouldn't a) know what the product was or b) understand its composition. These items are man-made and easy to recognise because you'll *never* see them growing out of the ground or on a tree.

Considering we've never had so much choice, why then are more people than ever suffering with malnutrition? Is it because their diet is primarily made up of items devoid of any natural nutritional value? No-one can expect to thrive indefinitely on a diet of dead food.

My definition of good food is found in the isles resembling the old-fashioned greengrocers. No labels required here because we recognise the majority of foods as having grown out of the ground or on trees.

Natural food is real food. It comes in a rainbow of colours packed with macronutrients - carbohydrates, fat, protein; micronutrients – vitamins, minerals; antioxidants and phytonutrients. Real foods are appealing to the eye, nose, touch test and makes our mouth water.

Eating these ripe, seasonal, local foods make us feel satisfied hence they're known as 'good mood food'. They energise us making us feel connected and grounded because real food feeds our mind, body and soul.

Fast Food doesn't come faster than this because it requires little or no preparation. This is intuitive eating and eliminates the need to count calories because Mother Nature's foods are nutritionally balanced and perfectly packaged to meet all our needs.

Q. What % of your groceries fall into the 5Ps and natural foods category?

A.

When perfection rather than food is the real issue

"Those with addictive personalities have higher levels of dopamine in their brains, which causes them to turn to certain substances for comfort."
—Professor David Nutt

People with addictive personalities tend to have certain common traits, not least because they live double lives. They often have successful careers. Nonetheless, confident appearances mask their low self-esteem. They suffer high levels of stress because they feel fraudulent and worry about being found out as not perfect.

They tend to be intelligent, impulsive decision makers, enthusiastic about new things, creative, funny and impatient. They are highly sensitive, and prone to feeling anxious. They avoid or find confrontation difficult.

Their dispensation is to pleasers, so they make great listeners despite being critical and judgemental of themselves. Their arguments are either black or white. Their views oscillate from one extreme to the other and their view of life is either brilliant or depressive. Consequently, their 'you're either with me or against me' controlling attitude comes across as aggressive.

They dislike authority and appear arrogant. Being perfectionists, they have self-destructive compulsive behaviours. They are angry and fearful unable to measure up to their own exacting ideals. Consequently, they struggle to fit in socially so often appear withdrawn, or unwilling to participate.

Q. What issue(s) is your secret relationship with food hiding that you feel unable to cope with?

A.

How to interpret the signs

"Dealing with physiological causes means psychological causes are easier to address."—Harvey Diamond

Don't wait until disordered eating spirals out of control. Seek help as soon as you recognise your eating habits are masking something else.

Be aware that getting help for others is never easy because they may be a) in denial b) not ready to confront themselves. In the meantime, it's important to adopt healthy food habits and be a good role model around children.

Potential signs:

- Obsessing about body weight, shape or size.
- Controlling who eats what, when and where.
- Yo-yo dieting or transitions to ever stricter regimes.
- Excessive use of laxatives, diuretics, internal cleanses, colonics, detoxing regimes.
- Lacks trust to eat what they want, when they want.
- Knows the calorie content of everything and constantly weighs food or self.
- Pre-occupied with food morning, noon and night i.e. grazes.
- Withdrawn and lethargic, or over exercises.
- Changes in physical appearance or behaviour i.e. avoiding eating in public.
- Appears shaky/ faint or behaves agitated / defensive.
- Is always cold.
- Suffers bowel related issues / bloated stomach.

- Regular sore throats.
- Experiences difficulties sleeping.
- Thyroid issues.
- Eats fast and consumes large amount of foods.
- Has low blood pressure / pulse.
- Has a limited food choice.
- Dental issues.

Q. Which signs resonate with you and why?

A.

What's *your* story?

"All addictions turn from pleasure to dependency."
—Anthony Giddens

Now may be a useful time to treat yourself to a new journal specifically dedicated to unraveling your individual relationship with food.

Answer one of the below questions honestly and intuitively each day over the course of a month. Write as much as necessary to gain an understanding of the complexity of your response.

Periodically, re-visit this self-analysis questionnaire and keep adding to your initial answers. More thoughts will come to you as your consciousness becomes awakened to how your past contributed to your present situation.

Assuming you're doing this exercise because you don't want more of the same in your future. Becoming mindful about what you're thinking, feeling and doing hereon in will help you create your healthier future.

- What age were you when you first became aware of the mind, food, body connection?
- Which inner you are you constantly battling with, a fat or a thin one?
- How many years have you been hungry?
- What rules / rituals do you have about food?
- What is your definition of diet?
- Which foods occupy your mind the most?
- What's your first and last daily thought?
- What are your biggest fears around food?
- How do you typically celebrate or reward yourself?
- How satisfied are you with your weight and body shape?
- What has to happen for you to be happier, healthier, sexier, more confident?
- What area of your life is 'on hold' until you achieve your ideal weight / body shape?

- How does weighing yourself influence your mood?
- How many times a day do you eat in-between meals?
- Which is true for you, food is associated with pleasure, pain, other?
- What foods do you have emotional attachments too and why?
- How judgmental are you about your food habits?
- What's your attitude when you fall off the wagon and how do you get back on track?
- How does food as a coping mechanism work for you?
- What are your top food triggers and how did they originate?
- How do the seasons or other people's moods influence you?
- What are your good mood / bad mood foods?
- How would you describe your portion control?
- What are you not expressing when you self-sabotage with food?
- What are the payoffs to changing and not changing your food habits?
- What's sabotaging you from being your ideal weight / shape?
- Which is more important, image or your health?

- What will you be, do and have when you've achieved your ideal weight / shape?
- What would your perfect meal include and who would you share it with?
- How will your family and friends describe your legacy?

Which solutions?

"Addiction to food is the same as addiction to morphine, just as dangerous and just as hard to withdraw from." —Herbert Shelton

There is growing awareness of holistic therapies that work for people committed to being free of disordered eating. Accessibility to a wide-ranging choice of supportive treatments also helps us establish and maintain healthier diets and lifestyle habits.

Examples include but are not limited to:

- Thought Field Therapy (of which Emotional Freedom Technique is a derivative of)
- Neuro-Linguistic Programming (NLP)
- Cognitive Behavioural Therapy
- Group Therapy / Workshops
- Coaching & Mentoring
- Regression Therapy

- Inner child Therapy
- Magnet Therapy
- Hypnotherapy
- Acupuncture
- Reflexology
- Kinesiology
- *My personal favourites are Coaching; Thought Field Therapy; Meditation and drinking wheatgrass which immediately dissolves cravings.*

Here are some self-help / distraction techniques that benefited me (of which there are hundreds);

- Detox using fresh vegetable juice to cleanse at a cellular level (and cleanse my palette).
- Colonics to speed up eliminate of toxins.
- Transition to a higher green and living foods plant based diet, including wheatgrass.
- Eat when experiencing real hunger after first drinking a glass of water.
- Practicing food combining to improve assimilation of nutrients.
- Not eating when emotionally unbalanced.

- Keeping a food mood journal to chart progress.
- Chanting, meditating and mudras.
- Promise no more deprivation diets.
- Developing compassion for self and others who struggle with food issues.
- Eating mindfully using chopsticks or with cutlery in the opposite hand.
- Eating in silence to savour the look, smell, texture and taste of food.
- Appreciating the journey food took to reach the plate.
- Affirmations and visualisations.
- Ensuring congruency between thoughts, words, deeds and actions.
- Accepting no-one is perfect so don't add a guilt trip to a binge trip.
- When falling off the wagon, get back on board *before* the next meal.
- Learning to interpret the body's needs for water and then stay hydrated.
- Being inspired by others who have already achieved success.
- Staying away from negative people.

- Exercise like rebounding, yoga and running for charity.
- Listing the benefits of becoming healthier to maintain a focused attitude.
- Chunking down goals into short, med and long term.
- Making eating a special occasion; setting the table using the best of everything.
- Chewing slowly allows our stomach time to communicate with our brain.
- Information is power, become educated by reading everything on your condition.

Q. When will you implement solutions?

A.

When foods your drug of choice

"It's amazing how pervasive food it. Every second commercial offers food. Every second TV episode involves a meal. You can't walk ten feet without seeing or smelling food. I'm acutely aware of food and its omnipresence is astounding." —Adam Scott

Food is the obvious choice to have a secret relationship with. It's legal, highly accessible and it's an inexpensive habit to fund.

Children learn early in life that the only thing they can control is what goes in and out of their bodies. Therefore, food becomes a useful controller. Growing up we discover that comfort eating helps us deal with difficult emotions, challenging people and problematic situations.

However, the obstacle with disordered eating compared to other compulsive behaviours lies in the fact that we have to eat to live. Meaning there is no escaping its presence unlike other addictions (drugs, alcohol etc.) whereby circumstances are improved by changing the environment. Someone suffering with a food addiction has their six senses (mind, eyes, ears, nose, taste, touch) stimulated 24/7 and it's torture!

We're bombarded with food from kiosks and vending machines. Food's on offer at petrol stations; schools; work; hospitals; on all modes of transport; at every entertainment venue, even at the gym.

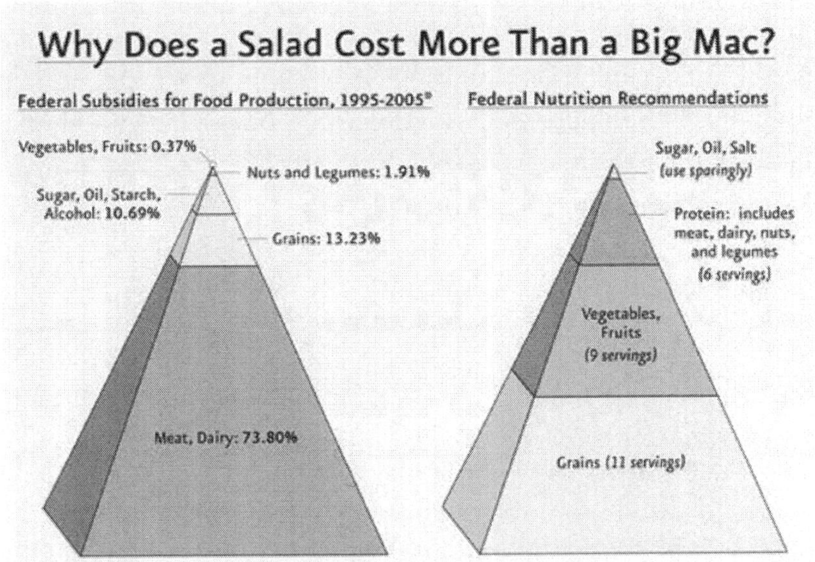

http://www.pcrm.org/good-medicine/2007/autumn/health-vs-pork-congress-debates-the-farm-bill

No wonder disordered eating, malnutrition, hypersensitivity and food allergies are widespread. Food items with the 5Ps are cheaply provided and temptingly ready to eat. Surely something's wrong when a hamburger is produced cheaper than an apple!

Q. How does food help control your situation?

A.

Why I eat when I'm not hungry?

"All addictions begin as psychological to tranquilise anxiety."
—R Callahan

Whatever the situation, there is always a 'payoff'. If there wasn't, we'd move out of our own way and think, do or say something different. Therefore, it's useful to get clear about your motives around food.

My payoff for under eating was primarily about feeling in control. My payoff for overeating was to numb repressed feelings. That and the fact I simply like eating!

It's only when improved payoffs are identified as being *greater* than existing payoffs that transformation occurs. Your secret relationship with food may also be more about you being addicted to the ritual of seeking pleasure or pain rather than the food itself.

Q. What payoffs does disordered eating give you?

A.

When the prognosis is 'one day at a time'

"A useful thing I was told when entering treatment was I wasn't a person trying to become good. I was a sick person trying to get well."
—Darren Littlejohn

Recovering or cured? That's an interesting question for which I've found no conclusive evidence. Whilst I'm not convinced an addict (regardless of their drug of choice) is ever cured. It would appear the longer the compulsion remains untreated, the harder and longer it takes to recover. Additionally, the health consequences become more serious.

When you've identified your 'triggers', think how you could respond differently in future to ensure a healthier outcome (after all the definition of madness is repeating something yet expecting a different outcome).

One of my triggers is conflict. When I'm upset I used to binge and purge. Now I meditate or journal instead. By establishing healthier responses to what upsets me (you will identify your own distraction techniques), I found falling off the health wagon became less frequent and the severity of the fall also lessens.

Q. On a scale of 1 – 10 (1 is poor 10 is perfect) how would you rate your relationship with food, where would you like to be?

A.

When will you kiss your secret goodbye?

"The food you eat is either the safest most powerful form of medicine, or the slowest form of poison." —Dr. Ann Wigmore

The absorbing thing with secrets is they fill a gap. When you've experienced any secret relationship that has been enduring, intimate and intense, giving it up inevitably means a period of withdrawal. The complexity of which will determine your recovery.

As I progressively relinquished my secret relationship with food, I channelled my addictive needs into shopping. Eventually, I merged my additive urge to shop with my desire to retrain as a holistic health practitioner. When I felt the urge to self-sabotage my body, I distracted myself by buying nutrition books thus feeding my mind instead.

I literally spent hours browsing the internet, totally absorbed in finding exactly the right book. By learning to respond differently to my habitual craving, I eventually produced a different outcome. I gave myself permission to relax around food, gradually, the power it had over my mind started to weaken.

I became passionate about helping others recover their vitality as I was doing. I also learnt the importance of expressing myself honestly. Today, I'm more in control of my mind than it is of me.

So if you like me find that tackling your secret relationship with food creates another compulsive behaviour to fill the gap. Just make sure you channel that energy into something that serves your healthier goals.

Q. Which healthier habits will eliminate self-sabotage?

A.

Where to now?

"We're all looking for personal freedom to freely express ourselves. 1st we have to master self-awareness, 2nd master transformation, 3r master intent." —Don Miguel Ruiz

You are where you are today *because* of your experiences, without them, you wouldn't be who you are so celebrate that. Learning to accept yourself exactly as you are is an important part of your recovery. This chapter proves you're not alone in your struggle with food and there's light at the end of the tunnel.

You've been challenged to identify the signs and give a name to your secret relationship with food. I've shared details of my journey back to health while you've been exploring yours. We've labeled our triggers, pinpointed our payoffs and put them into context. Now we understand food isn't the only contributory factor.

It's clear that eating real food improves our mood and we've touched on some practical solutions to help reclaim responsibility for your health. Now it's time to expand your thinking. To successful rebuild physical and emotional health, diet needs to be supported by the following lifestyle habits:

✓ Drink pure water to stay hydrated.

✓ Breathe fresh air to oxygenate your blood.

✓ Expose your skin and eyes to sunshine daily for much needed vitamin D3.

- ✓ Peace of mind ensures adequate rest and sleep to rebuild and revitalise your body.
- ✓ Exercise to strengthen your frame.
- ✓ Fast when your body needs help doing what it does best, heal.

Adopting this balanced health strategy is the only way to ensure a future of vitality and longevity. Where the Crown Princess Victoria of Sweden, Elton John, Joan Rivers, Sharon Osbourne, Oprah Winfrey, The Spice Girls succeed, you can too.

All you have to do is be willing to change one meal at a time; have an attitude of abundance; choose wisely and become addicted to life instead of food. Final word goes to Julia Cameron "*when we alter our relationship with food; we alter our relationship with everything.*"

Q. How will your attitude / behaviour differ hereon in?

A.

For more information that includes a book recommendation list, web resources and my food mood journal please contact me directly.

DON'T FORGET, YOU ARE WHAT YOU EAT.
I NEED TO EAT A SKINNY PERSON.

THE PROFESSIONAL WOMAN NETWORK

Training and Certification on Women's Issues

Linda Ellis Eastman, President & CEO of The Professional Woman Network, has trained and certified over two thousand individuals to start their own consulting/seminar business. Women from such countries as Brazil, Argentina, the Bahamas, Costa Rica, Bermuda, Nigeria, South Africa, Malaysia, and Mexico have attended trainings.

Topics for certification include:

- Diversity & Multiculturalism
- Women's Issues
- Women: A Journey to Wellness
- Save Our Youth
- Teen Image & Social Etiquette
- Leadership & Empowerment Skills for Youth
- Customer Service & Professionalism
- Marketing a Consulting Practice
- Professional Coaching
- Professional Presentation Skills

If you are interested in learning more about becoming certified or about starting your own consulting/seminar business contact:

The Professional Woman Network
P.O. Box 333
Prospect, KY 40059
(502) 566-9900
lindaeastman@prodigy.net
www.prowoman.net

Women's Empowerment Series

Breaking Free Overcoming Self-Sabotage
Creating a Blue Print for Inner Change: Tools for Personal Growth
Tapping into Your Inner CEO Self-Leadership
Leaders in Pearls: Becoming a Change Architect
Releasing Strongholds: Letting Go of What is Holding You Back
The Power of a Woman: Embracing the Woman Within
How to Break the Glass Ceiling Without a Hammer
The Power of Change: Reinvent Yourself at Any Age
Life is an Attitude. The Power of Positive Thinking
Transformation: Reinventing the Woman Within
Learning to Love Yourself: Self-Esteem for Women
A Journey Within: Self-Discovery for Women
The Woman's Handbook for Self-Confidence
Remove the Mask! Living an Authentic Life
The Woman's Handbook for Self-Empowerment
Becoming Your Own Best Friend
The Self-Architect: Redesigning Your Life

The African American Library

Single and Loving It! Secrets for the SINGLE African American Sister
Boys to Men The Guide for African American Boys
Sister to Sister A Guide for African American Girls
Bruised But Not Broken
Learning to Love Yourself: A Handbook for the African American Woman
Wellness for the African American Woman: Mind, Body & Spririt
Life Skills for the African American Woman
Raising African American Boys
Raising African American Girls

Living Your Vision and Purpose

The Professional Woman Network - Book Series

Becoming the Professional Woman
Customer Service & Professionalism for Women
Self-Esteem & Empowerment for Women
The Young Woman's Guide for Personal Success
The Christian Woman's Guide for Personal Success
Survival Skills for the African-American Woman
Overcoming the SuperWoman Syndrome
You're on Stage! Image, Etiquette, Branding & Style
Women's Journey to Wellness: Mind, Body & Spirit
A Woman's Survival Guide for Obstacles, Transition & Change
Women as Leaders: Strategies for Empowerment & Communication
Beyond the Body! Developing Inner Beauty
The Young Man's Guide for Personal Success
Emotional Wellness for Women Volume I
Emotional Wellness for Women Volume II
Emotional Wellness for Women Volume III
The Baby Boomer's Handbook for Women

Youth Empowerment Series

Raising Healthy Children in an Unhealthy World
The Teen Handbook for Self-Confidence

These books are available from the individual contributors, the publisher (www.pwnbooks.com), www.amazon.com, and your local bookstore by request.